LITERATURE AND
THE ENVIRONMENT

LITERATURE AND THE ENVIRONMENT

*Edited by George Hart
and Scott Slovic*

Exploring Social Issues through Literature
Claudia Durst Johnson, Series Editor

GREENWOOD PRESS
Westport, Connecticut • London

Library of Congress Cataloging-in-Publication Data

Literature and the environment / edited by George Hart and Scott Slovic.
    p.cm.—(Exploring social issues through literature, ISSN 1551–0263)
   Includes bibliographical references and index.
   ISBN 0–313–32149–3 (alk. paper)
   1. American literature—History and criticism. 2. Environmental
literature—History and criticism. 3. Environmental protection in literature. 4.
Environmental policy in literature. 5. Ecology in literature. 6. Nature in
literature. I. Hart, George. II. Slovic, Scott, 1960– III. Series.
PS169.E25L58 2004
810.9'3556—dc22   2004009204

British Library Cataloguing in Publication Data is available.

Library of Congress Catalog Card Number: 2004009204
ISBN: 0–313–32149–3
ISSN: 1551–0263

First published in 2004

Greenwood Press, 88 Post Road West, Westport, CT 06881
An imprint of Greenwood Publishing Group, Inc.
www.greenwood.com

Printed in the United States of America

The paper used in this book complies with the
Permanent Paper Standard issued by the National
Information Standards Organization (Z39.48–1984).

10 9 8 7 6 5 4 3 2 1

The editors and publisher gratefully acknowledge permission to use the following:

"Salvation" (excerpts), "In the Woods" (excerpt), and "Protesting at the Nuclear
Test Site" (excerpts) by Denise Levertov, from *The Life Around Us,* copyright
© 1992, 1996 by Denise Levertov. Used by permission of New Directions Publishing Corporation.

"The Bath" (excerpt), "For the Children" (excerpt), "Front Lines" (excerpt),
"Control Burn," "Mother Earth" (excerpt), and "As for the Poets" (excerpt) by
Gary Snyder, from *Turtle Island,* copyright © 1974 by Gary Snyder. Used by permission of New Directions Publishing Corporation.

Excerpts from Denise Levertov's Papers are courtesy of the Department of Special
Collections, Stanford University Libraries. © The Denise Levertov Literary Trust,
Paul A. Lacey and Valerie Trueblood Rapport, Co-Trustees.

Contents

Series Foreword

Exploring Social Issues through Literature was developed as a resource to help teachers and librarians keep pace with secondary school curriculum developments in the language arts such as integrated studies and teaching literature across the curriculum. Each volume in the open-ended series confronts an important social issue that has both historical ramifications and contemporary relevance to high school students. The initial topics developed for the series reflect the 'hot button' issues most requested by educators. Themes—such as environmental issues, bioethics, and racism—encompass a considerable body of literature. The books in this series provide readers with an introduction to the topic and examine the differing perspectives offered by authors and writers from a variety of time periods and literary backgrounds.

This resource was developed to address students' needs and appeal to their interests. The literary works selected range from standard canonical works to contemporary and multicultural adult fiction that would be familiar to teens and to young adult fiction. Many titles are found on curriculum reading lists; other considerations in selection include pertinence, interest level, subject and language appropriateness, and availability and accessibility of the text to the non-specialist. The authors of these volumes, all experts in their fields, also sought to include a wide spectrum of works offering as many differing perspectives on the issue as possible.

Each volume begins with an introductory essay tracing the historical and literary developments related to the identified social issue. The chapters provide brief biographical information on the writer and present critical analysis of one or more work of literature. While the focus of the chapters is generally full-length fiction, it is not limited to that and may also include poetry, short stories, or non-fiction—such as essays or memoirs. In most chapters works are arranged chronologically to reflect the historical trends and developments. In other cases works are grouped according to thematic sub-topics. The analysis includes discussions of the work's structural, thematic and stylistic components and insights on the historical context that relates the work to the broader issue. Chapters conclude with bibliographic information on works cited and a list of suggested readings that may be helpful for further research or additional assignments.

Educators looking for new ways to present social issues will find this resource quite valuable for presenting thematic reading units or historical perspectives on modern problems of conflict. Students of literature as well as general readers will find many ideas and much inspiration in this series.

Introduction

Scott Slovic and George Hart

The phrase "literature and environment" came into common use among literary scholars in the United States and abroad in the early and mid-1990s when the scholarly organization called "The Association for the Study of Literature and Environment" (acronym "ASLE") and the journal *ISLE: Interdisciplinary Studies in Literature and Environment* were created. Although the phrase "literature and the environment" is still sometimes used, many critics prefer the more inclusive idea of approaching literature in a way that explores the relationship between literary expression and *all* environments rather than focusing more narrowly on the interest in and concern for "*the* environment" (the world beyond human affairs) in literary expression. The word "environment" literally means "surroundings," as in the German equivalent "*Umwelt*" (or "around-world").

Although writers in North America and throughout the world have always been interested in interactions between humans and the landscape, flora, and fauna, literary scholars and other specialists in the arts and humanities (the visual and performing arts, history, philosophy, and related disciplines) have traditionally concentrated their studies on human expression and human experience, seldom considering the ramifications of human behavior for the larger planet and the impact of "nature" on human experience. Of course, there have been notable exceptions to this rule. In his recent book called *A Century of Early Ecocriticism*, David Mazel collects brief examples of "proto-ecocriticism," works of literary scholarship in America and England from 1864 to 1964 that address the representation and consideration of nature in literature. Individual critics, such as Norman Foerster and

Perry Miller, performed important studies of nature and the American imagination during the early decades of the twentieth century. In 1964, Leo Marx published his landmark study *The Machine in the Garden*, exploring the pastoral tradition (attitudes toward rural experience in opposition to urban experience) and focusing on the role of technology in nineteenth- and twentieth-century American literature.

Interest in the natural world is nothing new among literary artists. Not only is traditional Native American oral narrative permeated with references to plants, animals, astronomy, natural elements, and specific places, but the earliest European explorers to arrive in North America, such as Alvar Nuñez Cabeza de Vaca (who traveled from what later became Florida along the Gulf of Mexico into Mexico between 1524 and 1534), filled their reports with interesting descriptions of the physical world and the native people on this continent. Some people are inclined to point to later writers such as Henry David Thoreau, the author of such works as *A Week on the Concord and Merrimack Rivers* (1849) and *Walden* (1854), as the originators of the tradition of American writing about nature, but this view is mistaken. Many writers between the sixteenth and eighteenth centuries, including Jonathan Edwards and Cotton Mather, wrote fascinating treatises, sermons, and meditations about the natural world. However, in the mid-nineteenth century interesting shifts began to occur in American environmental writing. Thoreau and his contemporaries began to write about social and environmental concepts together, demonstrating that human experience necessarily includes relationships to other human beings and to the larger planet. For instance, in *Walden*, a work that recounts Thoreau's two-year experiment in simple living on the shores of Walden Pond near his hometown of Concord, Massachusetts, the author explicitly places his narrative in the context of the festering American social problem of slavery. Thoreau set up house at Walden Pond from 1845 to 1847. Just months before Thoreau moved to the pond, abolitionist author and former slave Frederick Douglass published his *Narrative of the Life of Frederick Douglass, An American Slave, Written by Himself*. Thoreau frames his investigation into the possibility of living a simple and "deliberate" life in proximity to nature within the context of "slavery," including both institutional slavery in the American South and the kind of slavery that results from indebtedness, overwork, and unnecessarily complicated social and professional ambitions.

Until the early decades of the nineteenth century, American authors of European descent tended to feel that their new society lacked the sense of human history that could generate a proper literary and artistic perspective. In "The Author's Account of Himself" at the beginning of his 1819 *Sketch Book* (a story collection that included such classic pieces as "The Legend of Sleepy Hollow" and "Rip Van Winkle"), Washington Irving noted America's "fine scenery" (712) but asserted that "Europe held forth all the charms of storied and poetical association...the accumulated treasures of age" (713)—literally, ruined castles and other old buildings. A few decades later, however, Americans began to appreciate the relatively unique advantages of the American continent—at least in relation to Europe: namely, the vast and seemingly inexhaustible stretches of scarcely populated land, including huge numbers of wild animals, endless forests, and magnificent rivers and lakes. Thomas Cole, the distinguished American landscape painter, wrote the following in his 1836 "Essay on American Scenery":

> The essay, which is here offered, is a mere sketch of an almost illimitable subject—American Scenery; and in selecting the theme the writer placed more confidence in its overflowing richness, than in his own capacity for treating it in a manner worthy of its vastness and importance.
>
> It is a subject that to every American ought to be of surpassing interest; for, whether he beholds the Hudson mingling waters with the Atlantic—explores the central wilds of this vast continent, or stands on the margin of the distant Oregon, he is still in the midst of American scenery—it is his own land; its beauty, its magnificence, its sublimity—all are his; and how undeserving of such a birthright, if he can turn towards it an unobserving eye, an unaffected heart! (568)

Even today, in the early twenty-first century, there are still those in the United States who look at this country and the rest of the world as if nature were inexhaustible and pristine, despite the phenomenon of the industrial revolution, which from the early nineteenth century through the present has radically depleted a broad range of natural resources, contributed to the extinction or endangerment of numerous plant and animal species (through direct killing or through habitat destruction), and spewed vast quantities of toxins into the environment (many of them located especially close to poor and relatively disempowered communities). For the most part, Thoreau tended to look toward wild nature as an antidote to the ills and excesses of human civilization. In his famous essay "Walking," he stated, "In Wildness is the preservation of the World" (112). He did not say much about the potential diminishment of nature.

However, between the 1870s and the second decade of the twentieth century, the writer and activist John Muir helped to launch the tradition of American environmental activism and showed that writers could be artists and social activists at the same time. Muir became particularly famous for his efforts to preserve Yosemite Valley in California and for his many books and articles about wilderness adventures and spectacles in California, Alaska, and other regions of North America and the world. He cofounded the Sierra Club and became its first president in 1892. One of the major environmental battles of Muir's life was his effort to protect the Hetch Hetchy Valley in the Sierra Nevada mountains of California from being dammed and used as a water reservoir for the city of San Francisco. In the conclusion to his 1912 book *The Yosemite,* Muir wrote:

> "Hetch Hetchy water is the purest of all to be found in the Sierra, unpolluted, and forever unpollutable." On the contrary, excepting that of the Merced below Yosemite, it is less pure than that of most of the other Sierra streams, because of the sewerage of campgrounds draining into it, especially of the Big Tuolumne Meadows camp-ground, occupied by hundreds of tourists and mountaineers, with their animals, for months every summer, soon to be followed by thousands from all the world.
>
> These temple destroyers, devotees of ravaging commercialism, seem to have a perfect contempt for Nature, and, instead of lifting their eyes to the God of the mountains, lift them to the Almighty Dollar.
>
> Dam Hetch Hetchy! As well dam for water-tanks the people's cathedrals and churches, for no holier temple has ever been consecrated by the heart of man. (201–2)

As in the passage above, Muir knew how to use his eloquent voice for practical, political purposes when necessary. Even though he lost the battle to save Hetch Hetchy, his passionate writings are among the most famous examples of an American author recognizing the potential damaging effects of human behavior on the natural world. Amazingly, in recent years, a new initiative has emerged among environmentalists in the American West, seeking to remove the Hetch Hetchy Dam and restore the valley gradually to its natural condition. This is a western example of the "rewilding" phenomenon that other writers, such as John Elder in Vermont, have observed in different regions of the country (see Elder's *Reading the Mountains of Home* [1998] for a narrative of the return to natural forest conditions in New England during the late twentieth century).

Throughout the twentieth century, many notable American authors highlighted the natural environment, and particularly the relationship between human beings and the physical world, in their writings. Mary Austin, for instance, published her important book about the arid regions of the American Southwest and southeastern California, *The Land of Little Rain,* in 1903. Henry Beston, on the other side of the continent, published his classic meditations on Cape Cod, *The Outermost House,* in 1928. Sigurd Olson produced several beautiful volumes of essays about the lake country of northern Minnesota in the 1940s and 1950s, including *The Singing Wilderness* (1956). Meanwhile, Marjorie Stoneman Douglas wrote about the Florida Everglades; her beautiful paean to that unique part of the world, *The Everglades: River of Grass,* appeared in 1947. In American poetry of the first half of the twentieth century, Robinson Jeffers bridges the gap between an activist-writer such as John Muir and postwar writers such as Edward Abbey and Gary Snyder. In 1948 he published a controversial volume of poetry, *The Double Axe,* which presented a "philosophical attitude" called "Inhumanism." Jeffers described this attitude as "a shifting of emphasis and significance from man to not-man" (xxi), which is, in short, an early expression of "biocentrism."

Other core environmental ethics were given their first contemporary expressions during the mid-century. One of the major works of American environmental writing, Aldo Leopold's *A Sand County Almanac,* was published in 1949 and articulated his famous "Land Ethic": "A thing is right when it tends to preserve the integrity, stability, and beauty of the biotic community. It is wrong when it tends otherwise" (224–25). In the 1940s and 1950s, Loren Eiseley created renewed interest in the literary genre of the personal essay with his meditations on evolution and human experience, collected in *The Immense Journey* (1957) and subsequently in several additional volumes.

The modern era of American environmental activism, environmental literature, and environmental scholarship (especially in the arts and humanities) began to emerge in the early 1960s, with the publication of Rachel Carson's *Silent Spring* in 1962. Carson's eloquent and scientifically formidable exposé of the effects of the pesticide DDT on the environment and human health prompted immediate, high-level attention within President John F. Kennedy's administration and emboldened environmental scientists and activists throughout the United States. Two years later, with the help of author Wallace Stegner, who served as writer-in-residence with the U.S. Department of the Interior, a federal law called the Wilderness Act was crafted and passed by Congress, supporting the preservation of wild regions across the continent. Stegner later collected his 1961 "Wilderness Letter" and other important writings about nature in his 1969 book, *The Sound of Mountain Water.* Some scholars have designated Edward Abbey's 1968 hybrid work of fiction and nonfiction, *Desert Solitaire: A Season in the Wilderness,* as the cornerstone of modern American environmental writing, pointing to its combination of political and epistemological meditations, its complexity of moods and voices, and its ironic, proto-postmodern view of the indeterminacy of verbal representations of the world. A few years later, Abbey produced another of his best-known works, the novel *The Monkey Wrench Gang* (1975), which related the wilderness antics and eco-sabotage efforts of a small band of nature lovers in the West—this book inspired activist Dave Foreman to establish the radical organization Earth First! in 1980.

Coming in the wake of the first Earth Day celebration, which occurred in 1970, the 1970s were a time of energetic artistic ferment in the social-activist and environmentalist communities. Three Pulitzer-Prize-winning books were published in this decade—Annie Dillard's *Pilgrim at Tinker Creek* and Gary Snyder's *Turtle Island* in 1974 and Peter Matthiessen's *The Snow Leopard* in 1978—that would become modern classics of American environmental literature. Other major environmental publications of the late 1960s and 1970s include Ursula K. Le Guin's ecological fantasy, *The Earthsea Trilogy* (1968, 1971, and 1972) and Leslie Marmon Silko's novel, *Ceremony* (1977). Le Guin's novels show the spread of ecological ideas into contemporary popular culture, while Silko's novel explores the social and psychological effects of militarism and environmental degradation among Native American communities in the American Southwest.

One of the reasons for the emergence of a formal community of scholars interested in literature and environment during the 1990s was the recognition that many of the finest contemporary authors in the United States and abroad were devoting their thoughts and words to exposing the destructive relationships between humans and nature and reimagining the place of human beings on this planet in order to make it possible to avert catastrophic fates for ourselves and other species. Barry Lopez's National-Book-Award-winning *Arctic Dreams: Imagination and Desire in a Northern Landscape* (1986) was one of the landmark publications of the 1980s, along with such notable volumes as William Kittredge's *Owning It All* and Rick Bass's *Wild to the Heart,* both published in 1987. Dozens of contemporary writers in North America are among the leading figures in this field, including Homero Aridjis, Margaret Atwood, Wendell Berry, Joseph Bruchac, John Daniel, Alison Hawthorne Deming, David James Duncan, William L. Fox, Ray Gonzalez, Joy Harjo, Robert Hass, John Hay, Linda Hogan, Denise Levertov, Bill McKibben, W.S. Merwin, Farley Mowat, Gary Paul Nabhan, Richard K. Nelson, John Nichols, Mary Oliver, Simon J. Ortiz, Robert Michael Pyle, Pattiann Rogers, Scott Russell Sanders, Rebecca Solnit, Luci Tapahonso, Terry Tempest Williams, Edward O. Wilson, Ann Zwinger, and many, many others, in addition to those mentioned earlier.

Some of these writers have made a special effort to help modern Americans appreciate their physical presence in the world, believing that sensory attunement to nature will help us to understand that ecology is not merely an abstract concept but a material phenomenon with practical implications for the future of life on this planet. One of the fine articulations of this perspective comes in Scott Russell Sanders's 1987 essay "Speaking a Word for Nature":

However accurately it reflects the surface of our times, [literature] that never looks beyond the human realm is profoundly false, and therefore pathological. No matter how urban our experience, no matter how oblivious we may be toward nature, we are nonetheless animals, two-legged sacks of meat and blood and bone dependent on the whole living planet for our survival. Our outbreathings still flow through the pores of trees, our food still grows in dirt, our bodies decay. Of course, of course: we all nod our heads in agreement. The gospel of ecology has become an *intellectual* commonplace. But it is not yet an *emotional* one. For most of us, most of the time, nature appears framed in a window or a video screen or inside the borders of a photograph. We do not feel the organic web passing through our guts, as it truly does. While our theories of nature have become wiser, our experience of nature has become shallower.... Thus, any writer who sees the world in ecological perspective faces a hard problem: how, despite the perfection of our technological boxes, to make us feel the ache and tug of that organic web passing through us, how to situate the lives of characters—and therefore of readers—in nature. (226)

In other words, Sanders writes to help his readers feel and appreciate their own naturalness, their involvement with the physical world, the more-than-human world. We are animals—nothing more or less. And yet we strive increasingly to suspend ourselves above nature, to enclose ourselves within human-constructed spaces and technologies, to establish abstract, virtual relationships with other people, other species, and even with the natural resources we rely upon for our daily existence.

Other contemporary writers, while acknowledging the significance of our physical experience of the world, have tended to focus on the social ramifications of environmental degradation. One of the most famous examples of recent American environmental writing, and a key instance of socially conscious literature, is Terry Tempest Williams's 1991 *Refuge: An Unnatural History of Family and Place,* which considers the human health effects of nuclear testing in the Nevada desert during the 1950s and early 1960s. Toward the end of the book, in the scathing epilogue titled "The Clan of One-Breasted Women," Williams writes:

> In Mormon culture, authority is respected, obedience is revered, and independent thinking is not. I was taught as a young girl not to "make waves" or "rock the boat". . . .
>
> For many years I have done just that—listened, observed, and quietly formed my own opinions, in a culture that rarely asks questions because it has all the answers. But one by one, I have watched the women in my family die common, heroic deaths. We sat in waiting rooms hoping for good news, but always receiving the bad. I cared for them, bathed their scarred bodies, and kept their secrets. I watched beautiful women become bald as Cytoxan, cisplatin, and Adriamycin were injected into their veins. I held their foreheads as they vomited green-black bile, and I shot them with morphine when the pain became inhuman. In the end, I witnessed their last peaceful breaths, becoming a midwife to the rebirth of their souls.
>
> The price of obedience has become too high. (285–86)

While Williams's book focuses on the specific situation of her family in the state of Utah, the broader implication is that some environmental changes (such as changing water levels in the Great Salt Lake) must be accepted and others (such as contamination through nuclear testing) are unnecessary and avoidable and should be resisted through political action and political art. Here, at the intersection of environmental imperatives and political possibilities, the environment becomes a "social issue," and the authors and books that we examine in this volume all come to this crossing with a commitment to both earth and society.

The purpose of *Literature and the Environment* is not to provide an encyclopedic survey of major American environmental texts. Readers will quickly notice that the earliest work presented here is Mary Austin's *The Land of Little Rain,* published in 1903. Scholars familiar with the field of environmental literature will immediately think of major texts that we have elected not to examine here. However, this small sample covers an equitable range of works by male and female authors (five men, six women); includes six works of nonfiction, three works of fiction (counting Le Guin's trilogy as a single work), and two collections of poetry; and offers at least one sample of Native American literature (Silko's *Ceremony*). Most of the books introduced in this volume will be immediately recognizable as famous examples of twentieth-century American environmental writing that explores broad or specific social issues; other works, such as Ursula K. Le Guin's *The Earthsea Trilogy* and Denise Levertov's *The Life Around Us,* may come as surprises, although both Le Guin and Levertov are commonly recognized as major contemporary authors.

We hope this book will whet the appetite of students and teachers to read beyond the range of works and authors represented in this introductory selection. Because we have been able to offer only a small sample of detailed treatments in this book, we provide a list of suggested additional readings —including primary texts, anthologies, and scholarly books.

A NOTE ON THIS PROJECT

In 2001, I received a message from Lynn Araujo of Greenwood Press, inviting me to consider preparing a manuscript for the press's new series, Exploring Social Issues through Literature. Lynn was interested in finding someone to help with a manuscript specifically on exploring environmental issues through literature. This immediately seemed like a good idea to me, but I knew I was already overcommitted, so I turned to a group of my closest colleagues and asked for help.

Nine of my fellow faculty members in the Graduate Program in Literature and Environment at the University of Nevada, Reno (UNR), decided to work together on the project, and George Hart—who was an NEH post-doctoral fellow at UNR at the time—agreed to co-edit the project with me.

The Association for the Study of Literature and Environment (ASLE) was started in October 1992 and currently has approximately 1,000 members in the United States, plus independent branches in Japan, the United Kingdom, and Korea and branches-in-the-making in Germany, Australia, and New Zealand. American students interested in pursuing studies in this field can certainly do so at virtually any college or university where literary study is available—that is to say, just about any liberal arts institution. ASLE members are on the faculty at hundreds of American colleges and universities; other teachers and scholars work in this field without formal association with ASLE. Students or teachers interested in finding out more about ASLE and about the field in general should take a look at the ASLE Web site: www.asle.umn.edu.

Several universities in the United States have developed special areas of concentration in environmental literature and ecocriticism— the University of California at Davis, the University of Nevada at Reno, and the University of Oregon come most quickly to mind. Nevada offers undergraduate courses in literature and environment, but the literature and environment program is, at this time, focused on graduate students working at the M.A. and Ph.D. levels. For further information, about Nevada's literature and environment program, please see the Web site: www.unr.edu/cla/lande/main.html. All royalties earned through sales of this book will be given directly to the literature and environment program and will help to support our various activities, including visits to Reno by environmental scholars and writers such as those featured in this book.

In the introduction and in the list of suggested additional readings, George and I have tried to indicate that environmental literature and ecocriticism (or environmental studies more broadly) are vast and varied fields, currently thriving but also built upon substantial historical foundations. The eleven authors featured in this introductory volume—Mary Austin, Loren Eiseley, Rachel Carson, Wallace Stegner, Denise Levertov, Edward Abbey, Ursula K. Le Guin, Gary Snyder, Barry Lopez, Leslie Marmon Silko, and Terry Tempest Williams—are all commonly recognized as major figures in American environmental literature and all are well known for exploring social and environmental issues in their literary work.

We hope that the introductory overviews we've provided here will be helpful to students and teachers interested in the social and environmental aspects of these particular authors and texts, but we also hope that this collection will serve to inspire readers to delve further into this vibrant and important area of literature and literary scholarship.

Scott Slovic

BIBLIOGRAPHY

Cole, Thomas. "Essay on American Scenery." 1836. *The American Landscape: A Critical Anthology of Prose and Poetry.* Ed. John Conron. New York: Oxford UP, 1973. 568–78.

Elder, John. *Reading the Mountains of Home.* Cambridge: Harvard UP, 1998.

Irving, Washington. "The Author's Account of Himself." *The Norton Anthology of American Literature.* Ed. Nina Baym et al. 2nd ed. Vol. 1. New York: Norton, 1985. 712–14.

Jeffers, Robinson. *The Double Axe and Other Poems.* 1948. New York: Liveright, 1977.

Leopold, Aldo. *A Sand County Almanac and Sketches Here and There.* 1949. New York: Oxford UP, 1987.

Mazel, David, ed. *A Century of Early Ecocriticism.* Athens: U of Georgia P, 2001.

Muir, John. *The Yosemite.* 1912. Garden City, NY: Doubleday, 1962.

Sanders, Scott R. "Speaking a Word for Nature." *Secrets of the Universe.* Boston: Beacon, 1987.

Thoreau, Henry David. *A Week on the Concord and Merrimack Rivers.* 1849. Orleans, MA: Parnassus Imprints, 1987.

———. *Walden.* 1854. Princeton: Princeton UP, 1971.

———. "Walking." 1862. *The Natural History Essays.* Ed. Robert Sattelmeyer. Salt Lake City: Peregrine Smith, 1980. 93–136.

Williams, Terry Tempest. *Refuge: An Unnatural History of Family and Place.* New York: Pantheon, 1991.

1

Mary Austin,
The Land of Little Rain (1903)

Mary Webb

In 1888, an Illinois-born young lady of 20 moved with her family to the strange and exotic desert of southern California. There she began to explore and celebrate a land she would later consider sacred, a land she, like other Americans, knew only vaguely through dime westerns and cowboy novels of the late nineteenth century. Mary Hunter Austin was the first woman writer to champion the desert Southwest. She found inspiration in the fragility and compelling solitude of the desert and a profound interest in writing about its inhabitants. *The Land of Little Rain,* a collection of literary essays, was published in 1903, when Austin was 35 years old. In her first and most successful book, Austin makes clear the themes that pervade many of her 30 published works: her love of the land and respect for the creatures in it. Austin came to know the desert of Southern California at a time when most Americans regarded deserts as hostile and forbidding places.

Born in Carlinville, Illinois, in 1868, to George and Susannah Hunter, Austin developed an early affinity for nature and an unusual—even mystical—appreciation for its power. Some fifty years after her childhood, Austin recalled a moment at age six when "earth and sky and tree and wind-blown grass and the child in the midst of them came alive together with a pulsing light of consciousness" (qtd. in Finke 15). Her outdoor experiences as a child would set the stage for her appreciation of nature and her need to experience its solitude. After her father's early death, the family migrated west to California in 1888. There, despite late nineteenth-century Victorian constraints on feminine behavior, Austin's keen observations, appetite for botanical research, and willingness to walk around her new environment taught her what the desert had to offer. For a young woman raised in the humid environment of Illinois, this world was new and enchanting, with open spaces and far horizons. Her biographers note that Austin made sure to carry a ten-cent notebook, so impressed was she upon first viewing the startlingly beautiful and demanding landscape (Finke 24). Between wild stage rides and the hardships of homesteading, this young woman explored a sometimes frightening landscape, staying up nights to watch the nocturnal animals under the full moon or taking the reins when a stage driver got sick. Austin scholar Melody Graulich notes that Austin wanted, in *The Land of Little Rain,* to "express her feeling about the desert West, a feeling she had never seen described" (*Western Trails,* 20). Throughout *The Land of Little Rain,* readers will hear the words of a woman writing before her time, exhorting us to protect the solitude and fragile nature of the unknown desert.

SYNOPSIS

In *The Land of Little Rain,* Austin brought to the reading public of the early twentieth century its first encounter with the Great American Desert, through an unusual blend of literary sketches that honor and give voice to Native American and Hispanic cultures. Austin roused readers' awareness of a world where, for centuries, people lived in harmony with the desert environment. *The Land of Little Rain* is a lyrical work that anticipates the sentiments found in much of the nature and environmental writing of the twentieth century. The book takes as its primary thesis a celebration of the gifts given by the desert: the "compensations, deep breaths, deep sleep, and the communion of the stars," as Austin notes in the last paragraph of the opening essay (8). Edward Abbey, a well-known environmental writer of the twentieth century, wrote in his 1988 introduction to *The Land of Little Rain* that Austin's collection is

> a book about earth, sky, weather, about some of the plants and animals that survive and reproduce among those elemental and elementary events, and about a few of the human beings who once lived in what now seems, from our urbanized point of view, like something close to an original state of nature. (Austin ix)

Austin shares with readers her passionate love of nature and its intricately tied relationships; she tells stories of old stage drivers and miners, croaking ravens and coyotes. On her walks through the isolated spaces of the desert she encountered people from many cultures and became acquainted with women and men from the Paiute and Shoshone tribes. She found a way to tell their stories by listening to the medicine men, the Indian basket makers, and Mexican villagers.

Readers of the twenty-first century will understand Austin's point of view, through essays that focus on the country and its power. Note the direct address as she describes the land of little rain to her readers: "Here are the long heavy winds and breathless calms on the tilted mesas where dust devils dance, whirling up into a wide, pale sky. Here you have no rain when all the earth cries for it, or quick downpours called cloud-bursts for violence" (2). Readers will note Austin's interest in the land itself, not its defeat. This insight leads to a kind of vision, a celebration of the land's resilience, as exemplified in this longer passage from "My Neighbor's Field":

> It is interesting to watch this retaking of old ground by the wild plants, banished by human use. Since Naboth drew his fence about the field and restricted it to a few wild-eyed steers, halting between the hills and the shambles, many old habitues of the field have come back to their haunts. The willow and brown birch, long ago cut off by the Indians for wattles, have come back to the streamside, slender and virginal in their spring greenness, and leaving long stretches of the brown water open to the sky. In stony places where no grass grows, wild olives sprawl; close-twigged, blue-grey patches in winter, more translucent greenish gold in spring than any aureole. (49–50)

Like Austin, modern readers know all too well the perils of living beyond our planet's environmental means. We read and hear daily accounts of vanishing wetlands, overcrowded cities, and the threat of global warming. A *New Yorker* opinion column, written just after the November 2002 elections, sounds clear echoes of Austin's warnings:

> Once a forest is cut down, or a stream is filled in with waste, or a wildlife refuge is opened up to oil drilling, it's virtually impossible to undo the damage—at least, in our lifetime, or our children's, or our children's children's. By now, we have become practically inured to these sorts of losses and depredations, skimming past news about the hole in the ozone, or the latest mysterious fish die-off, or the recent study warning that as many as half the planet's species are in danger of extinction. (Kolbert 36)

The Land of Little Rain still resonates with us one hundred years after the book was published, because twenty-first century readers see what population pressure and industry have enacted upon the land, even in remote areas such as the deserts of the Southwest. Visitors to the Grand Canyon, for example, have seen the air quality (many hundreds of miles from automobile-locked cities) in the canyon degrade, especially since the 1970s. This slim collection of essays offers important advice about living with aridity, and it describes how inhabitants of Austin's beloved "long, brown land" have adapted to that land, with its scant rainfall and its harsh conditions.

In the opening title essay, Austin sets the pattern that the book will follow, as she presents an overview of the "land of lost rivers, with little in it to love; yet a land that once visited must be come back to inevitably" (2). Detailing with a keen eye, the lives of birds, coyotes, and cattle, Austin notes how a pair of meadowlarks will stand ("droop" is the word she uses) above their nest in an effort to keep their eggs shadowed from the sweltering midday desert sun. Another description catalogs the scavengers that circle the iron-colored hills and the cattle, dying of thirst after patiently eking a living from the sere landscape:

> Cattle once down may be days in dying. They stretch out their necks along the ground, and roll up their slow eyes at longer intervals. The buzzards have all the time, and no beak is dropped or talon struck until the breath is wholly passed. (18)

A sympathetic observer, Austin details desert creatures' movements, excluding none, not even the smallest or least significant. In each description, her viewpoint is direct, unsentimental, even austere.

Austin devotes several essays to Native Americans—both women and men, Paiute and Shoshone—who lived for many hundreds of years in the Owens Valley. In "The Basket Maker," readers encounter Seyavi, the woman who weaves baskets, and her people who live off the land in the Owens Valley. Austin shows us how the native people learned to harvest river mussels, marsh roots, and pinyon nuts. She weaves in subtle information about actual historical events that native people, such as Seyavi's, endured. The taking of the Owens Valley by whites in the 1860s is one such example of a real incident that outraged Austin enough for her to include it. In "The Basket Maker," we read of the Paiute Indians, who had begun using the Owens River to irrigate land to grow food. When the whites arrived, they took this most arable land from the Indians and drove about 150 of them into Owens Lake to drown (Reisner 61). Austin, using the traditional Indian names for the places, recounts this event in the opening paragraph of "The Basket Maker." She retells the story without opining a moral lesson. Readers gather the subtle message that Seyavi, the character on whom this particular essay focuses, knew the land well enough to survive.

Austin's essays draw attention to signs of native inhabitants, particularly in "Water Trails of the Ceriso." In this essay, Austin spends several detailed paragraphs depicting how the various ground-dwelling birds find and use the scarce water. She concludes the essay with a description of a "water mark" built by the Shoshone, a kind of rock arrangement that travelers in that country would use to orient themselves to the spring, to find water. Austin gives voice to a people then silenced, detailing the work of "an older, forgotten people" (15).

In her final sketch, "The Little Town of the Grape Vines," Austin centers the reader's attention on the Hispanic towns and their particular importance in the California desert: "Where [the town] lies, how to come at it, you will not get from me," she tells us. Rather, Austin describes customs and holidays of Mexican-American culture to bring the town alive. Thus readers celebrate with her and experience a place where, "all the speech is soft, all the manners gentle; where all the dishes have *chile* in them, and they make more of the Sixteenth of September than they do of the Fourth of July" (101). This passage and the essay that follows emphasize Mexican culture and its Independence Day, along with the people who inhabit the "Little Town of the Grape Vines." In her characterizations, Austin did much to dispel cultural stereotypes of the early twentieth century.

HISTORICAL CONTEXT

Several inspirations combined to shape Austin's perspective in *The Land of Little Rain*. One was her fascination with the desert landscape and its inhabitants; another was Austin's awareness of the desert's fragility, which came to her early on from her direct experience of trying to live off of the arid desert in the midst of a severe drought. Austin and her Illinois family, used to the green, fertile land of the Midwest, found themselves struggling to make a living—by farming—from a drought-locked landscape. Austin's autobiographical *Earth Horizon* tells the story of the deprivation pioneer families like hers suffered: "For the settlers on the Tejon [the desert region near Bakersfield], there was not so much as a mess of greens to be raised or gathered" (qtd. in Zwinger 24).

The hardships and tolls taken on hundreds of other migrants who had come west provided the opportune moment for U.S. government–backed projects that would bring water and population to "that long, brown land." In *The Land of Little Rain,* Austin warns us of the implications of such manipulations of the land, specifically in the essay "Other Water Borders." In this essay, Austin describes how easily the delicate balance of the desert ecosystem can be disrupted when water crosses desert land for irrigation. She has first-hand knowledge of these effects:

> With the water runs a certain following of thirsty herbs and shrubs. The willows go as far as the stream goes, and a bit farther on the slightest provocation. They will strike root in the leak of a flume, or the dribble of an overfull bank.... Given a new waterway in a barren land, and in three years the willows have fringed all its miles of banks; three years more and they will touch tops across it. (86–87)

Austin learned how pervasive the effects of manipulating desert water could be. As a result of her family's attempt to homestead desert land, she grew intimately familiar with the rhythms of the desert.

Austin was then quite simply horrified by the swift and brutal changes she saw being enacted on the land that she'd grown to know and love. The most visible of these changes was the demise of the Owens River, which was diverted into a channel to quench the thirst of Los Angeles, some 250 miles away. In a series of ironic coincidences, *The Land of Little Rain* was published in 1903, the same year that the United States Reclamation Service (later known as the Bureau of Reclamation) was formed. The Reclamation Service was created to help the United States "reclaim" arid lands west of the 100th meridian. Austin would write about living in balance with the land while federal laws and offices (such as the Bureau of Reclamation) promoted a shifting in that balance by irrigating desert land. She wrote, "Not the law, but the land sets the limit," in the *same year* that Reclamation engineers began to investigate diverting the Owens River. This trend in the western United States, of diverting water to irrigate desert land, was an idea that grew out of John Wesley Powell's survey of arid land and exploration of the Grand Canyon in the 1870s. Austin's essays depict the ways in which the monumental act of building dams to irrigate desert land would distort Powell's notion of conservation. At the time, the United States wanted to populate its vast west, and the Bureau of Reclamation thus had its mandate to begin building dams on western rivers. *The Land of Little Rain* emphasizes what an enormous impact on the land humans have through irrigation of arid lands. Austin wrote, "It is difficult to come into intimate relations with appropriated waters; like very busy people they have no time to reveal themselves" (83).

Besides the effects of drought and Austin's direct experience with living on the land, other inspirations combined to shape Austin's perspectives in *The Land of Little Rain*. A longing for solitude and an early awareness of and sensitivity to the hardships that many women of her time period endured became focal points in all of Austin's work. As a child, Austin observed the effects of Victorian women's constrained lives, probably without fully understanding what she saw. From observing that these women did not have access to birth control to seeing how they were victimized by the (sometimes) brutal expectations of Victorian husbands, Austin internalized the importance of independence for women. Austin's adolescence was populated by women who came to her mother for health care; often physically debilitated by endless child-bearing and household duties, they were forced to depend solely on their husbands for their livelihood. Austin saw her own mother, following the death of her husband George Hunter, struggle to get her widow's pension. Susannah Hunter worked as a home nurse to support the family, but despite Susannah's support of women's independence, she and Mary would battle over Mary's desire for intellectual stimulation through books and writing. Her mother felt that too much time spent in the world of the imagination would isolate her daughter and make it hard for her to find a marriage partner. Mary felt books were the most important thing and had grown up reading her father's books, a remarkable enough accomplishment for a young lady of the 1880s. At age seven, she declared to her supportive father that she wanted to write books herself. Austin's interest in the world of books already set her apart from the traditional Victorian young lady.

Besides a keen interest in the lives of women and in the land, Austin's need for solitude helped to train her eyes on the natural world. She was largely self-taught and learned the names of insects, plants, and animals as she observed them. After the family's move to California, Austin became acquainted with General Edward Beale, an early pioneer to the area, who had also served as Superintendent of Indian Affairs in California and Nevada. According to biographer Augusta Finke, Beale spent hours talking with Austin, teaching her about the history and folklore of the area, "even making available government reports on geological and botanical surveys" (Finke 45). The following passage from "Water Borders" exemplifies Austin's way of observing and then understanding botany, in this case, the life of a fir tree:

> It goes without saying that a tree that can afford to take fifty years to its first fruiting will repay acquaintance. It keeps, too, all that half century, a virginal grace of outline, but having once flowered, begins quietly to put away the things of its youth. Year by year the lower rounds of boughs are shed, leaving no scar; year by year the start-branched minarets approach the sky. A fir-tree loves a water border, loves a long wind in a draughty canon, loves to spend itself secretly on the inner finishings of its burnished, shapely cones. Broken open in mid-season the petal-shaped scales show a crimson satin surface, perfect as a rose. (83)

The Land of Little Rain demonstrates how its author moved into the unfamiliar world of the Tejon country, observed and recorded it, and then learned about what she'd seen. In her later autobiographical work, *Earth Horizon*, Austin notes how starved she was for food and company, upon moving to the desert. Both the physical deprivation of homesteading, with very little fresh food, and the psychological aloneness she felt nearly brought her to the point of mental collapse. She had lost her appetite, could not sleep, and could find no one with whom to share her experiences, as she describes her state in the following:

> Her trouble was that the country failed to explain itself. If it had a history, nobody could recount it. Its creatures had no known life except such as she could discover by unremitting vigilance of observation; its plants no names that her Middlewestern botany could supply.... Until these things elucidated themselves factually, Mary was spellbound in an effort not to miss any animal behavior, any bird-marking, any weather-signal, any signature of tree or flower. (qtd. in Zwinger 24)

Austin goes on to describe her discovery of wild grapes in a remote canyon, on which she feasted for weeks, thus curing herself of her literal malnutrition. Physically restored by the fresh fruit, she also found sustenance and spiritual healing in the perfect design of what she observed in the natural world. She describes an almost sacred discovery, that of "a poor appetite of any sort being cured by its *proper food;* that there was something you could do about unsatisfactory conditions...and that was getting out to hunt for the remedy" (italics mine; qtd. in Zwinger 28). Austin's early experiences in the desert would forecast the way in which she took strength from the hours spent alone and how quickly she learned to trust her own vision. She understood that she would be a writer, no matter what might happen—and indeed, plenty did happen. She survived a disappointing marriage, the trauma of raising (and then institutionalizing) an autistic child, and her eventual divorce, largely because of the strength she could draw from the land, its solitude, and her writing.

STYLISTIC ANALYSIS

Austin's ability to observe the natural world shows readers of *The Land of Little Rain* again and again how much there is to learn from the desert, as well as how easily dismissed that arid land and its people were at that time. Readers should understand that Austin's style of writing reflects her time period of one hundred years ago: it is more formal sounding and is sometimes difficult to read. The length of sentences makes the reader work a bit to get through passages of description and comprehend what the author sees. The following example shows how Austin brings the reader's vision right down to ground level, literally, in her description of "water trails":

> By the end of the dry season the water trails of the Ceriso are worn to a white ribbon in the leaning grass, spread out faint and fanwise toward the homes of gopher and ground rat and squirrel. But however faint to man-sight, they are sufficiently plain to the furred and feathered folk who travel them. Getting down to the eye level of rat and squirrel kind, one perceives what might easily be wide and winding roads to us if they occurred in thick plantations of trees three times the height of a man. It needs but a slender thread of barrenness to make a mouse trail in the forest of the sod. To the little people the water trails are as country roads, with scents as signboards. (9)

Note the arrangement of words and their effect on the reader: "It needs but a slender thread of barrenness to make a mouse trail...." The sentence requires a kind of suspension or pause in the reader's comprehension. An impatient reader might scroll right past the sentence and lose the remarkable image of a mouse's track in the grass. Note also the combination of colloquial phrases with the longer syntax, making the sentences seem simple (plain language) and yet complex (longer sentences) at once.

Another stylistic marker is Austin's use of *be verbs,* in this case "is." In this short passage, Austin forecasts what would become a central thesis of twentieth-century environmental writing but does so with sentences all turning on the verb "to be": "Man *is* a great blunderer going about in the woods....The cunningest hunter *is* hunted in turn, and what he leaves of his kill *is* meat for some other. That *is* the economy of nature, but with it all there *is* not sufficient account taken of the works of man. There *is* no scavenger that eats tin cans, and no wild thing leaves like disfigurement on the forest floor" (italics mine; 22). In characteristic Austin style, the long sentences and the six uses of "is" tend to weary a reader who longs for action verbs.

Other examples contrast with stronger verbs, personification, and metaphor: "It is enough occupation, when no storm is brewing, to watch the cloud currents and the chambers of the sky. From Kearsarge, say, you look over Inyo and find pink soft cloud masses asleep on the level desert air; south of you hurries a white troop late to some gathering of their kind at the back of Oppapago...highest up in the air, drift, unshepherded, small flocks ranging contrarily" (99). While readers may find these comparisons quaint—clouds as troops hurrying away— this passage demonstrates Austin's use of comparison to render the vast drama of a desert sky. Her direct address, using "you," and an unsentimental kind of personification, bring the reader closer to what the text describes. Other uses of personification are more sentimental and present inanimate objects (trees, meadows, grasses) with almost mystical qualities. As seen in an earlier citation, Austin portrays the silver fir as having very human and even seductive characteristics: "A fir-tree loves a water border, loves a long wind in a draughty canon, loves to spend itself secretly" (83). Here Austin combines the parallel grammatical structure, in repeating phrases with "loves," with strong verbs to help the reader imagine the power of that tree.

As these examples show, *The Land of Little Rain* uses a variety of stylistic methods to draw readers in and allow them to experience the compelling world that Austin sought to celebrate and protect. She spoke to readers of the early twentieth century in a different style, one that employed traditional comparisons like personification. Some of Austin's personification includes a sacred-sounding element, such as this one in "The Streets of the Mountains," where Austin describes the high Sierra peaks as "terrible.... When those glossy domes swim into the alpenglow, wet after rain, you conceive how long and imperturbable are the purposes of God" (70). Here, readers get a sense of Austin's appeal, especially to readers of one hundred years ago. The direct address (you), the tone of formality (terrible, as in inspiring terror), and the implication of knowing God through nature would have likely roused her readers' attention and gained their interest. Her message both then and now is the same: we must take care not to dismiss the land.

CONCLUSION

The sampling from these essays in *The Land of Little Rain* offers some context for understanding Austin's point of view and style. A woman writer of vision, she managed to escape the restrictions placed on Victorian women, and in doing so, she would encourage readers to appreciate the most insignificant of creatures and least visible of cultures. She celebrated the land and its people. The final essay about the Little Town of Las Uvas closes with a wonderful exhortation that invites readers to visit this Mexican-American hamlet and see its residents' existence in relation to the earth:

Come away, you who are obsessed with your own importance in the scheme of things. Come away by the brown valleys and full-bosomed hills to the even-breathing days, to the kindliness, earthiness, ease of El Pueblo de Las Uvas. (107)

All the essays in this collection will set readers straight: there is much to discover in the desert's emptiness, not the least of which is the solace the author found in its solitude. That solace proved to be the strongest inspiration for *The Land of Little Rain*. Always one to wander outside and see what might be happening in the natural world, Austin, through the essays in this slim volume, will catch readers' hands to show them the ways in which "that long brown land lays such a hold on the affections" (6).

BIBLIOGRAPHY

Austin, Mary. *The Land of Little Rain*. 1903. New York: Viking/Penguin, 1988.

Finke, Augusta. *I-Mary: A Biography of Mary Austin*. Tucson: U of Arizona P, 1983.

Graulich, Melody, ed. *Western Trails: A Collection of Short Stories by Mary Austin*. Reno: U of Nevada P, 1987.

Graulich, Melody, and Elizabeth Klimasmith, eds. *Exploring Lost Borders: Critical Essays on Mary Austin*. Reno: U of Nevada P, 1999.

Kolbert, Elizabeth. "Sound of a Tree Falling." *The New Yorker* 18 Nov. 2002: 36.

Reisner, Marc. *Cadillac Desert*. New York: Penguin, 1987.

Stegner, Wallace. *Beyond the Hundredth Meridian*. New York: Penguin, 1953.

Zwinger, Ann, ed. *Writing the Western Landscape*. Boston: Beacon, 1994.

2

Loren Eiseley, *The Immense Journey* (1957)

Kathleen Boardman

A collection of thirteen interconnected essays about evolution, *The Immense Journey* begins with a commentary on fossils and on the origins of life in water. It ends with speculations about the place of humankind in the continuous unfolding of life upon this planet. First published in 1957 by Random House, the book is not a specialized treatise for scientists or a textbook for students; neither is it a defense of evolutionary theory aimed at creationist skeptics. Rather, it is written for the thoughtful layperson who is curious about evolutionary biology and anthropology, who appreciates a well-crafted prose style, and who is intrigued by questions about the origins and meaning of life. Proceeding on the assumption that educated people know and generally accept Darwin's theory but don't necessarily understand all its workings and implications, author Loren Eiseley sets out to explain evolution in terms that the general reader will find comprehensible and interesting. He illustrates with examples from his personal experience with the natural world, speculates on the future based on his scientific knowledge of the past, and meditates on the spiritual significance of the restless, changing forms of life on Earth. In short, this book is meant to delight as well as instruct. To that end, it draws on the humanities as well as the sciences to chronicle the "immense journey" of life in a world of infinite possibilities.

An influential and unusual book for its time, *The Immense Journey* uses vivid language to discuss a rich variety of living forms—fish, birds, plants, amphibians, mammals, primates, *Homo sapiens* (the human species), and even the possibility of life elsewhere in the universe. The essays illuminate such topics as the beginnings of life in water, the adaptation of species to new or difficult environments (like the ocean depths), the impact of angiosperms (flowering plants) upon life on Earth, the origins of the human brain, and the impact of pedomorphism (extended childhood) upon the development of that brain. Ranging backward and forward in time, from inferences about past eons to speculations about future millennia, the book touches on important Darwinian concepts—inheritance, variation, competition, natural selection, divergence, and extinction. It also explains more recent discoveries about human evolution.

The essays in *The Immense Journey* may be read and enjoyed separately. Indeed, most of them appeared originally as articles in such publications as *Harper's Magazine, American Scholar,* and *Scientific American.* Several—most notably "The Flow of the River," "The Judgment of the Birds," "The Bird and the Machine," and "How Flowers Changed the World"—have been republished in anthologies many times since the book's first appearance. However, reading the essays one after another, as a book, makes it possible to evaluate the range of Eiseley's background as an anthropologist and paleontologist. It also becomes easier to delve into the topics of most concern to him: the passage of time and the tremendous change that comes with it, the "place" of humans on this planet and their impact upon it, and the mystery of life that makes living beings more than just machines.

CRITICAL RECEPTION

Loren Eiseley was 50 years old the year *The Immense Journey* was published. Not only was it his first book, but it also proved to be the best known and best selling of the dozen books of nonfiction prose he wrote for popular audiences between 1957 and his death in 1977. (He also produced four volumes of poetry, two of which were published posthumously.) In fact, *The Immense Journey* is still in print, still with the same publisher. According to Eiseley's biographer, editors had originally expected only a modest success for this somewhat unusual nonfiction book of lay science (Christianson 291–92). Although the dust cover of the original edition proudly proclaimed the author as "an imaginative naturalist" who explored "the mysteries of man and nature," the editors still worried that the book might contain too much imagination and not enough science. Nevertheless, early critical reception was positive, with high praise for the book's eloquence, imagination, point of view, images, and ideas. Although some professional scientists later began to criticize Eiseley's style and approach, literary people and the general public consistently appreciated his poetic language and the accessible but accurate information he provided. For example, one early reviewer of *The Immense Journey* complimented Eiseley for "pressing his hands against the confining walls of scientific method" and for being able to "look beyond science into the realm of the spirit" (Dubkin 12). Prominent nature writer Joseph Wood Krutch also noticed one of the most haunting features of the book: "the wonderful paradox of Man trying to grasp what eludes him just because he is himself part of it" (5).

BIOGRAPHICAL BACKGROUND

The Immense Journey was written, essay by essay, during the decade before its publication; but we might say it evolved even more slowly and over the course of its author's life. Born in 1907 in Lincoln, Nebraska, Loren Eiseley was a solitary child with a difficult family life. However, living at the edge of town gave him an opportunity to explore ponds and fields and take notice of all the wild creatures dwelling in the marginal areas between country and city. A relative introduced him to the exhibits of mammoth and dinosaur fossils at the museum on the University of Nebraska campus in Lincoln. In high school he declared an ambition to become a nature writer, and in college he wrote poetry and essays for *Prairie Schooner*, which was at that time a campus literary magazine. Eiseley also had an opportunity to join two summer fossil-gathering expeditions on the High Plains of western Nebraska and eastern Colorado and Wyoming. Such experiences provided material for essays like "The Slit," where our author finds himself face to face with a fossil skull in a rock cleft, and "The Flow of the River," where he tells about floating down the Platte, the wide, shallow river that bisects the state of Nebraska. After dropping out of school several times and riding the rails during the Depression, Eiseley completed a bachelor's degree in anthropology and English at the University of Nebraska and then went on to the University of Pennsylvania to earn a master's degree and doctorate in anthropology. Postdoctoral studies provided background in physical anthropology and a specialization in early man.

Let's pause here for a word about "man." Today, in the early twenty-first century, we use inclusive language in our published writing: we avoid using "he" when we are referring to females as well as males, and we rarely use "man" or "mankind" when we discuss prehistoric peoples or human beings of today. However, as a writer and scientist whose training and career were situated solidly in the mid-twentieth century, Eiseley was not unusual in his use of "man" and "he" to refer to people in general. Most scientists and professors of his time were male, and in most cases they thought primarily of males when they wrote "man." Eiseley went a bit further, using the singular "man" also to evoke *Homo sapiens'* uniqueness, solitariness, and even loneliness among the creatures of the natural world. Thus, to enjoy reading Eiseley for his style and insights, it is important first to acknowledge his male-centeredness as a product of his culture and personal background, and then to move on without letting his use of "man" interfere with other interesting features of his style and content.

In the late 1940s, after holding professorial positions in Kansas and Ohio, Eiseley became professor of anthropology at the University of Pennsylvania and curator of early man at the university's museum. In his academic career, he had engaged in scientific and scholarly research that resulted in some monographs and articles written for professional colleagues. But he was still a *writer*—inclined toward poetry and essays—as well as a scientist. In the early 1940s, Eiseley had decided to try his hand at writing about science for a popular magazine, and "The Folsom Mystery," based on his research on Ice Age hunters and their prey, appeared in the December 1942 *Scientific American*. The positive response was encouraging, and soon he was regularly submitting articles to *Harper's Monthly* (now *Harpers*) and finding enthusiastic readers. In his autobiography, *All the Strange Hours* (1975), Eiseley tells about a turning point, a time when he began to think consciously about what was happening in his writing and decided to push further in the direction of what he called "the concealed essay, in which personal anecdote was allowed gently to bring under observation thoughts of a more purely scientific nature" (177). This "concealed essay," informed by his scientific training as an expert on early man and shaped by his experience as a poet, became his trademark. Editors began to suggest that Eiseley pull some of his magazine articles together into a book on nature and evolution. He agreed that this would be a good idea, and after several years of revising previously published essays, establishing connections among them, and writing new material, he finished *The Immense Journey*.

HISTORICAL CONTEXT

The book appeared nearly a hundred years after Darwin's *Origin of Species* (1859) but only twelve years after the dropping of atomic bombs on Hiroshima and Nagasaki and just at the beginning of the U.S.–Soviet "space race." Certainly, the most vital discussions of evolutionary theories and the nature of evolutionary processes had been largely completed in the nineteenth century. And, despite continuing controversies between so-called creationists and evolutionists in the twentieth century, the cutting-edge discussions of evolution's religious and spiritual implications had already taken place several generations before *The Immense Journey* saw print. Eiseley reanimates the discussion of evolutionary theory by clarifying some of its philosophical implications and by reevaluating some of the claims made by earlier scientists. He also sketches the history of the scientific discoveries and debates that took place in the decades immediately before and after Darwin's book appeared. Certainly Darwin was not the only scientist working on the question of evolution, and Eiseley draws readers' attention to a number of others, especially Alfred Russel Wallace, a codiscoverer of the principle of natural selection. Indeed, Eiseley's second book, which appeared the year after *The Immense Journey*, was *Darwin's Century* (1958), a careful look at the history of evolutionary science in the nineteenth century.

In "The Maze," the middle essay of *The Immense Journey*, Eiseley also outlines some continuing controversies among scientists, and between evolutionary scientists and anti-evolutionists. The details of human evolution are sketchy, he says, because the fossil record is so fragmentary. Anti-evolutionists point to this sketchiness as evidence of the shortcomings of evolutionary theory, while evolutionists see it as a cause for curiosity, wonder, and further research. Eiseley leaves it at that. But his placement of this chapter at the center of the book suggests that the maze of evolutionary paths and possibilities lies at the very center of evolutionary theory, and of life itself.

Although discussions of evolution had cooled somewhat by the mid-twentieth century, American ambivalence about science and technology was at its height. On the one hand, science was the miracle worker: diseases had been overcome, wars won, unknown places explored, and the standard of living raised, all through the practical application of scientific discoveries. On the other hand, science had also unleashed the potential for mass destruction on an unheard-of scale. Living in the shadow of the "A-Bomb," Americans began thinking about the possible end of life on Earth, caused not by some natural disaster but rather by man-made weapons. For better or worse, science was on nearly everyone's mind. A few weeks after *The Immense Journey* appeared, the USSR launched Sputnik I, the first artificial satellite to orbit the earth, and the United States responded with a patriotic fervor to "catch up" with the Communists, resulting in an unprecedented emphasis on science in the school systems and in popular culture. Many non-scientists began to feel that, as a result of the postwar burgeoning of science and technology in the Western world, their knowledge of science was woefully inadequate. And yet scientific specialization wasn't yet so advanced (or didn't seem so) that lay people felt it was hopeless even to try to catch up in their understanding of science and technology.

The Immense Journey evokes the excitement of scientific discovery. Like the evolution of life on earth, science has itself become an "immense journey" because each answer raises at least one new question. For example, paleontologists' discoveries about the rapid evolution of the human brain raise new questions: why did this brain evolve so fast? Why did this "instrument" appear before its possessor needed it in order to survive? At the end of every scientific quest, there is always a new mystery, and Eiseley is pleased, or at least content, with that. However, he is not happy with the arrogance of the scientists of his day, or with science's inability or refusal to see its own limitations. To make it clear that scientists, far from having an edge on the truth, are subject to the same cultural values and prejudices as other people, *The Immense Journey* provides examples of the impact of racism and colonialism upon scientific "knowledge" about humanity in the nineteenth century. Eiseley notes that while we may be able to see our predecessors' blind spots and foolish mistakes, we are probably unable to see our own. He also argues that modern science has been too "man-centered" (or *anthropocentric*), with the result that the contributions and welfare of other life on the planet have been ignored. Finally, Eiseley critiques modern science's refusal to see beyond quantities and measurements and into the spiritual realm of life. While he conveys his enthusiasm for *scientific method* (close observation and the making and testing of hypotheses) as a way of searching for knowledge, he eloquently criticizes the arrogance of *scientism* (the assumption that science has, or will eventually have, all the answers to every question worth asking). Scientists who claim to have the only way to the truth and who spurn any help or input from other "cultures" (such as philosophy or the arts) are foolishly proud and even dangerous.

Through most of his career, Eiseley was personally affected by a widening gap between the "two cultures" of science and the humanities. Some professional colleagues even criticized him for spending too much time researching in libraries and writing for lay audiences but too little time doing fieldwork and writing technically for the scientific community (see for example Buettner-Janusch 9). At the time, combining the scientific and the literary in one's writing was even more suspect than it is today. But the literary way of writing about nature and science suited Eiseley's particular talents, inclinations, and background. In addition, he became convinced that it was wrong to continue to separate the "two cultures" and to excise feeling and poetry from scientific prose. He believed society needed to balance the analytic tendencies of science—the need to separate and categorize everything in order to understand it—with a more poetic way of understanding, by synthesizing, connecting, and unifying our experience of the world. Eiseley was an "antimaterialist": to him, there was more to life than just "matter" or physical substance. There was also mind or spirit, and the spiritual aspects of nature could be better expressed in literary than in scientific writing.

THEMATIC SECTIONS

As we begin to interpret *The Immense Journey,* we may divide its thirteen chapters into three thematic sections dealing, respectively, with early life forms, human evolutionary development, and the meaning of life. The first five chapters feature life before the appearance of humankind. They introduce concepts like evolutionary time, the principle of organization, and the adaptability of flora and fauna. These early chapters explain processes like evolutionary succession: more complex animals and plants develop from simpler forms, and overspecialized living beings tend to die out when conditions change. In describing these principles, Eiseley emphasizes the restlessness of life, "its eternal dissatisfaction with what is" (37), and its consequent adaptation to new environments.

The fourth chapter of this first section centers on the story of "The Snout," a poorly specialized "bog-trapped failure"(56) that three hundred million years ago moved out of the ooze and onto land as lakes and streams died up, causing the extinction of many more specialized water creatures. If the Snout had not come ashore and developed a brain with cerebral hemispheres, *Homo sapiens* would not exist, at least not in the form we know. This story is familiar, and the fish-with-legs has become a popular contemporary symbol of Darwinian evolutionary theory. But Eiseley goes on to remind us that nature is "still busy with experiments" (47) and that "there are things still coming ashore" (54). Humans do a fairly good job of looking at the past, but they tend to stop with the present. Eiseley emphasizes that the future stretches ahead at least as far as the past stretches behind us, and, given what we know about all the changes in life and environment that have occurred in the past, we ought not to be too sure about humanity's part in that future. Evolutionary processes are not confined to the past; they occur in the present and will continue as long as life exists in the universe.

The next five chapters focus on humankind, the rapid development and dominance of *Homo sapiens*, and the future prospects of humanity. This section poses far more unanswered questions than the first. Eiseley explains that evolutionists disagreed, and still disagree, on the reasons for the rapid development of the human brain in size and complexity. Darwin insisted that it developed gradually through competition and natural selection, while Wallace, his contemporary, noted huge, unexplained "leaps" in human brain development and argued that natural selection alone could not account for them. Perhaps the explanation was at least partly cultural, Wallace suggested: humans could communicate and form communities, and these human communities, in turn, hastened human evolution. Although some of Wallace's theories had been disproved by the time Eiseley was writing, Eiseley shared his impulse to look beyond the strictly biological explanations for humankind's uniqueness.

This second group of essays includes "The Dream Animal," one of two pieces not previously published elsewhere in some form. The title refers to *Homo sapiens*, the only species to have developed language and self-consciousness. Because of language, human beings "escaped out of the eternal present of the animal world into a knowledge of past and future" (120); also because of language, human culture could provide some of the advances and adaptations that would ensure the survival of the species. Humanity no longer had to rely on evolutionary processes. On the other hand, the human brain is a mixed blessing: because of the self-awareness that comes along with consciousness, the human species is unique, alone, and lonely in the animal world. In an often-quoted passage from this chapter, Eiseley evokes the beginning of human consciousness and the simultaneous onset of human loneliness:

> For the first time in four billion years a living creature had contemplated himself and heard with a sudden, unaccountable loneliness, the whisper of the wind in the night reeds. Perhaps he

knew, there in the grass by the chill waters, that he had before him an immense journey. (125–26)

For Eiseley, *Homo sapiens'* distinction is not its cleverness or its domination of the earth—but rather its loneliness. Humans tend to assume that the world was made—or evolved—for their use and enjoyment. The human ego, Eiseley says, can hardly grasp the idea that for many eons the world existed very nicely without this species and that the universe might be entirely indifferent to its coming and going. Thus, Eiseley believes, it is crucial that we understand the magnitude of the earth's geologic age, because as long as we fail to see time and evolution in perspective, we will continue to be *anthropocentric;* that is, we'll continue to see "man" as the goal of evolution, and we'll continue to satisfy our human needs at the expense of all other life on the planet. The self-centeredness, or species-centeredness, of humanity has made us not only lonely but also dangerous. In spite of his professional interest in the history of humankind, Eiseley resists the species egotism that separates human beings from other life on the planet: we are only "one of the many appearances of the thing called Life" (59).

The last three chapters of *The Immense Journey* explore the mystery of life. By this point, Eiseley has explained all the key terms and concepts that we need in order to understand how evolution works; but because his interest extends beyond the material, he also discusses the philosophical implications of evolutionary theory. Throughout the book, Eiseley outlines his disagreement with the ways many other scientists, philosophers, and theologians have explained the meaning of life, in light of the discoveries of evolutionary science. Some have seen a randomness in nature: that is, although evolution follows certain natural principles and patterns, it is purely chance that the various species developed exactly as they did, and even the appearance of *Homo sapiens* is a random event. Another group argues in favor of determinism: that is, through all the changes and developments in life forms throughout eons and eons, the final product was always meant to be "man." A third group, the mechanists, say that despite the complexity of life and the development of living forms, a living organism is no more than a sophisticated machine. It can be explained entirely in chemical or physical terms. Especially in these last three chapters, Eiseley argues against randomness, determinism, and mechanism—and urges his audience to keep their eyes open to the mysteries of life. As literary critic Andrew Angyal points out, in these last chapters evolution becomes not just a process of nature but a potent metaphor:

through this metaphor, Eiseley "implies that there is something mysterious, purposeful, even transcendent about these apparently random events in the natural world" (32). In addition, if we understand evolution correctly, we also begin to comprehend that ours is a world of infinite possibility.

In "The Secret of Life," the last essay in the book, Eiseley contrasts his method of seeking the secret of life with the methodology of laboratory scientists. Like an old-fashioned naturalist, Eiseley walks into the woods and fields in autumn, looking for evidence of life in its many ingenious forms: seeds and seed pods, metamorphosing caterpillars, grasshopper legs. He examines the "discarded machinery" (197) of life in hopes of discovering the secret of life. These autumn investigations of the countryside parallel, of course, his earlier work as a field paleontologist, which he describes in "The Slit," the opening chapter. A paleontologist, an expert on fossils, is also observing the discarded machinery of life in order to discover something about life.

On the other hand, laboratory scientists, both Soviet and American, aim to create life in the lab, or they isolate the ingredients of life, the chemicals or vitamins that are necessary to sustain life. While he insists that he respects their efforts, Eiseley emphasizes that even if they succeed in creating life (which he does not expect to see), the "secret of life" will still elude them. The lab scientists' questions tend to be mechanistic: what combination of chemicals and reactions will yield "life"? Eiseley's questions are different: he wants to know "in what way it is managed" (209) that dust and particles come to pursue the "devious plans and symmetries" of life forms. He would like to find out, but doesn't expect to find out, "what strange forces at the heart of matter" (209) regulate the heartbeats of tiny mammals and the distinctive forms of each plant. Even if we could reverse time and speed it up, so that we could experience the evolutionary process in reverse, we could not at any stage describe the "how" and "why" of our body's functions. The secret of life will remain a secret, but, at least for Eiseley, it is worthwhile to puzzle and wonder over that enigma of life.

After 46 years, science and technology have moved far beyond the activities described in *The Immense Journey*. Scientists have made further discoveries in the area of human evolution, and "life" is being created and cloned in laboratories on a greater scale than Eiseley might have imagined. However, his vision of the complexity and mystery of life, and his evocation of the restlessness and constant creativity of evolutionary process, remain fresh, largely due to his distinctive writing style. Eiseley manages to explain difficult concepts clearly, present specific examples vividly, and use his sentence structures to create the thoughtful depth and dynamic movement that are so important to his treatment of his subject matter.

These three sentences from "How Flowers Changed the World," one of the most highly regarded essays in the book, suggest the lyrical rhythms of Eiseley's prose style and his use of examples:

> Without the gift of flowers and the infinite diversity of their fruits, man and bird, if they continued to exist at all, would be today unrecognizable. Archaeopteryx, the lizard bird, might be snapping at a beetle on a sequoia limb; man might be a nocturnal insectivore gnawing a roach in the dark. The weight of a petal has changed the world and made it ours. (77)

The passage reinforces a major theme of the book: that change is constant in the world and that evolution might have pursued many alternative paths—and might yet take them. In addition, the sentences express wonder in the presence of the natural world as we experience it. In such ways, Eiseley not only explains evolution as seen through the lens of physical anthropology but also combines his profound sense of the passage of time and his vivid sense of the importance of an individual moment.

Like the classic essays of Michel de Montaigne, Eiseley's essays often begin with or center themselves on a personal experience, usually a small everyday happening that suggests a question or concept that the essayist explores in hopes of gaining insight. This exploration proceeds not just through further attention to the personal experience but also through research that might bear on the case: scholarly study, wide reading, fieldwork, and so forth. This process also echoes the work of Sir Francis Bacon, the seventeenth-century English scientist and essayist whom Eiseley studied and greatly admired. Each essay in *The Immense Journey* moves from the specific to the abstract, emphasizing vivid images rather than abstract theories. This technique allows an audience to join Eiseley vicariously on his journey of discovery.

For example, "The Slit," the first chapter in the volume, begins with a personal experience: as a "bone hunter" on a paleontological expedition, Eiseley has gone down into a "slit" in the rocks and found himself face to face with a skull set in a geological layer older than *Homo sapiens*. "We stared a little blankly at each other, the skull and I" (5), he remarks, and then reports his next vivid impression: excavating this fossil, he could suddenly picture himself as a fossil. Moving on from the personal experience and the flash of insight, Eiseley discusses the knowledge drawn from his scientific research and his background as a paleontologist so that he can credibly assert that "we are all potential fossils still carrying within our bodies the crudities of former existences" (6). Like Montaigne's, Eiseley's essayist-voice is personal in tone, skeptical, yet capable of wonder. Like Bacon, he sounds scientifically informed and self-assured, yet he can put aside the empiricism of science to respond with awe to the mysteries in the natural world.

One way he does this is by capturing the strange in the "natural." Repeatedly, he tells us that we all take too much for granted: we are so used to the world as it is that we fail to see its "queerness," its miraculousness. We need to develop the ability to "see from a strange inverted angle" (167) and encourage a taste for the marvelous. In "The Judgment of the Birds," one of the best-known essays in *The Immense Journey,* Eiseley provides several striking examples of his own ability to see beyond the commonplace and view the world from an inverted angle. First he tells about waking up early in a New York hotel tower and looking out the window to see thousands and thousands of wings as pigeons float out among the spires and cupolas of the city in the first light of dawn. After experiencing a strange feeling of dislocation, he has this insight: one of humankind's greatest creations, a world-class city, does not really belong to "man" at all. In the second example, a crow, having become disoriented in a thick fog, is flying too low and suddenly emerges almost face to face with Eiseley. This time it is the crow that sees from the inverted angle; believing himself to be flying high in the sky, he squawks in horror at the sudden appearance of a freak of nature—a giant man, or a floating man. Eiseley next describes an experience with "flying chemicals." Alone in the badlands, standing among the lifeless chemicals that streak the rocks, he looks up to see a large flock of small birds pass noisily overhead. Their small bodies contain the same substances as those in the rocks—calcium, iron, phosphorus, carbon—but they are full of life. Eiseley describes this as a miracle.

"The Judgment of the Birds" draws its title from yet another example, a story of the judgment of living beings in favor of life. Eiseley narrates his chance observation of a gathering of birds in a clearing. (No scientist could ever set this up as an experiment, he reminds us, but a good scientist would always be ready to observe.) A raven has just caught and eaten a nestling, and, drawn by the cries of the parent birds, many small birds flutter into the clearing, making little cries of protest and misery. Eiseley then describes the transcendent moment when the birds deliver the "judgment of life against death" (175) by beginning to sing.

Eiseley continues the celebration of life in the following chapter, "The Bird and the Machine," also a well-known and often-republished essay. Here he approaches the wonder of life from a different angle and provides only a single extended example. He tells the story of a pair of sparrow hawks, one of which he had captured on an expedition for a zoo. After a night of captivity in the field, the imprisoned mate was taking one last look at the bright sky when Eiseley, on an impulse, released it. As the hawk disappeared into the sky, Eiseley heard the cry of its mate, which had been circling and watching for hours. From this long-ago experience, Eiseley concludes that although evermore-sophisticated machines may be able to do many of the things that living beings do, and do them better, "the machine does not bleed, ache, hang for hours in the empty sky in a torment of hope to learn the fate of another machine, nor does it cry out with joy nor dance in the air with the fierce passion of a bird" (193). Such an idea has often been expressed, and just as often dismissed as "sentimentality." (Eiseley himself received this sort of criticism from some scientists.) But for many readers who continue to enjoy Eiseley's work, his style brings the message home, reemphasizing the mystery and miraculousness of life.

BIBLIOGRAPHY

Angyal, Andrew J. *Loren Eiseley*. Boston: Twayne, 1983.

Buettner-Janusch, John. Rev. of *The Firmament of Time*. *American Anthropologist* 65 (June 1963): 9.

Christianson, Gale E. *Fox at the Wood's Edge: A Biography of Loren Eiseley*. New York: Holt, 1990.

Dubkin, Leonard. Rev. of *The Immense Journey*. *New York Times* 1 Sept. 1957: 12.

Eiseley, Loren. *All the Strange Hours: The Excavation of a Life*. New York: Scribner's, 1975.

———. *Darwin's Century: Evolution and the Men Who Discovered It*. New York: Doubleday, 1958.

———. *The Immense Journey*. New York: Random House, 1957.

———. *The Lost Notebooks of Loren Eiseley*. Ed. Kenneth Heuer. Boston: Little Brown, 1987.

Krutch, Joseph Wood. Rev. of *The Immense Journey*. *New York Herald Tribune Book Review* 25 Aug. 1957: 5.

3

Rachel Carson, *Silent Spring* (1962)

Jane Detweiler

With the publication of her fourth book, *Silent Spring* (1962), Rachel Carson found a surprisingly wide audience for her concerns about the overuse of chemical pesticides. Her previous books—*Under the Sea-Wind* (1941), *The Sea around Us* (1951), and *The Edge of the Sea* (1955)—had been quite successful, bringing Carson worldwide recognition. But these best sellers were lyrically descriptive, evoking the intricate ecologies of the oceans with fascinating stories about Carson's beloved Maine coast, helping readers to envision (and care about) the crabs, snails, and sea anemones living in tide pools. These books were not about an abstract, invisible, and terrifying chemical threat. So, when Carson was invited to write about the dangers of pesticides, she faced some difficult tasks. First, she needed to make the complicated, systemic threat of certain chemicals understandable. She had to avoid alienating her popular audience by using too much dry and academic explanation, or by oversimplifying her material and thus seeming to talk down to readers. Second, she wanted to encourage the reading public to care about the birds, animals, and "non-pest" insects (like butterflies and bees) that were negatively affected by efforts to eliminate insects that consumed crops, annoyed humans, or spread diseases. Along with being beautiful and valuable in their own right, these creatures were the "canaries in the mine" whose deaths signaled impending danger for humans and the world's ecosystems. Finally, and perhaps most importantly, Carson needed to confront general ideas (largely supported by industry and the government) that pesticides were absolutely necessary to preserve agriculture and prevent disease—and that they were safe to use widely and indiscriminately.

Far from being safe, *Silent Spring* argued with much research support, pesticides steadily accumulated in the bodies of animals who ate plants and other animals. And, as animals at the top of this food chain, human beings were likely to experience heavy exposure at all points in the process of pesticide use (from development, to testing, to application, to drinking contaminated groundwater, to consumption of plants and animals as food).

As a work of nonfiction, *Silent Spring* demonstrates how Carson met her writerly challenges with a blend of literary descriptions and anecdotes woven together with clear, understandable scholarly discussions of chemistry, biology, and ecology. In addition, the book includes the political, cultural, and economic history of pesticide development and use that readers must consider. Opening with a "fable for tomorrow," *Silent Spring* balances evocative descriptions of past and present natural beauty and careful discussions (often with diagrams of complex molecular structures) of chemistry. It also presents a substantial amount of observation-based evidence, from professionals and public citizens alike, in the form of brief stories that predict a grim future. The sense of impending danger builds through the book's exploration from under the ground up, so to speak. After first examining the potential long-term pollution of aquifers, Carson then follows the progress of pesticides through the soils, plants, and onward to birds, to animals, and, ultimately, to the very humans who used DDT or other pesticides in the first place. Meanwhile, she points out the greatest irony of all: the insects that were the target of the pesticides develop a resistance to these chemical agents, and almost every other part of the ecosystem sickens or dies before the pests do. In closing, Carson repeats the call to action she has threaded through the entire book and makes several suggestions about the "other road" her reader might take by using alternative methods of pest control (for example, natural predators and bacterial diseases that kill a particular problem insect) and by pressuring industries and governments to protect the environment.

HISTORICAL BACKGROUND

Readers in this new millennium may have some difficulty understanding what a radical statement *Silent Spring* was in 1962 and how readers might have experienced its challenge to easy, but strongly believed, assumptions of those times. In the early 2000s, such things as "organic" (no pesticides used) produce, the "environmental movement," product safety warnings, as well as the very existence of the Environmental Protection Agency are all commonplaces. We know these things so well, at least in part, *because* Carson's work was published and shocked its readers into action. Many of those readers in the post–World War II period grew up watching public service announcements that proudly illustrated how pesticides had improved the world by preventing insect-caused problems. Some readers, way back then, knew family members or friends who had contracted diseases (like malaria) from mosquitoes before pesticides were widely used to control these insects. Most readers at that time were able to buy larger amounts of unblemished, inexpensive fruits and vegetables at the grocery store than they had before the war because insect damage had been reduced. A fair number of those readers might have even run or played in the spray from pest-control trucks that rumbled down their own neighborhood streets, since these vehicles and their cargo were perceived as being beneficial—and it was fun to chase them. For other readers who worked in postwar agriculture, the promise of various chemicals (pesticides, herbicides, and fertilizers) seemed to have been kept, since a given farm might have seen increased crop yields and profits from sales once insects and weeds had been reduced. And, for most Americans, the potent combination of scientific advances and industrial strength *had* delivered a safer world just a few years previously.

In response to World War II, the 1940s had seen the United States power up innumerable factories to build war materiel, develop many new chemicals and plastics, and even harness atomic power for various purposes (for example, weapons and power-generating plants). Afterward, these tremendous industrial forces were shifted to producing consumer goods that the average citizen had only *dreamed* of purchasing during the Great Depression and the war. And then, at war's end, the new Communist threat lurked behind what Winston Churchill had just recently termed the "Iron Curtain" across Eastern Europe. Popular knowledge seemed to hold that, since scientific research and new technologies had helped to defeat the Axis powers, and then helped to restore war-torn Europe and Asia, the average Joe or Jane had to trust that technological innovations again would be sure protection against menacing Communist nations. From the vantage point of many Americans in the late 1940s and onward through the Cold War, Soviet Russia was seen as aggressively building its own atomic weapons, sending up suspicious satellites like Sputnik, and all the while fostering revolutions in other countries, installing friendly regimes, or simply invading and then governing those nations from Moscow. There were also Communists to fear in the vast and massively populous nation of China, since the new People's Republic of China seemed to be exporting its revolution to other Asian countries. The Berlin Airlift, the Korean War, and the Cuban Missile Crisis were instances in which the United States and its allies confronted such "Communist aggression." In popular culture as in government, this threat was viewed as being very real; further, it was considered to be as pervasive within the United States as it was in, say, Cuba or the Eastern Bloc countries. Responses to the perceived danger of Communist spies ranged from mild (spontaneous public demonstrations of patriotism and democratic spirit) to extreme (the McCarthy investigations and trials of suspected Communists; "blacklisting" of civil servants, journalists, and actors for being "un-American"). In this political atmosphere of fear and suspicion, it was difficult to abandon one's trust in powerful economic and government entities that had been powerful protectors in the past. It was equally hard to question the "gifts" of science, industry, and technology that had vastly improved the living conditions for most Americans (for example: single-family housing; air conditioning; radio, telephone, and television communications; automotive transportation; ample food; superior medical care; high industrial employment rates).

Yet, with an increasing number of alarming bird and fish kills in the late 1950s, many American voices rose to question the need for (and safety of) the large-scale pesticide spraying. These citizen voices faced powerful resistance: pesticide use was pushed with intensive marketing, governmental support, and substantial financing by the chemical industry. As Houghton Mifflin editor Peter Brooks remembers *Silent Spring*'s beginnings, in 1958 he asked Rachel Carson to write a serious book on pesticides because he knew citizens who resisted aerial DDT spraying for the gypsy moth, tent caterpillar, and mosquito infestations in areas of the Northeast (Brooks 228–29; Lear 131; Waddell xii–xv). There had also been a pesticide poisoning scare related to cranberries, and the juice products made from those berries, that had been contaminated (Lear 358–60). Brooks knew that Carson had a scientific background as a trained biologist and a good reputation as a publications editor for the Fish and Wildlife Service (she was the first woman to take and pass the federal civil service examination). She also had demonstrated, over and over, the personal concern about the natural world to carry out such a substantial and controversial project. Brooks knew that only an internationally known science writer—and one with several best sellers—could handle a project of this magnitude. Rachel Carson was the perfect choice for taking this difficult message to the reading public.

Already deeply concerned, and having tried to publish magazine articles on the topic to no avail, Carson agreed with her editor, Brooks, that it seemed only a book would allow the space for the appropriate, substantial research evidence on the topic. Also, book publishers at that time had the kind of freedom necessary to deal with a controversial issue; because of their production costs and constant need for advertising support, magazines apparently were much more at the mercy of the major chemical industries. As Carson considered writing the book, she remembered all the appeals for help she had received from concerned citizens, like Olga Owens Huckins, who was horrified by the agonized deaths of songbirds in her own backyard birdbath and robins in the local woodlands after a forced aerial pesticide spraying. These various requests were part of what prompted Carson to write the manuscript that became *Silent Spring* (Carson xiiv; Lear 315). With the same strong sense of the interrelated natural world that marked her other books—and all her professional efforts as a government biologist—Carson acknowledged the importance and necessity of such a project. As she had written to the editors of *Ladies Home Journal*, trying to interest them in her early research, she noted that the danger

of these chemical poisons—some of great toxicity—is only beginning to be assessed in its relation to the lives and welfare, not only of the whole community of animals in the area subjected to ground and aerial sprays, but of the human population as well. There exists already, however, a large body of well documented evidence that these highly toxic poisons, as presently used, represent an alarming threat to human welfare, and also to the basic balance of nature on which human survival ultimately depends. (qtd. in Lear 317)

From 1958 to 1962, Carson dove into that "large body of well documented evidence" to make her case, knowing full well that she faced well-financed and politically powerful opponents. As she wrote to Brooks, "There would be no peace for me if I kept silent," since

The time had come when it must be written. We have already come very far in our abuse of this planet. Some awareness of this problem has been in the air, but the ideas had to be crystallized, the facts had to be brought together in one place.... Knowing the facts as I did, I could not rest until I had brought them to public attention. (Brooks 228. See also Freeman 463, 518)

Silent Spring was a consuming and difficult project for Carson, who found out late in its progress that she had steadily advancing breast cancer. Persevering amidst many painful and exhausting medical treatments, this dedicated science writer encountered all the strong reactions, both negative and positive, that she had fully expected upon publication of her book. Serialization of certain chapters in the *New Yorker* and excerpts in other publications gave the chemical industries notice of just what was going to be included in the book, and spokespeople for their interests responded vehemently, even viciously. One letter writer responded to a *New Yorker* installment by suggesting that Carson's indictment of "the selfishness of insecticide manufacturers probably reflects her Communist sympathies.... We can live without birds and animals but, as the current market slump shows, we cannot live without business" (Davidson 18). Carson's prose style was brutally parodied, and, as an "unhappy spinster," she was accused of caring less about starving humans than about a few dying sparrows. In a number of news articles, editorials, and letters, her scientific approach was criticized and her reporting of particular studies characterized as overly biased and self-serving. Major industrial companies, like DuPont and Monsanto, threw their advertising campaigns into high gear, attempting to discredit Carson and to undercut her statements with counterevidence from their own researchers. One company (Velsicol Chemical Company, maker of chlordane and heptachlor) even threatened to sue her publisher before the book appeared, sending a letter that suggested *Silent Spring* might provide cause for legal action because of its disparaging claims about particular chemicals made by this manufacturer (Lear 416). At the same time, state and federal governments seemed at war with themselves and each other. Some public health, agricultural, and wildlife management agencies supported pesticide use or diminished its dangers; others just as vigorously opposed the spraying or pointed out its hazards.

However, Carson's arguments also drew strong support, from the grass roots all the way to the White House. Consumers bought her book in record numbers (it was a national bestseller and also a Book-of-the-Month Club selection), and President John F. Kennedy endorsed its findings by setting several investigations and agencies in motion pursuing the leads *Silent Spring* presented. Leading public figures (Abraham Ribicoff, Robert Kennedy, William Proxmire, E. B. White), scientists (Loren Eiseley, H. J. Muller, Roland Clement, Clarence Cottam, Frank Egler, Edwin Way Teale), and professional organizations (the American Medical Association) joined Carson's longtime allies like the National Audubon Society. Together, these political actors used the tremendous impact of *Silent Spring* to push hard for all those protections that Americans of today now consider obvious: clean food and water; safe chemicals and other products; wild areas preserved from contamination; care in disposing of sewage, chemicals, or nuclear wastes; and so forth. Carson, who died of her cancer shortly after the first edition of *Silent Spring* appeared, would doubtless have been proud to know that support for her position grew steadily. Since 1962, her book has never been out of print, and it has continued to be a central text in the contemporary environmental movement worldwide.

Carson's arguments are as strong today as they were forty years ago, which is certainly one measure of a truly profound scientific contribution. As Al Gore notes in his introduction to a recent edition of *Silent Spring*, this piece of nonfiction "came as a cry in the wilderness, a deeply felt, thoroughly researched, and brilliantly written argument that changed the course of history. Without this book, the environmental movement might have been long delayed or never have developed at all" (Carson xv). If the book's discussions about the dangers of pesticides now seem "just common sense," this is another measure of how important and influential *Silent Spring* has been. Contemporary citizens have, in a very real sense, learned from Rachel Carson *how* to think deeply, carefully, and long-term about any choices or actions that might affect the environment.

A RHETORICAL ANALYSIS

Many scholars have considered why *Silent Spring* was so successful, and why it has continued to be so influential. Since this book is not, strictly speaking, a "literary" text (like a novel, short story, or poem), perhaps the best way to consider its continuing appeal is to follow these scholars and to study its rhetorical strategies. Although the word "rhetoric" is often used today to diminish the importance of political statements (for example, "His arguments are just empty rhetoric"), the study of rhetoric or argumentation has, since classical Greece, focused on "the available means of persuasion in a given situation" (Aristotle). From a rhetorical standpoint, we might examine how Rachel Carson was able to persuade her readers in the general public so effectively in order to get them to accept that pesticides posed dangerous risks. She was trained as a professional biologist, and she could never lose sight of the professional scientists, politicians, and intellectuals who would test her arguments and her data very carefully. Yet she also had to *translate* into everyday terms all the complicated scientific and historical evidence that nonprofessional readers would need to understand before they could make the decisions *Silent Spring* called upon them to make. As a highly effective "popularizer" (a professional who writes for a popular readership), Carson found the right combination of rhetorical strategies to make all that dry scientific information into an argument. She crafted a persuasive case that would move her general public readers into political action to save the natural world and ultimately themselves.

One kind of rhetorical strategy Rachel Carson used quite skillfully was to blend stories into her scientific evidence. Greg Myers, a rhetorical scholar, has pointed out that a natural science popularizer must shift out of a professional mode that is distant, objective, and timeless in the sense that whatever is described seems taken out of human experience and out of history. Instead, the popularizer must capture readers' attention with stories that illustrate a natural process in a way that places the reader "right in the action." Consider these two examples:

- A *"professional science"* description: "Elephants respond aggressively when threatened."
- A *"popular science"* description: "The old bull elephant with the broken tusk charged my Land Rover when I wandered too near to his herd, which was lingering by the water hole."

In the first example, the writer refers to elephants as a nonspecific, universal group and thus emphasizes a seemingly timeless "scientific law" being described here. The writer is entirely absent from the statement: there is no "I" observing the generic elephants. This statement captures a very broad observation to be shared with other professional scientists and is also one that readers might find in a science textbook. In the second example, the writer refers very specifically to one identifiable animal and does so in ways that locate the writer as an observer in a particular place and time. A scientist "I" risks the old bull elephant's wrath. In this way, the writer also places the reader more in the

scene by making the observed process (the elephant's charge) more of
a narrative, or story, that is easy to envision. This kind of portrayal
might be found in popular science magazines like *Nature, National
Geographic,* or *Discover,* where a nonprofessional reader will learn
about new scientific advances or recently discovered places or animals.
Both of these descriptions assume an intelligent, informed reader—a
reader with a particular level of existing knowledge on the topic and
who expects certain kinds of portrayal based on the kind of information source being consulted. When we read a science textbook, we
look for different kinds of information, presented in different ways,
than we do when we pick up *National Geographic:* this second kind of
publication has a more personal voice, more lively photographs, and
more storytelling than the first does.

Rachel Carson had learned through long experience as a popular science writer how to appeal to readers in the general public. These readers had responded well to her other books, in which she had described
the beauty of the sea, salt marshes, tidal areas, and beaches. She had
been able to capture readers' imagination by sharing her own love of
specific places and telling about particular animals that lived there.
However, with the manuscript that became *Silent Spring,* Carson wrote
about many different landscapes, some of which she didn't personally
know. She had to include necessary but dry information about chemistry, with lots of research study data and expert opinions. She also described a huge, almost invisible threat in which readers weren't inclined
to believe. To buy into her frightening arguments, readers had to question industry and the government, when these organizations had provided protection from enemies and incredible improvements in the
general standard of living during post–World War II times.

Carson's first and boldest narrative gesture opens *Silent Spring.*
Rather than opening with a theoretical discussion of chemicals in the
environment, or even a careful description of a dying animal's physi-
ology, Carson crafts a truly new kind of appeal to her audience. She
appropriates the "universal" treatment usually given to examples of
scientific laws but blends this with a very old form of fiction. In a very
nonscientific move, her first chapter, "A Fable for Tomorrow," offers
a short projection, a sketch of an *imaginary* American town. This fic-
tionalized ordinary scene starts out in fairytale fashion, full of pastoral
beauty:

> The town lay in the midst of a checkerboard of prosperous farms,
> with fields of grain and hillsides of orchards where, in spring,

white clouds of blossom drifted above the green fields. In autumn, oak and maple and birch set up a blaze of color that flamed and flickered across a backdrop of pines. Then foxes barked in the hills and deer silently crossed the fields, half hidden by the mists of the fall mornings. (Carson 1)

In a few short paragraphs, however, "a strange blight" falls on the land, and all the living creatures sicken: "Everywhere was the shadow of death. The farmers spoke of much illness in their families" (Carson 2). Knowing that her readers were primed to expect the sorts of epidemics that had routinely swept through communities before the discovery of vaccines and antibiotics, Carson then drops her bombshell: this is no naturally occurring "silent spring." The insects, birds, and animals were devastated by the "white granular powder [that] ... had fallen like snow upon the roofs and lawns, the fields and streams. No witchcraft, no enemy had silenced the rebirth of new life in this stricken world. The people had done it themselves" (Carson 3). Having thus set the stage with a hypothetical extreme case, Carson then points out that, although no actual town had experienced all of the illnesses, deaths, and stillbirths that her fabled town had, some towns in America had certainly suffered one or more of them (3). The questions she deftly raises then: Why? Why has this happened? What might happen if her readers take no action?

In the remaining chapters of *Silent Spring*, Carson then answers her own question by alternating exposition (facts, figures, expert testimony, explanations) with storytelling (illustrations, examples, process descriptions, anecdotal observations) presented in a compelling "popularizer" style. Beyond the "fable" of the first chapter, Carson includes many vivid images to flesh out her scientific claims. For example, in a chapter titled "Needless Havoc," she presents several examples of how pesticides used to combat a problem either did not accomplish this goal, or caused much more widespread damage than the problem, or both. The Japanese Beetle—termed a nuisance insect because it damaged crops and suburban plantings but never in devastating amounts—is Carson's case in point. Telling the story of this insect's accidental introduction and rapid spread in North America (a native of Asia, it had no natural predators in this new area), the chapter details the huge pesticide programs deployed in various states, alternating with records of tremendous bird and fish kills. In Michigan's effort to control this minor pest, Carson writes, a cheap pesticide called aldrin was dropped copiously and indiscriminately from low-flying planes (90), in such large amounts that its granules looked like snow (91). This pesticide program resulted in bird kills all around De-troit and in human illnesses among workers exposed in the aerial ef-fort: "nausea, vomiting, chills, fever, extreme fatigue, and coughing" (Carson 91). Another township in the Midwest, similarly treated with this pesticide, recorded an 80 percent death rate for songbirds that had been banded and researched by birdwatchers. In Sheldon, Illinois, a similar program using the pesticide dieldrin (a chemical 50 times as potent as DDT) produced widespread death, which Carson sketches out with lists of the dead: insect-eating birds (robins, meadowlarks, pheasants, grackles, starlings who ate the insects or bathed in rain pud-dles) and small mammals (squirrels, muskrats, and farm cats that ate the dead animals or simply licked their own fur and feet) (93). But Carson, the expert popular science writer, leaves readers with a truly horrifying description that burns an image of death's process into our memory. She wonders whether the question of pesticide use is just sci-entific, or also moral (99), and then quotes from reports that scientists made on the Sheldon incident. These observers noted the strong evi-dence of chemical poisoning:

> The mute testimony of the dead ground squirrels, which "exhib-ited a characteristic attitude in death. The back was bowed, and the forelegs with the toes of the feet tightly clenched were drawn close to the thorax. The head and neck were outstretched and the mouth often contained dirt, suggesting that the dying animal had been biting at the ground." (100)

Perhaps readers would have been persuaded by all the statistics and lists, and felt sorry for all the dead birds and mammals that had been counted, but Carson winds up her chapter with an image that under-lines her moral questions: is it right for us to use chemicals that can do this to a small animal that has done us no harm? Is it right to spread a pesticide of questionable effectiveness against the Japanese Beetle, when it is so violently "effective" as a killer of other creatures? How can we call ourselves a *civilized* culture, if we kill so heedlessly in this way?

These samples from *Silent Spring* offer some hints of what made Rachel Carson's arguments so effective in 1962, when the very idea of pesticides as dangerous was frighteningly new. Most readers would not have considered the facts—which simply were not generally known—nor would they have any personally compelling stories to help them understand the trail of causes and effects that Carson traced. Yet her precise blend of statistics and stories, "fable" and fact, set in motion a broader environmental movement that, within a decade, had pushed for the Environmental Protection Agency and a large number of laws and programs that now protect us all. Those laws and programs have been effective, and Carson's cautious, skeptical attitudes about human interventions in the environment have come to be more prevalent, if not dominant, in our culture. The species most affected by DDT, like the brown pelican, the bald eagle, and the California condor, have been protected from excessive pesticide use and reintroduced into the wild. The "general readers" Carson addressed have become much more savvy about chemicals in the environment—and in their own bodies. The government and industries are much less cavalier about damaging the ecosystems around us than they were in the 1950s and 1960s.

However, Rachel Carson would surely warn that the political work of environmentalists is never done. Despite the tremendous advances in environmental protection, we readers need to keep on choosing "the other road" *Silent Spring* sets out, for all the reasons that this powerful book examines in such excruciating scientific detail and with such profoundly lyrical description. In its final pages, Carson leaves us with the imperative that we retain a crucial awareness

> that we are dealing with life—with living populations and all their pressures and counter-pressures, their urges and recessions. Only by taking account of such life forces and by cautiously seeking to guide them into channels favorable to ourselves can we hope to achieve a reasonable accommodation between the insect hordes and ourselves. (296)

In this way, humans can move beyond the "Stone Age" (297) view of the world as simply existing for our use; with Rachel Carson, we can evolve to viewing natural environments as our home and the creatures in them as our equals in the right to live and flourish.

BIBLIOGRAPHY

Brooks, Peter. *The House of Life: Rachel Carson at Work*. New York: Houghton, 1972.
Carson, Rachel. *Silent Spring*. New York: Houghton. 1962.
Davidson, H. Letter. *The New Yorker*. 20 & 27 Feb. 1995: 18.

Freeman, Martha, ed. *Always, Rachel: The Letters of Rachel Carson and Dorothy Freeman, 1952–1964.* Boston: Beacon, 1995.

Lear, Linda. *Rachel Carson: Witness for Nature.* New York: Holt, 1997.

Myers, Greg. *Writing Biology: Texts in the Social Construction of Scientific Knowledge.* Madison: U of Wisconsin P, 1990.

Waddell, Craig. *And No Birds Sing: Rhetorical Analyses of Rachel Carson's Silent Spring.* Carbondale: Southern Illinois U P, 2000.

4

Wallace Stegner, *The Sound of Mountain Water* (1969)

Michael P. Cohen

The materials Wallace Stegner collected for *The Sound of Mountain Water* reveal him at the most creative and productive era of his life, demonstrating his elegance of expression and his importance as a writer. In these essays he articulated emerging ideas of environmental preservation in the mid-century western United States.

In terms of history, these essays reveal the gestation period of the Wilderness Act, itself discussed and advocated by a group of conservationists including David Brower, Aldo Leopold, and Howard Zahniser, especially in the era following World War II. Stegner's own struggles of conscience reveal him as an acute observer of the West who saw the problems of rapid development of natural resources. He found federally designated wilderness an important solution to the awkward and dangerous social and economic changes rapidly transforming the western landscape. His defense of wilderness in "Wilderness Letter"—entitled "Coda: Wilderness Letter" for this volume—is surrounded by other concerns that these essays explore.

HISTORICAL CONTEXT

Stegner does not pretend to stand outside of history. His committed position reveals many of the predicaments of those who are interested in the environmental history of the United States, who believe that the historical ideas and practices of the past must always be seen as determining the treatment of the environment in the present, who believe that old myths won't work but who also believe that no one can escape the legacy of past ideas.

Stegner's analysis of environmental problems and his positions on environmental issues are not separable from his sense of participation in the historical, contemporary, and personal history of the cultural West. His arguments for wilderness are connected to his works of fiction and history because he refuses to keep them separate: consequently he is truly interdisciplinary because he is a committed writer. He writes about environment as a cultural issue in which all of our acts are implicated.

Stegner cannot abstract western history or an objective view of environment from his own personal experience; for him all knowledge is local in its beginnings, situated in a place and evoked through concrete experience. Yet he is thoroughly committed to larger abstract cultural institutions for which he speaks. He speaks not only for himself but also for conservation groups like the Sierra Club. In a larger sense, he speaks for the value of universities and libraries and for culture in the American West.

In his fusion of concerns about the natural and cultural evolution of the American West, he ask for reconciliation, for the delicate working out and accommodating of the shape of the culture to meet and adjust to the realities and the aesthetics of the place. Stegner speaks for nature and for culture and for their two-way transaction, the interdependence of both on each other.

He accepts the responsibility for living and writing in a changing world and for participating fully in public discussions about the directions of its change. In particular, he reveals his debt to his mentor, Bernard DeVoto in "The West Emphatic: Bernard DeVoto," and this essay tells us a great deal about the tradition of environmental rhetoric he inherited and passed on.

STRUCTURE AND CONTEXT

The structure and intentions of *The Sound of Mountain Water* became paradigmatic for his later collections; all of them mediate between personal reminiscence, historical meditations, literary assessments, and at the center, focus on ethical responsibilities of Americans to their landscape. Indeed, his environmental values and his mode of expressing them changed very little over his career.

Nevertheless, this volume falls within the context of his earlier and later nonfiction writings about Americans within their landscape. These writings began with *Beyond the Hundredth Meridian* (1954) and *This is Dinosaur* (1955). Stegner's way of thinking is precisely described by one of his key titles: *Wolf Willow: A History, a Story, and a Memoir of the Last Plains Frontier* (1962). His thinking of Americans and their environment continued with *The Gathering of Zion* (1964). The most concise statement of his views is in *The American West as Living Space* (1987), and the last collection he produced, *Where the Bluebird Sings* (1992), is remarkably similar in structure to the collection *Marking the Sparrow's Fall* (1998), in progress when he died and edited by his son, Page. Each retrospective collection begins with history, places conservation at the center of the volume, and ends with essays on western writers.

Stegner's prose style is distinct, personal, and direct, unashamedly cast in the first person for reasons that become clear. The early essays in *The Sound of Mountain Water,* several written in the 1940s, are less sure of themselves than later ones become; as he gets older, he becomes more moralistic, more sure of himself, and sometimes more simplistic in his arguments.

STYLISTIC ANALYSIS

Since his death in 1993, several influential collections about Stegner have appeared, some as tributes, and some that attempt to assess his importance as a commentator on the West. Essays collected in these volumes attempt to establish Stegner as more than what Yvor Winters once called him, a "Western Realist" (Benson, *Wallace Stegner* 338). Individual tributes often focus on his qualities "as a man," emphasizing such qualities as "kindness, courtesy, responsibility, and hard work" (Benson, *Lemonade Springs* xii). Terry Tempest Williams speaks of his dignity, his steadiness, his wisdom, his civility (Introduction, *Crossing to Safety* xvii). Charles Wilkinson speaks of Stegner's integrity and authenticity, as a writer and a man ("Wallace Stegner and the Shaping of the Modern West," Meine 8). Many commentators are directly indebted to Stegner's generosity toward younger writers; we owe him a great debt because of his personal encouragement, and we must credit our own ability to write about the West to his sharp eye for accurate and authentic writing. Speaking for a new generation of western historians, Patti Limerick speaks of him as "a guide we have in common" ("Precedents to Wisdom," in Page Stegner and Mary Stegner 28).

Yet some acknowledge differences from his views and style. Eliott West notices how traditional Stegner's view of the wilderness is, and how he sought a "unified vision of the American West" ("Wallace

Stegner's West, Wilderness, and History," Meine 87, 85). Stegner's version of the West *is* being revised, as is evidenced by Donald Worster's recent book, *A River Running West: The Life of John Wesley Powell* (2001), which gives a more complex version of Powell than Stegner provided in 1954.

But about Stegner's central theme, aridity, most are in absolute agreement. Our West is the region beyond the 100th meridian; it begins with the mountains; its feel, as he writes, includes "a dryness in the nostrils, a cracking of the lips, a transparent crystalline quality of the light...a new palette of grey, sage-green, sulphur yellow, buff, toned white, rust red, a new flora and fauna, a new ecology" (*Sound* 13). Aridity is an absolute geographical fact. "The West's ultimate unity is its aridity" (15). Water is scarce; precious little precipitation falls as snow on the high mountains; it flows down toward the places where life can exist. Consequently, the title, *The Sound of Mountain Water*, is complex in its personal, geographical, historical, and policy-making implications: it contains a central paradox. The sound of water is the sound of life in a region where life is tenuous, and depends on a limited resource. The sound of mountain water is sweet because it is the sound of a rare and essential source of life here, not given with generosity.

THEMATIC AND RHETORICAL COMPONENTS

One of Wallace Stegner's generosities was to provide articulation for the environmental values of his generation. He spoke to the sense of duty to place, and its value. In all of his works of nonfiction, he expressed his uneasiness with the direction of progress. His ambivalence begins with his membership in the West as a cultural region: he claimed to be an insider but also claimed to be rootless. So Stegner's environmental essays: they are about the cultural West and speak to the causes of his generation, providing a foundation for the ones we might write.

At the center of *The Sound of Mountain Water's* "Coda: Wilderness Letter" is its profession that wilderness is "part of a geography of hope." Written in 1960, as part of the campaign for the Wilderness Act of 1964, the essay is revered and quoted, and it is also critiqued for its abstract and anthropomorphic rationale. President Kennedy's Secretary of the Interior, Stewart Udall, loved the essay and enlisted Stegner in the writing of *The Quiet Crisis* (Benson, *Lemonade Springs* 40).

Having its own literary geography, one that includes more than wilderness alone, the essay is surrounded by questions of water and aridity, questions of myth and history of the West, by the sound of water, and by the silences of its absence. It is preceded by excursions into places of the West and it is followed by discussions of western writers. The book is shaped according to his own mapping of the West beyond the 100th meridian, from place to conception of place, to historical and literary representations of the place.

Stegner inherited his ideas of the West from John Wesley Powell and refined them—indeed he was writing his Powell biography during the time that he first published several of these essays. Stegner's ideas of the West embody now-contested ideas about the region as a frontier, a term grounded in arguments made by Frederick Jackson Turner. Stegner's arguments are also Turnerian.

In 1892, Turner wrote "On the Significance of the Frontier in American History," and announced a crisis of discontinuity between open and closed Wests, between the freedom of the wilderness and what followed, a damaging transition from individualism to mass society. Stegner's views sometimes suggest that he belatedly applies the Turnerian view of the end of the frontier to mid-century America, and it is true that much of Utah, in particular, in 1940 was still frontier by the census criteria of 1890. Stegner seemed to live uneasily in both Wests at the same time.

Reading his essays rhetorically allows us to explore the strengths and limitations of Stegner's formation of arguments for wilderness, particularly his use of Turner's ideas in them. So these arguments have a tradition. Edward Abbey, once Stegner's student at Stanford, insists that wilderness needs no defense, only defenders, while more recently William Cronon, in "The Trouble with Wilderness," argues that wilderness is entirely a cultural construction. Stegner refused to be part of that argument. He says both and then turns to matters of human value and ethical responsibility to the land.

"Wilderness Letter" came from Stegner's pen at a time of crisis in the West, and as Eliott West has observed, Stegner's theme in other essays, especially "History, Myth, and the Western Writer," is crisis. West also notes that Stegner's version of the crisis of western identity "*has* to be taken, in fact—in two ways. It refers both to what the West is and to who westerners are" (Rankin 63). The crisis is part of a process of mutual shaping.

So there is no separating Stegner's West from his westerner. There is a kind of ecology between the two. Stegner himself believed in neither rugged individualism nor mass society; he wished to see neither an all-wild West nor an entirely developed landscape, and in these "neithers and nors" lay the ambivalence that was so productive to his thought. Consequently, Stegner sees both crisis and hope in his "geography of hope." That vision of ecological process allows him to be more flexible and more constructive than Turner.

In other words, Stegner has more than separate ideas about this mutual shaping; he reveals the dynamic between the natural and cultural West.

Stegner's honesty has never been in question, nor has his good will, nor his generosity. His knowledge often required that he second-guess the wilderness leaders he served with his pen. For instance, the wilderness movement chose to oppose the dam proposed for Dinosaur National Monument but not the dam proposed for Glen Canyon. To Stegner, Glen Canyon was not *The Place No One Knew: Glen Canyon on the Colorado,* as the Sierra Club had entitled its book with Eliot Porter's photographs that elegized the lost canyon, and he said so. But he "didn't push it," after the Sierra Club and The Wilderness Society set their priorities (Cohen 178; Thomas 175–77). There is honesty in his openness in presenting his program and in compromising with his institutional allies; that openness allows a critique of these positions.

The tone and syntax of *The Sound of Mountain Water* reveals how ambivalent Stegner was about the West and about his place, or our place in it, about the extent to which generational divides found him on one or another side of the ridge that held headwaters from rivers flowing in separate directions. He was caught between traditional and modern concerns, was neither an anti-modernist nor a modernist, neither perfectly hopeful and of a community, nor hopelessly despairing and willing to own membership in an alienated generation.

We continue to revere and critique. Particularly interesting is the argument between Ann Ronald and J. J. Benson centering on Stegner's ideology (For Ronald, "Stegner and Stewardship," see Rankin 87–103; for Benson, "Evaluating the Environmentalist," see Benson, *Lemonade Springs* 45–60). But "Wilderness Letter" continues to be useful, because it reveals the kinds of arguments that were made in 1960, the kinds of arguments that could be made at the time, and consequently the tradition of these arguments that might ground our own. It is a kind of landmark. Read carefully, it is about more than Stegner and is about those who cared about the mutual process.

For as Dan Flores has commented, speaking of Stegner's *The American West as Living Space,* we tend to carry Stegner's books as we travel through the West, and carry his ideas too, as if they were sacred texts: "I suspect I am like a lot of others in internalizing Stegner's ideas that way" (Rankin 75). Flores echoes Stegner's style in his own sentence: he has managed to echo the voice, using the kind of syntax Stegner himself might have used, to create Stegner's careful, unassuming, and tentative grasping after certainty in a place of crisis. This is the voice. This is what matters.

Because Stegner cared about books and admired makers of books, it is fitting that the concluding essay of *The Sound of Mountain Water* is a formal talk given at the opening of a public library. Such a conclusion reminds us of his literary allegiances. The title of his book, is, after all, metaphorical. The metaphor suggests or even insists on our asking about the way a writer might speak for a landscape, or for what is sometimes called a resource, as a scarce cultural lifeline and why this approach might have more power than treating landscape only as natural. While purists worry about anthropocentrism in his writings, Stegner did compose a viable wilderness idea, and though there is trouble in it, his strategy is worth scrutinizing.

CULTURAL CONTEXT

How a western writer feels about the people who utilize the scarce resources matters immensely. One might compare Stegner's essay, "Born a Square" in *Sound* with "Walter Clark's Frontier," written twenty years later and collected in *Bluebird*. "The thesis of this piece," Stegner writes in "Born a Square," "is that the western writer is in a box with booby traps at both ends" (170). At one end is "an inadequate artistic and intellectual tradition," and at the other end is a set of attitudes and values "destructive of his own," that come from an East-Coast literary tradition "that appears to specialize in despair, hostility, hypersexuality, and disgust" (172). Stegner imagines the western writer as a "native-white-Protestant second-or third generation immigrant kind of boy," who grows up in fresh air, in a western city of pre-industrial sort (172). He is faced with a litany of offensive modernist attitudes. Stegner seems to violate every canon of political correctness when he speaks of eastern literary folk as "Expatriots, beats, faggots, junkies," Southerners, Negroes, and Jews, whose "special masochism" the westerner is not likely to understand (174, 175). In a comment that anticipates by inversion his later idea that it is useful for the eastern intellectual like Leslie Fiedler to show up in the West for a while, as long as he doesn't stick around, Stegner says "the western writer should go away and get his eyes opened, and then look back" (183). Nevertheless, the westerner, as a denizen of "the New World's last chance to be something better," has an imperative to avoid the "Russian-Jewish tradition of emotional volatility. With the highest respect for Bellow, I have to throw in with Hemingway, at least on this issue, because I grew up in stiff-upper-lip country. We have the obligation to be ourselves, even when it seems we are squares" (184).

Consequently, he treats Clark, who was a native of Reno, as a westerner like himself, native to a place where all life depends on a single mountain stream. As in the former essay, "Born a Square," Stegner speaks of himself when he speaks of Clark: "For he could not forget, and neither can I, that the western experience is more than personal; it is part of the process of civilization building" (*Bluebird* 180).

Elizabeth Cook-Lynn has pointed out in *Why I Can't Read Wallace Stegner*, that to believe that western experience was "part of the process of civilization building," was to absent the Native American and to claim indigenousness for the European immigrant. Stegner does say that "The western naïveté of strenuousness, pragmatism, meliorism, optimism, and the stiff upper lip is our tradition" (*Sound* 184). He does believe that he and his colleagues had personally witnessed the end of the frontier, the end of a certain process, and the beginning of another, a single, unified process, unique to his generation's "western experience." Further, when he speaks optimistically of the West, in an unrevised passage that concludes the introduction to *Sound* in the 1969 and 1980 editions, he produces a kind of muted boosterism for utopian western possibilities. "Born a Square" ends on the note of hope: "This is not exhortation, neither is it prophesy. It is only, since I am from the west and incorrigible, hope" (185). The last sentence of "Coda" ends with the geography of hope. The concluding passage of the introduction to *Sound* includes *hope* as the key term:

Angry as one may be at what heedless men have done and still do to a noble habitat, one cannot be pessimistic about the West. This is the native land of hope. When it fully learns that cooperation, not rugged individualism, is the quality that most characterizes and preserves it, then it will have achieved itself and outlived its origins. Then it has a chance to create a society to match its scenery. (38)

What reason for hope, why is it native, and how might a society match its scenery? Is civilization building that goes on in the American West by some process different from anywhere else? Is civilization building a universal human enterprise? Is the test of a society that it somehow live up to the scenery in which it is embedded, that the aesthetic promise of the landscape is the standard by which it might be judged?

Clearly, Stegner is committed to high civilization, to libraries, and to reasoned discourse, to concrete acts, and not to mystical revelations; he believes that westerners should build something worthy of the resources used for construction. All of these are values that good students must question. It is easy to assent and hard to criticize, because Stegner's uneasiness about the West so gracefully evokes our own that we tend to assimilate it too easily without asking whether it is truly the same uneasiness that we feel, or something different, with different grounds, and from a distant time, not like our own.

When he considered the historical context for "Wilderness Letter"—in an essay for *Living Wilderness* (1980) that was later republished in *Marking the Sparrow's Fall* (1998)—Stegner pointed out that in 1960, the situation was as follows:

> When I wrote my "wilderness letter" to David Pesonen 20 years ago, I had probably been prompted to do so by David Brower. He was usually the cattleprod that woke me from other preoccupations and from my workaholism and directed my attention to something important. In this case what he woke me to was close to my heart. . . . The Wilderness Bill, already debated for years and the subject of hundreds of official pages, had not yet passed. The ORRRC report, with its inventory of what remained of our outdoors and its promise of reorganization of the bureaus managing it, seemed a good place to put in a word. (117)

As usual, Stegner is rather humble about his own contribution: "By luck or accident or the mysterious focusing by which ideas whose time has come reach many minds at the same time, my letter struck a chord" (117). Of the wide dissemination of the letter, as he said, "I take this as evidence not of special literary worth, but of an earnest, world-wide belief in the idea it expresses" (118).

He also points out that he did not attempt all arguments for wilderness but focused on one. "I was prepared to argue for the preservation of wilderness not simply as a scientific reserve, or a land-bank, or a playground, but as a spiritual resource, a leftover from our frontier origins that could reassure us of our identity as a nation and a people" (119). In other words, he does not confront all arguments but chooses a pragmatic handle, the American character, and places his argument within the shared mythology of the frontier.

In 1980, he also recognizes the way he had located his argument in a specific place, and by implication suggests that all arguments about wilderness must be rooted in place, and must be focused on places that the author values: "I spoke with some feeling about the deserts of southern Utah—Capitol Reef, the San Rafael Swell, the Escalante Desert, the Aquarius Plateau" (119). He focused on personal places and used a personal voice, but we may ask whether the place evoked the argument or whether the argument used specific place to buttress its structure.

The voice of the essay, quintessential Stegner, does not change over the years, despite what he wrote twenty years later, "Returning to the letter after 20 years, I find that my opinions have not changed. They have actually been sharpened by an increased urgency" (118). That his opinions have not changed and that his voice had not changed as a result of increased urgency tells us something of his unchanging loyalties to the wilderness idea and to civility and decorum. Speaking for wilderness, he uses an unassuming style, informal, unique, not quite matter-of-fact, but decisive, as in passages like the following: "It is good for us when we are young, because of the incomparable sanity it can bring briefly, as vacation and rest, into our insane lives. It is important to us when we are old simply because it is there—important, that is, simply as an idea" (147).

Stegner's "wilderness *idea*" (146) does not distinguish between a specific place designated by the government as wilderness and the idea of wilderness. It is partly humanistic: "I want to speak for the wilderness idea as something that has helped form our character and that has certainly shaped our history as a people" (146). It is a counter to what Stegner fears, "the Brave New World of a completely man-controlled environment" (147). Yet in an era when many writers were producing Jeremiads, full of gloom and doom, Stegner chose a rousing conclusion: "We simply need that wild country available to us, even if we never do more than drive to its edge and look in. For it can be a means of reassuring ourselves of our sanity as creatures, a part of the geography of hope" (153).

Strangely enough, Stegner explores ideas primarily about culture here, the development of society in the West. To understand the evolution of these ideas, one must see his own cultural background.

CULTURAL BACKGROUND

Bernard DeVoto and Wallace Stegner grew up in Utah as outsiders; they had similar concerns; they became close colleagues and confidantes; and DeVoto impelled Stegner to enter public controversies about the West. Stegner wrote an admiring biography of DeVoto, *The Uneasy Chair* (1974). Their chief concerns began within the cultural world that formed them in Utah.

In an August 1934 *Harper's* article, "The Plundered Province," DeVoto first spoke of the West as "innocent victim of an empire building financial colonialism run out of Wall Street" and aided and abetted by the "governmental stupidity" of Washington. "Looted, betrayed, sold out, the Westerner is a man whose history has been just a series of large scale jokes" (Thomas 37). Thus he began his career as a columnist by serving as a spokesman defending western public lands from eastern capitalism. But he could not portray westerners as innocent victims for long; his rhetoric shifted from blaming eastern financiers for the plundering of the West's resources to later attention toward homegrown despoilers, particularly the group later called the Sagebrush Rebels of Utah and Nevada, who wanted all federal lands ceded to the individual states, who would then dispose of them to private entrepreneurs.

Stegner conceived the history of his place in a different way: "I have an exaggerated sense of place," he told an interviewer in the1980s,"I also have a feeling that my personal experiences are all I surely know, and these experiences are very likely to be rooted in places" (42). For Stegner, more than for DeVoto, these places were more likely to be natural, not cultural. Stegner also admitted in an interview, "I don't suppose I missed history...until I was at least middle aged and then I realized that I didn't have a single place to which I could refer myself" (50). In part Stegner was speaking of his relationship as an outsider to Mormon culture, but he also spoke of the human condition; after all, the Wilderness Act of 1964 defines wilderness as "a place where man is a visitor, but does not remain" (Nash 200–37). Consequently, the western paradox is internal and biographical in these writers, especially acute in Stegner. As John Thomas writes, in *A Country in the Mind: Wallace Stegner, Bernard DeVoto, History, and the American Land,* "The legacy bequeathed to DeVoto and Stegner took the form of a Western paradox composed of paired opposites: endless space and confining space; openings and barriers; belonging and rootlessness; opportunities and limits; freedom and constraint; dream and fact" (59). Stegner is urban and wants civilization, yet he disdains civilization that comes from the East; he detests the modern and hopes western culture will keep its distance from the modern and develop independently; the idea of the West as plundered province and as a colony is someplace beyond his desire to preserve wilderness.

His personal experience was not only local but also national. "There were two powerful constraints on environmental thinking in the early fifties; McCarthyism and the Republican developmentalism" (Thomas 140). Eisenhower's Secretary of Interior McKay linked these explicitly in 1953, when he said, "I have no sympathy for those mistaken souls who preach our forests should be socialized and turned over...for...stewardship" (146). Stegner and DeVoto saw America faced with big money versus big government and states' rights versus people's rights, and they chose. Maybe this was a choice of evils, but they lined up with big government as protector of the people's rights (159).

Many western legislators, like Patrick McCarren of Nevada, spoke for both the Sagebrush Rebellion and for McCarthyism. From the DeVoto/Stegner perspective, these two movements attacked free speech and democratic government and promised to damage the natural and cultural roots of Americans. Also, a stand for states' rights allied them to racists in the southern states. Thinking about the "Wilderness Letter" in 1980, Stegner wrote:

> The Sagebrush Rebellion is the worst enemy not only of long-range management of the public lands, but of wilderness. If its counterpart in the 1940s had won, we would have no wilderness areas at all, and deteriorated national forests. If it wins in the 1980s we will have only such wilderness as is already formally set aside. Federal bureaus are imperfect human institutions, and have sins to answer for, and are not above being influenced by powerful interests. Nevertheless they represent the public interest, by and large, and not corporate interests anxious to exploit public resources at the public's expense. (Stegner, *Marking the Sparrow's Fall* 119)

Though we might speak of Stegner and DeVoto as environmentalists, like others of their era, they spoke of themselves as "conservationists." Our justification for using the term "environmentalist"—normally reserved for the period after 1970—is premised on their theories of geographical determinism and on their recognition of environmental limits to the growth of civilization in the West. In other words, they believed that geography determined destiny, "the physical confrontation of the High Plains and Rocky Mountains which shaped the behavior of the diverse peoples who crossed them or settled there" (Thomas 60, 61). Geographical determinism leads Stegner to recognize and focus on limits, particularly as a result of aridity: "Aridity alone makes the various Wests one." Consequently, writing western history meant writing environmental history, where environment was a strong character in every story and often played a determining role. As historians they were committed to teaching environmental lessons, as, about the "legacy of limits" (62). As Stegner put it, "You may deny it for a while. Then you must try to engineer it out of existence or adapt to it."

CONCLUSION

However, in the 1950s, in the world of McCarthyism and Sagebrush Rebellion where McKay could argue that conservation was Communism, where states' rights became a strategy to continue racism, only certain arguments could be made about public policy in the public domain.

"A place is nothing in itself," Stegner wrote in "The Marks of Human Passage," his introduction to *This Is Dinosaur*, "It has no meaning, it can hardly be said to exist, except in terms of human perception, use, and response" (15). Such an approach has led many critics to speak of Stegner's anthropocentrism. But he also wrote, on the previous page, "We live in an Antibiotic Age, and Antibiotic means 'against life.' We had better not be against life. That is the way to become as extinct as the dinosaurs" (14).

Stegner made a conscious decision to frame his arguments in terms of human welfare and human decisions; his perspective is unashamedly anthropocentric, civilized, and cultured. When Stegner spoke for wilderness, he chose to speak for his community and generation; he chose to be a man of his time. Further, his essays were often commissioned by the Sierra Club and The Wilderness Society. Leaders of these groups discussed appropriate strategies for such arguments, at

Sierra Club Biennial Wilderness conferences in the 1940s and 1950s, and decided quite explicitly not to make biocentric arguments but to speak for stewardship and the human value of wilderness (Cohen 126–29). They were of their time and spoke to the 1950s. Consequently, Stegner crafted arguments within these parameters; speaking for his generation's communal decisions, he reflected their constraints as much as his own, constraints revealed in his choice of tone and content, his approach and discovery of arguments first evident in the book *This Is Dinosaur*. Stegner's arguments reflect choices of the newly emerging wilderness movement, and these choices gave us the Wilderness Act of 1964. We must honor Stegner's choice to serve his cultural and institutional community not as an iconoclast but as an advocate for constructive change.

BIBLIOGRAPHY

Benson, Jackson J. *Wallace Stegner: His Life and Work.* New York: Viking, 1996.

———. *Down by the Lemonade Springs: Essays on Wallace Stegner.* Western Literature Series. Reno: U of Nevada P, 2001.

Cohen, Michael. *The History of the Sierra Club, 1892–1970.* San Francisco: Sierra Club Books, 1988.

Cook-Lynn, Elizabeth. *Why I Can't Read Wallace Stegner and Other Essays: A Tribal Voice.* Madison: U of Wisconsin P, 1996.

Cronon, William. "The Trouble with Wilderness." *Uncommon Ground.* Ed. William Cronon. New York: Norton, 1996. 69–90.

Etulain, Richard W., ed. *Conversations with Wallace Stegner on Western History and Literature.* Foreword by Stewart L. Udall. Rev. ed. Reno: U of Nevada P, 1996.

Meine, Curt, ed. *Wallace Stegner and the Continental Vision: Essays on Literature, History, and Landscape.* Washington, DC: Island Press, 1997.

Nash, Roderick, *Wilderness and the American Mind.* New Haven: Yale UP, 1967.

Rankin, Charles E., ed. *Wallace Stegner : Man and Writer.* Foreword by Stewart L. Udall. Albuquerque: U of New Mexico P, 1996.

Stegner, Page, ed. *Marking the Sparrow's Fall: Wallace Stegner's American West.* Ed. with a Preface by Page Stegner. New York: Holt, 1998.

Stegner, Page, and Mary Stegner, ed. *The Geography of Hope: A Tribute to Wallace Stegner.* San Francisco: Sierra Club Books, 1996.

Stegner, Wallace Earle, 1909–. *Beyond the Hundredth Meridian: John Wesley Powell and the Second Opening of the West*. Introduction by Bernard DeVoto. Lincoln: U of Nebraska P, 1954.

———. *The Sound of Mountain Water*. 1969. Rev. ed. Garden City, N.Y: Doubleday, 1980.

———. *The Uneasy Chair: A Biography of Bernard DeVoto*. Garden City, N.Y.: Doubleday, 1974.

———. "The Geography of Hope." *Living Wilderness*, 1980.

———. *The American West as Living Space*. Ann Arbor: U of Michigan P, 1987.

———. *Crossing to Safety*. 1987. New York: Modern Library, 2002.

Stegner, Wallace Earle, and Wayne Owens, eds. *Wilderness at the Edge: A Citizen Proposal to Protect Utah's Canyons and Deserts*. Introduction by Wallace Stegner. Foreword by Wayne Owens. Salt Lake City: Utah Wilderness Coalition/Gibbs Smith, 1990.

Thomas, John L. *A Country in the Mind: Wallace Stegner, Bernard DeVoto, History, and the American Land*. New York: Routledge, 2000.

Worster, Donald. *A River Running West: The Life of John Wesley Powell*. New York: Oxford UP, 2001.

5

Ursula K. Le Guin,
The Earthsea Trilogy (1972)

Susan Palwick

Ursula K. Le Guin's *Earthsea Trilogy* consists of *A Wizard of Earthsea* (1968), *The Tombs of Atuan* (1971), and *The Farthest Shore* (1972). The scope of Earthsea in fact extends beyond these three books; Le Guin dates her own "first approach to and exploration of" Earthsea to two stories she published in 1964 (*Wind's* 65); in 1990 she published a fourth Earthsea novel, *Tehanu,* and in 2001 she published both *Tales from Earthsea,* a story collection, and *The Other Wind,* a fifth Earthsea novel. The present essay will discuss only the trilogy, as these novels form the core of the Earthsea canon; in addition to being the best known of the Earthsea stories, they are among the best known of all of Le Guin's writings.

LE GUIN'S WRITING

Le Guin's writing career has been varied and illustrious; she has published 19 novels, 9 story collections, 2 books of translation, 10 volumes of poetry, 12 children's books, 2 essay collections, screenplays, and sound recordings (Homepage). She has won more than 30 awards for her writing, including 2 Lifetime Achievement Awards, from the Pacific NW Booksellers Association and the L.A. *Times,* and a number of science-fiction awards, including multiple Hugos (awarded by the membership of the World Science Fiction Convention) and Nebulas (awarded by the membership of the Science Fiction and Fantasy Writers of America). Although Le Guin's work, especially her more recent writing, often blurs genre boundaries, she is best known as a writer of science fiction and fantasy, and *The Earthsea Tril-*

ogy has been hailed as a fantasy classic that appeals to many people who do not usually read fantasy. All three volumes won non-genre awards: *A Wizard of Earthsea* won the Boston *Globe* Horn Book Award for Excellence; *The Tombs of Atuan* won the Newberry Award; and *The Farthest Shore* won the National Book Award for Children's Books.

The Earthsea Trilogy, like Le Guin's other work, is deeply concerned with the ecological themes of wholeness and balance, of respect for the natural world and living things, and of the limits and proper uses of power. The novels are set in Earthsea, an invented world consisting of an archipelago of islands with a diversity of languages and cultures. The stories are separated by a number of years. Their common element is the wizard Ged, who begins as an apprentice in *A Wizard of Earthsea* and has become Archmage of Roke by the time we reach *The Farthest Shore.* Each novel is narrated from the viewpoint of a young person; each is a coming-of-age story leading the character, and the reader, into widening experience and wisdom. In *A Wizard of Earthsea,* the viewpoint character is Ged himself; in the other two novels, it is some-one else who learns from him, who helps him and is helped by him. In *The Tombs of Atuan,* Ged helps Tenar, the high priestess of an ancient cult, break free of the imprisonment of a belief system she never chose; in *The Farthest Shore,* the young prince Arren accompanies Ged on his quest to defeat a powerful wizard who is destroying magic itself. The scope of the trilogy becomes broader with each successive novel. In *A Wizard of Earthsea,* Ged must confront an opponent who turns out to be himself. In *The Tombs of Atuan,* the primary conflict is interpersonal, between Ged and Tenar. In *The Farthest Shore,* Ged and Arren must face a threat to the entire world.

This movement—from relationship with self, to relationship with another person, to relationship with society—parallels Le Guin's argument about the functions of fantasy in her 1975 essay "The Child and the Shadow." Here she claims that fantasy's use of myth and arche-type, rather than making it escapist—as many critics unsympathetic to the genre would claim—instead render it timelessly relevant. According to Le Guin, fantasy stories about imaginary worlds help children (and adults) learn to confront real-world injustice and evil. She em-ploys Jungian psychology to define "the shadow" as "all the qualities and tendencies within us which have been repressed, denied, or not used" (*Language* 64), and claims that "fantasy is the natural, the ap-propriate, language for the recounting of the spiritual journey and the struggle of good and evil in the soul" (*Child* 68). The task of fantasy, then, is to help the reader gain self-knowledge, "to see himself and the shadow he casts," so that he will be better equipped to confront the evils of the wider world, "the injustices and grief and suffering that we all must bear, and the final shadow at the end of all" (*Child* 70).

One of the stories Le Guin discusses in "The Child and the Shadow" is J. R. R. Tolkien's *The Lord of the Rings,* a work she loves and about which she has frequently written. When she wrote *The Earthsea Trilogy,* heroic quest fantasy had become immensely popular as the result of the publication of Tolkien's epic, which was first published in the mid-fifties but did not gain a wide readership until a decade later. Fantasy writer Peter S. Beagle, commenting in 1973 upon why it took Tolkien's work so long to attract attention, linked Tolkien's popularity to growing environmental awareness:

> The Sixties were no fouler a decade than the Fifties—they merely reaped the Fifties' foul harvest—but they were the years when millions of people grew aware that the industrial society had become paradoxically unlivable, incalculably immoral, and ultimately deadly.... [Tolkien] is a great enough magician to tap our most common nightmares, daydreams and twilight fancies, but he never invented them either: he found them a place to live, a green alternative to each day's madness here in a poisoned world.

Certainly the sixties saw a number of landmarks in environmental history, such as the first Clean Water Act (1960), the founding of the World Wildlife Fund (1961), and the 1962 publication of Rachel Carson's vastly influential *Silent Spring,* describing the danger of toxic chemicals to the environment. Le Guin's first two Earthsea stories, "The Word of Unbinding" and "The Rule of Names," were both published in 1964, the year Congress passed the Wilderness Act, and "The Word of Unbinding" reflects this cultural moment in being deeply concerned with place and landscape. In Le Guin's introduction to "The Word of Unbinding" in her 1975 story collection *The Wind's Twelve Quarters,* she observes that the story "reveals a certain obsession with trees, which, once you notice them, keep cropping up throughout my work. I think I am definitely the most arboreal science fiction writer" (*Wind's* 65).

THEMES

Environmental awareness in *The Earthsea Trilogy* expresses itself as an emphasis on wholeness and balance, seen in three prominent themes: 1) *reverence,* or the importance of studying things to learn what they are in themselves; 2) *interdependence,* not only in the connections between all that exists, but in the need to accept the shadow, the parts of ourselves and others we would choose to deny; and 3) *restraint,* not exerting power for change unless absolutely necessary, since changing one thing changes the entire world. These principles illustrate Le Guin's embrace of Taoism, the Eastern philosophy emphasizing the importance of balancing opposites: yin and yang, good and evil, light and dark. While Le Guin does not explicitly identify these concerns as environmental, they have clear connections to ecological thinking, which honors the natural world for itself rather than its use to people, stresses the interconnectedness and fragility of life on Earth, and urges hikers and other humans to tread lightly and leave no trace. In *The Earthsea Trilogy,* these themes appear stylistically as 1) a preoccupation with names, which reflect the namer's understanding of the named object; 2) the frequent use of contrasts and dualities that then resolve into wholes; and 3) the use of stillness and silence, of small motions rather than grand gestures. Le Guin is not a fantasy writer who relies on sword fights.

A WIZARD OF EARTHSEA

Late in *The Earthsea Trilogy,* Ged observes that, "wizardry depends on place . . . the weaving of spells is itself interwoven with the earth and the water, the winds and the fall of light in the place where it is cast" (*Shore* 71). Accordingly, *A Wizard of Earthsea* begins in a very specific place. "The island of Gont, a single mountain that lifts its peak a mile above the storm-wracked Northeast Sea, is a land famous for wizards" (*Wizard* 11). Within the first three paragraphs of the novel, we have learned three names for the central character: Duny, the name given to him by his mother and by which he is known as a child; Sparrowhawk, the name by which he will be commonly known as an adult; and Ged, his inner, secret name. The meaning of this multiplicity is not yet fully explained, but already we have a sense that what one calls something is important; that "magic consists in this, the true naming of a thing" (*Wizard* 59).

The child Duny's first major magical act, the deed that reveals his full talent to those around him, is to summon a mist to hide his island village from attacking invaders. Duny already knows that magic is worked with the stuff of the surrounding landscape, in this case the fog from the ocean. The boy's deed attracts the attention of Ogion, a wizard from the island of Re Albi, who comes to Gont, gives Ged his true name, and takes Ged to live with him and be his apprentice. Ged wishes to learn how to work powerful spells, but Ogion emphasizes the importance of watching and waiting: "Manhood is patience. Mastery is nine times patience. What is the name of that herb by the path?" (*Wizard* 28).

Ogion stresses magic as observation, a way of understanding the world. His teachings are at odds with the contrasting view of magic as control.

> In a land where sorcerers come thick, like Gont or the Enlades, you may see a raincloud blundering slowly from side to side and place to place as one spell shunts it on to the next, till at last it is buffeted out over the sea where it can rain in peace. But Ogion let the rain fall where it would. (*Wizard* 29)

Le Guin's use of the word "peace" here indicates that such control of the weather is a form of violence, coercion that refuses to allow the raincloud to express its true nature, which is to rain. But Ged, ambitious and impatient, repeatedly rebels against what he sees as Ogion's passivity. Seeking a spell of self-transformation among Ogion's books—for Ged, unhappy with what he is, seeks to become something else—he summons a whispering shadow, which terrifies and paralyzes him. Ogion dispels this apparition but gives Ged a stern warning about the nature of their craft, using contrast to emphasize the importance of balance:

> Have you never thought how danger must surround power as shadow does light? This sorcery is not a game we play for pleasure or for praise. Think of this: that every word, every act of our Art is said and is done either for good, or for evil. Before you speak or do you must know the price that is to pay! (*Wizard* 35)

Realizing that Ged is chafing against the narrow confines of Re Albi, Ogion offers him the choice to be sent to the School for Wizards on Roke Island, and Ged—who yearns for glory, although he loves Ogion—accepts.

At the school, Ged makes friends with the kind, gentle Vetch and enters into a rivalry with a student named Jasper. The school's curriculum, like Ogion's, emphasizes the importance of restraint; the Master Summoner, for instance, who teaches the pupils how to call to themselves "real powers, drawn from the immense fathomless energies of the universe," also shows them "why the true wizard uses such spells only at need, since to summon up such earthly forces is to change the earth of which they are a part" (*Wizard* 68). But Ged, not yet a true wizard, allows his rivalry with Jasper to goad him into attempting a very dangerous spell, a summoning of the spirit of the dead; in this Ged succeeds, but he summons more than he means to, rending the barrier between the world of the living and the dead. His shadow, his own death, escapes into the world; Ged is terribly wounded, and the mage Nemmerle, who restores the balance and closes the door that Ged has opened, sacrifices his own life in the process.

Ged spends most of the rest of the novel fleeing the shadow, the creature he summoned and cannot now escape. His denial of the shadow expresses itself more broadly in an unwillingness to face and accept what is. Trying to heal a friend's sick child, he refuses to accept the fact that it is the child's time to die: trying to fix what is not meant to be fixed, he nearly dies himself, and is recalled to life only by the soft touch of an animal, his pet otak, whose presence recalls Ged to life. Ged begins to grasp the lessons Ogion first tried to teach him about observation, interdependence, and silence.

It takes Ogion himself, however, to show Ged that his terror of the shadow comes from the fact that he has been fleeing it; he must turn and face it, refusing to set himself apart from this entity he has summoned just as he would refuse to set himself apart from the living creatures of Earthsea.

We see the theme of interdependence again when Ged, cast ashore on a remote island, finds an elderly man and woman who were clearly stranded there as children, and who have lost the use of language. These humble people give Ged food and drink, and the woman gives Ged a piece of a broken ring. To thank them for their hospitality, he sets a charm on their brackish spring, to guarantee good water. In *The Tombs of Atuan*, we will learn that the broken ring, which Ged considers of no account, is the lost half of the Ring of Erreth-Akbe, the greatest treasure in Earthsea and itself a powerful symbol of wholeness. Ged gains the ring through compassion and generosity, rather than force or skill; it comes to him because he has established a mutually nurturing relationship with two bereft fellow humans. Here we can already see how much he has changed from the boastful young apprentice who desired to do deeds of great power.

By the time Ged sets out to confront his shadow, accompanied by Vetch, he has fully learned to do only what is necessary, to favor silence over speech. He has learned that those who possess the greatest power are the most reluctant to use it.

Ged finally knows how to confront the shadow he summoned in his youthful pride, the shadow of his own death: "In silence, man and shadow met face to face, and stopped.... Ged reached out his hands, dropping his staff, and took hold of his shadow, of the black self that reached out to him. Light and darkness met, and joined, and were one" (*Wizard* 201). No longer trying either to control the shadow or to flee it, Ged names it with his own name, recognizing it as part of himself and reclaiming it, thus neutralizing its ability to terrorize him.

THE TOMBS OF ATUAN

A Wizard of Earthsea tells us that "Death is the dry place" (*Wizard* 152), and in *The Tombs of Atuan,* the second novel in the series, the landscape shifts from ocean to desert. Whereas Ged is given his true name after displaying power, the girl Tenar is given a false name—Arha—after being disempowered, taken from her home and subjected to a ceremony in which she is ceremonially killed. She has been chosen as the next high priestess of the Nameless Ones, ancient gods whose cult centers around an underground labyrinth. This maze of ceremonial tombs is Arha's exclusive domain, into which men are not permitted on pain of death. Whereas Ged, in *A Wizard of Earthsea,* needs to learn the value of silence, stillness, and darkness, they are nearly Arha's entire world.

We spend the first five chapters of the book learning about the cult and the labyrinth, as Arha does; Ged appears as a stranger, an intruder, relatively late in the book, taking the form of light—"the quivering radiance of the lighted cavern, life in the place of death" (*Tombs* 61)— in a place where light is not permitted. Arha traps Ged in the tombs. According to the rules of her cult, she should kill him immediately, but instead she has a series of conversations with him, thus learning about the outside world. Her fearful reaction to this news reveals that she values all the things Ged first rejected in *A Wizard of Earthsea,* that she is in some sense his opposite, the two of them becoming each other's shadow:

> It doesn't matter if there's oceans and dragons and white towers and all that, because you'll never see them again, you'll never even see the light of the sun. All I know is the dark, the night underground. And that's all there really is. That's all there is to know, in the end. The silence, and the dark. (*Tombs* 86–87)

Just as Ged and his shadow represented two halves of a whole, so do Ged and Arha/Tenar. Their complementarity is signaled in the plot by the fact that Ged has come to the Tombs of Atuan seeking the other half of the Ring of Erreth-Akbe, which contained nine Runes of Power; the Ring was broken across the Rune of Peace, which no one now knows how to write. "No king could rule well if he did not rule beneath that sign. . . . since it was lost there have been no great kings in Havnor" (*Tombs* 110). Whereas *A Wizard of Earthsea* focused on personal reconciliation, of Ged's acceptance of part of himself, *The Tombs of Atuan* deals with interpersonal reconciliation, of Arha's acceptance of Ged. Because their friendship will make whole the Ring of Erreth-Akbe, it holds out the promise of wholeness for the entire world, a theme explicitly addressed in *The Farthest Shore*.

Even as Ged promises Arha a release from prison and darkness, a journey into light and life, he reveals his own wisdom in not over-simplifying what he is offering her, in acknowledging that she will not leave pain and death behind:

> The Earth is beautiful, and bright, and kindly, but that is not all. The Earth is also terrible, and dark, and cruel. The rabbit shrieks dying in the green meadows. The mountains clench their great hands full of hidden fire. There are sharks in the sea, and there is cruelty in men's eyes. (*Tombs* 107)

Arha chooses wholeness and reclaims the name Tenar. She opts to forego her position of constrained, limited power in favor of freedom, which Le Guin emphasizes is a heavy burden. And yet the theme of interdependence remains constant, for Ged needs Tenar as much as she needs him. He cannot find his way out of the Tombs without her guidance, and she cannot find her way in the world without his. Each must heal the other's weakness; each must exert his or her own power and knowledge, and profit likewise from the power and knowledge of the other.

THE FARTHEST SHORE

Arren, the protagonist of *The Farthest Shore,* takes up at the point where we leave Tenar, having just begun a voyage of discovery. Appointed as a messenger by his father to the wizards of Roke, Arren has left his home in Enlad, for the first time becoming aware "of distance and diversity" (*Shore* 5). He brings the news that magic is running dry in Enlad, that those who try to say spells can no longer remember the words or can remember them but have lost faith in their meaning. Ged informs Arren that this is happening in other places as well. Some of the other wizards on Roke believe that the problem lies in a lack of human governance, for although the Ring of Erreth-Akbe has been made whole and the Rune of Peace restored, there is still no king in Havnor nor peace in Earthsea. But Ged believes the problem to be darker and deeper. "There is a weakening of power. There is a want of resolution. There is a dimming of the sun" (*Shore* 23). He therefore decides to take Arren with him on a quest to discover and confront the cause of the trouble.

Readers of the two previous novels, already steeped in Le Guin's philosophy of caution and restraint, will easily perceive how urgent Ged feels the matter to be, for when the Doorkeeper of Roke says, "And you would be up and doing," Ged answers simply, "I would" (*Shore* 23). Later in the novel, discussing with Arren the importance of doing only what is needful, he points out that this rule holds only as long as the balance is maintained. "But when the Balance itself is broken—then one considers other things. Above all, haste" (*Shore* 133).

And so the two set sail from Roke, seeking quickly to solve a problem whose source they do not even know. Here we see Ged using the wisdom he first acquired from Ogion in *A Wizard of Earthsea,* for rather than fleeing or ignoring the problem, he seeks to confront it. But despite the urgency of the quest, respect for the Balance remains paramount. Because the scale of *The Farthest Shore* has broadened to include all of Earthsea, it contains the trilogy's fullest expression of an ecological understanding, as Ged teaches Arren about human responsibility for the world:

> On every act the balance of the whole depends. The winds and seas, the powers of water and earth and light, all that these do, and all that the beasts and green things do, is well done, and rightly done. All these act within the Equilibrium....But we, insofar as we have power over the world and over one another, we must *learn* to do what the leaf and the whale and the wind do of their own nature. We must learn to keep the balance. Having intelligence, we must not act in ignorance. Having choice, we must not act without responsibility. (*Shore* 66–67)

Traveling among the islands of the Archipelago, Ged and Arren follow a trail of madness and despair, tracing it eventually to the work of a wizard named Cob who claims to offer eternal life, freedom from death. But one cannot evade death without also evading life, as Ged tells Arren. "Death and life are the same thing—like the two sides of my hand, the palm and the back. And still the palm and the back are not the same.... They can be neither separated nor mixed" (*Shore* 74).

Arren, if he becomes King, has the potential to restore the world to wholeness. Ged's temptation in *A Wizard of Earthsea* was evasion of death through a life of fearful flight; Tenar's temptation in *The Tombs of Atuan* was immersion in the safety of death without experiencing the plenitude of life. Arren's temptation is immortality, the terrible state of stasis that denies both life and death. Early in the novel, Ged observes that "When we crave power over life—endless wealth, unassailable safety, immortality—then desire becomes greed" (*Shore* 35). Much later, he tells Arren, "There is no safety, and there is no end. The word must be heard in silence; there must be darkness to see the stars. The dance is always danced above the hollow place, above the terrible abyss" (*Shore* 121). Arren's personal struggle in the novel, the source of his pain and growth, is the task of learning to differentiate genuine peace, the peace it will be his kingly task to create, from false peace, the costly security that holds danger at bay only by denying growth and life. We see this conflict in Arren's battle between his love for Ged and his desire to accept the lure of immortality, for he has heard Cob's promise and knows that "mages lived no longer than ordinary men. All their secret words could not put off for one hour the coming of their death" (*Shore* 99).

Arren needs to accompany Ged to the land of death itself, to the dry place, to learn that death is a place neither of terror nor of safety but of sterility and stasis:

> [The dead] were whole and healed. They were healed of pain and of life. They were not loathesome as Arren had feared they would be, not frightening in the way he had thought they would be. Quiet were their faces, freed from anger and desire, and there was in their shadowed eyes no hope. (*Shore* 173)

But he has also learned, from his travels with Ged, the source of true life and abundance. "I have given my love to what is worthy of love," he tells Ged. "Is that not the kingdom and the unperishing spring?" (*Shore* 165). Ged responds that it is, and the reader cannot help but remember the "unperishing spring" Ged created on the small island where he was given his half of the Ring of Erreth-Akbe.

When Arren and Ged at last meet Cob, they learn that his evil lies in denying the world by denying death: "Let all stupid nature run its stupid course, but I am a man, better than nature, above nature" (*Shore* 178). This directly contradicts the lesson Ged learned in *A Wizard of Earthsea*, that he must never set himself apart from nature. Cob, like Ged in the first novel of the trilogy, has succeeded in opening the door between the worlds, between life and death, but he cannot close it again. Unlike Ged, who learned to accept and embrace his own death, Cob acts only in denial of death, which is also a denial of nature, of the Balance. Ged articulates a vision of the world in which life and death are indeed like the front and back of a hand, inseparable, each meaningless without the other. Speaking to Cob of Erreth-Akbe's death—making the point that even the greatest heroes of Earthsea have died—Ged describes how Erreth-Akbe remains in the world:

> There, he is the earth and sunlight, the leaves of trees, the eagle's flight. He is alive. And all who ever died, live; they are reborn and have no end, nor will there ever be an end. All, save you.... You sold the green earth and the sun and stars to save yourself. But you have no self. All that which you sold, that is yourself. You have given everything for nothing. (*Shore* 180)

Ged, in contrast, willingly expends his own power to save the "green earth and the sun and stars;" he closes the door that Cob has opened, but in doing so he expends his own power, as Nemmerle did in *A Wizard of Earthsea* when he closed the door Ged had opened. Rather than taking the power of others in the service of evil, as Cob did, Ged forfeits his own power in the service of good. He demonstrates the lesson he has spent the book teaching Arren, that the only power worth having "is the power, not to take, but to accept" (*Shore* 138). He does not die, as Nemmerle did, but he is terribly weakened, and requires Arren's help to return to the world of the living.

Again we see the interdependence of characters, for Arren has needed Ged to teach him the wisdom he will need to be King, but Ged needs Arren to help him make the journey back to Roke. And we also see the importance of wholeness; Ged has indeed helped rid the world of evil, but he has been able to do so because he remembers and claims his early experience of error, which required him to confront evil within himself. His journey itself forms a whole, an unbroken circle like the restored Ring of Erreth-Akbe; from Roke, Ged returns to

Gont, the place where we first met him in *A Wizard of Earthsea*. Arren goes to Havnor to be crowned, to make good the promise of the Ring of Erreth-Akbe and restore peace to Earthsea, but Ged returns to his childhood home, where he will wander in solitude in the forests. "The Doorkeeper, smiling, said, 'He has done with doing. He goes home.' " (*Shore* 196).

CONCLUSION

What environmental lessons, then, does *The Earthsea Trilogy* have to teach us? It tells us that we must embrace the entire world, and ourselves within the world, and the worlds we contain, both light and shadow. It tells us that broken things can be mended only by confronting problems and taking action, but that any such action must be the smallest one that will be effective. It tells us that we must be afraid neither of life nor of death, for such fear will drive us to hoard and to waste, actions that upset balance and create disorder. The novels teach us that we must observe and learn to love the world before we attempt to shape it, and they tell us too that objects, technology, are worth nothing without the wisdom to use them well; the restored Ring of Erreth-Akbe cannot create peace without a king who has learned the difference between false and true peace, between fearful security and open-hearted acceptance. Although Le Guin has set *The Earthsea Trilogy* in an invented world of wizards and dragons, of islands that appear on no map we know, the stories are clearly relevant to our own Earth. We, like Ged and Tenar and Arren, must learn to respect balance, to love both the light and the darkness, and to honor stillness and silence.

BIBLIOGRAPHY

Beagle, Peter S. Introduction. *The Fellowship of the Ring*. By J. R. R. Tolkien. New York: Ballantine, 1973.

Le Guin, Ursula. *The Farthest Shore*. 1972. New York: Bantam, 1975.

———. *The Language of the Night*. New York: Putnam's, 1979.

———. *The Tombs of Atuan*. 1971. New York: Bantam, 1975.

———. *The Wind's Twelve Quarters*. 1975. New York: Bantam, 1979.

———. *A Wizard of Earthsea*. New York: Ace, 1968.

———. Homepage. 8 August 2002. <http://www.ursulakleguin.com/>.

6

Gary Snyder,
Turtle Island (1974)

George Hart

Turtle Island, published by New Directions in 1974, is Gary Snyder's fifth book of poetry. When it was published it presented his most complete statement to date on the environmental crisis, American culture, and the "old/new," ideal community that he saw emerging from the sixties counterculture. The poems show Snyder confronting mainstream American culture again after nearly a decade of living in Japan; they present his vision of a new society based on indigenous and primitive cultures living lightly and harmoniously on the earth; and they offer his personal experience homesteading on the western slope of the Sierra Nevada mountains as a model of this ecologically integrated life. Furthermore, five essays included with the poems explicitly address contemporary environmental issues such as energy shortages, pollution, and population growth, as well as express his ideas about the relationship of the poet to nature, how primitive cultures offer alternative ways of connecting with the land and animals, and what it means to have a bioregional understanding of place. *Turtle Island* constitutes the first single-volume collection of poetry to make a cohesive statement about the environment on multiple levels: social, political, aesthetic, personal, cultural, spiritual.

CRITICAL RECEPTION

Turtle Island appealed to a wide audience, but it was not received with universal praise. Kevin McGuirk points out that "it has generated the most criticism of any of his books.... The volume as a whole sets forth an explicit, sometimes militant ecopolitics" (261). When poets use their work to comment on political and social issues, they risk compromising their role as a creative artist by becoming a political activist. Although literary critics may have been put off by its "ecopolitics," *Turtle Island* was awarded the 1975 Pulitzer Prize for Poetry, a first for a book by a West Coast poet. *Turtle Island* was written and published during the first wave of environmental awareness and legislation—the first Earth Day (1970), the Clean Air Act (1970), and the Endangered Species Act (1973), for example—and many readers who embraced the book were looking for a poet who would address the issues and crises that they faced every day. However, the book's success notwithstanding, one of the most interesting questions to ask about the poems is whether or not they are good poems or simply political sloganeering. How does a poet write poetry that serves political and social purposes—raising awareness about the environmental crisis and proposing solutions to it—without compromising her or his artistic vision and poetic craft? Is the poet just an artist, or is she or he also a prophet, a teacher, a spokesperson?

BIOGRAPHICAL BACKGROUND

Gary Snyder was born in 1930 and he grew up on a small dairy farm in northwestern Washington state. He studied anthropology at Reed College in Oregon and later did graduate work in oriental languages at the University of California at Berkeley. In the early 1950s he worked as a fire lookout in the Pacific Northwest and on a trailcrew in Yosemite National Park. He participated in the West Coast Beat movement with other poets such as Phil Whalen, Lew Welch, Michael McClure, and Allen Ginsberg. The main character in Jack Kerouac's *The Dharma Bums,* Japhy Ryder, is a fictional portrait of Snyder at this time. In 1957, he signed onto the crew of an oil tanker, traveling around the seas of the Far East, and then spent most of the 1960s in Japan, studying Zen Buddhism. His travels in the American West, at sea, and in Japan form the basis of the poems in *Riprap* and *The Back Country; Myths and Texts* reflects his interest in anthropology and his experiences working as a logger; *Regarding Wave* focuses on his marriage to Masa Uehara, and their new domestic life together. Many of these experiences are also recounted in the essays and journal excerpts published in *Earth House Hold.* In 1969, Snyder and his family returned to California, and the poems in *Turtle Island* describe the poet's "reinhabitation" of his native country.

HISTORICAL CONTEXT

The broad social, political, and cultural context that forms the background for Snyder's personal experiences is the post–World War II era. As the United States gained power and wealth after the defeat of Germany and Japan, various social and political movements began to critique American culture from within—the civil rights movement, the women's movement, and the environmental movement. None of these groups was new: the abolitionist and temperance movements of the nineteenth century formed the basis for the civil rights and women's movements, and both groups had early twentieth-century correlatives in the New Negro and suffragist movements. The environmentalist movement emerged from the nineteenth-century Romantic philosophy, and the conservationist and preservationist movements of the early twentieth century. The 1950s are typically seen as a decade of conformity and affluence, but underneath the surface regularity, these groups were coming together and identifying the elements of American culture that needed to be changed. By the 1960s, these movements had formed a loose affiliation, in part united by their resistance to the U.S. war in Vietnam. The large number of young people who were involved in the protests against the war, racism, sexism, and environmental degradation constituted a subculture, or "counterculture," that saw itself as an alternative to the "fifties style" American mainstream way of life.

When Snyder returned to the United States, the sixties counterculture was at its peak. In "The Rediscovery of Turtle Island," the poet recounts how he learned about this "old/new" way of thinking about North America. "I first heard this continent called 'Turtle Island'…by a man who said his work was to be a messenger," Snyder writes. "He said that Turtle Island was the term that the people were coming to, a new name to help us build the future of North America. I asked him whom or where it came from. He said, 'There are many creation myths with Turtle, East Coast and West Coast. But also you can just hear it' " (*Place* 241–42). Snyder continues:

> As I reentered American life during the spring of 1969, I saw the use of the term "Turtle Island" spread through the fugitive Native American newsletters and other communications. I became aware that there was a notable groundswell of white people, too, who were seeing their life in the Western Hemisphere in a new way.…By 1970 I had moved with my family to the Sierra

Nevada and was developing a forest homestead north of the South Yuba River. Many others entered the mountains and hills of the Pacific slope with virtually identical intentions, from the San Diego backcountry north into British Columbia. They had begun the reinhabitory move.... Our new sense of the Western Hemisphere permeated everything we did. So I called the book of poems I wrote from that period *Turtle Island*. (*Place* 243)

STRUCTURAL AND THEMATIC COMPONENTS

The book is arranged in four sections: "Manzanita," "Magpie's Song," "For the Children," and "Plain Talk." The first three contain poems written in the late 1960s and early 1970s, and the last section comprises prose statements written for various occasions. The major statement in "Plain Talk" is called "Four Changes." This essay offers "a few practical and visionary suggestions" to remedy the social problems contributing to the environmental crisis of the time period: population, pollution, and consumption. The fourth suggestion concerns the "transformation" of the civilization that "has overshot itself and now threatens us with its inertia" (99). Each section explains "the condition," what it is and how it affects the social and natural environment, and suggests what action can be taken to remedy the situation.

According to scientist and activist Barry Commoner, the first law of ecology is that "everything is connected to everything else" (33) and naturally the conditions that Snyder addresses are all interrelated. What's more, the book itself obeys this principle because the poems in their way also describe the conditions and their impacts on the environment and offer examples of actions to make things better. In part three of "Four Changes," "Consumption," Snyder writes, "Man's careless use of 'resources' and his total dependence on certain substances such as fossil fuels...are having harmful effects on all the other members of the life-network....in fact mankind has become a locust-like blight on the planet that will leave a bare cupboard for its own children—all the while in a kind of Addict's Dream of affluence, comfort, eternal progress" (*Turtle Island* 97). Snyder connects this idea of waste to his own homesteading in a poem called "Affluence" (*Turtle Island* 50). The speaker of the poem describes the timber left behind "from logging twenty years ago," when it was cheaper to take the best logs and leave the rest. The remaining "still-hard limbs and twigs" create a fire hazard, and the speaker's chore in this poem is to remove it: "now burn the tangles dowsing / pokey heaps with diesel oil. / paying the price somebody didn't pay."

The poem that begins the "Magpie's Song" section, "Facts," is a numbered list of 10 facts that contribute to the environmental crisis; number two reads: "The U.S. has 6% of the world's population; consumes 1/3 the energy annually consumed in the world" (*Turtle Island* 31). In "Four Changes," and in poems such as "Affluence" and "Facts," Snyder presents his readers with arguments and examples just as environmental scientists and activists did at this time. Compare, for example, this passage from Paul Ehrlich's *The Population Bomb*, published in 1968:

> We, of course, cannot remain affluent and isolated. At the moment the United States uses well over half of all the raw materials consumed each year. Think of it. Less than 1/15th of the population of the world requires more than all the rest to maintain its inflated position. If present trends continue, in 20 years we will be much less than 1/15th of the population, and yet we may use some 80% of the resources consumed. Our affluence depends heavily on many different kinds of imports....Will other countries, many of them in the grip of starvation and anarchy, still happily supply these materials to a nation that cannot give them food? Even the technological optimists don't think we can free ourselves of the need for imports in the near future. (133)

Poets and writers often use a sense of crisis to convince their audiences to take action, to change their way of life before it is too late. The pollution and energy crises of the seventies came to pass, but many of Snyder's "facts" still hold true today. In a 1995 postscript to "Four Changes," Snyder writes, "Naïve and utopian as some of it sounds now, I still stand by the basics of 'Four Changes' " (*Place* 46).

However, as we will see in the poems, Snyder does not use this crisis to scare or manipulate his readers; for him, it is an imaginative tool for changing people's consciousness. Remarking on the energy crisis in 1973, Snyder explains,

> This is a marvelous time in which the nations of the world may get a new balance and a perspective on themselves—if it doesn't

degenerate into hysteria and short range crisis thinking. If we rush into a crisis mentality—totalitarian and draconian measures to keep cars running, and the houses heated to seventy-two degrees, and the GNP continually growing—then we will rip off nature. We should try to allay anxiety and spread confidence in the natural beauty of the human mind and the natural dignity of life at its normal, natural, ancient, slower pace. (*Real Work* 51)

Realizing that poetry and the arts are primary sites of creative change, and also considering people's resistance to hearing calls for change from their artists (the dilemma of the "poet as prophet" again), Snyder concludes: "I think that creative people, poets, religious people, if they wish to speak, have a message which is of great value now…although whether or not anyone will heed it is another question" (*Real Work* 51).

Often throughout the book, a poem will share a theme or topic with one of the essays, and it can be analyzed by its relation to that essay. Just as population, pollution, and consumption are interrelated social and environmental problems, and the answer to each and all involves the transformation of Western culture, so the poems present, implicitly and explicitly, versions of the transformation that the poet has tried to effect in his own life. One of the main themes throughout *Turtle Island* is the family. In "Four Changes," one of the proposed actions to take is: "Explore other social structures and marriage forms, such as group marriage and polyandrous marriage, which provide family life but many less children" (*Turtle Island* 93). Snyder, like many of his counterculture peers, viewed the nuclear family as one of the main culprits in the loss of the "old ways." In an essay on the communal aspects of the counterculture, Snyder writes: "The modern American family is the smallest and most barren family that has ever existed. Each newly-married couple moves to a new house or apartment—no uncles or grandmothers come to live with them. There are seldom more than two or three children. The children live with their peers and leave home early. Many have never had the least sense of family" (*Earth* 110–11). One of the poet's main goals is to get readers to think about family relationships in "new/old" ways.

Two of the most popular poems in *Turtle Island* focus on the transformation of the family. "The Bath" (12–14) portrays a vision of a family free of sexual and physical shame, in touch with their own bodies, as Snyder, his wife Masa, and their two sons, Kai and Gen, wash each other in the family's homestead sauna. At first, the speaker washes his eldest son, Kai, and realizes the identity of their bodies as father and son:

> And washing-tickling out the scrotum, little anus,
>   his penis curving up and getting hard
>   as I pull back skin and try to wash it
> Laughing and jumping, flinging arms around,
>   I squat all naked too,
>   *is this our body?*

The speaker repeats the question after his wife and younger son enter the sauna, and it becomes the refrain of the poem as the family's one-ness is affirmed in the cleansing ritual of the bath, transforming from a question to an affirmation: "*this is our body.*" Male and female, par-ent and child, share the same body, and it is the body of the earth as well. The other poem, "Prayer for the Great Family" (24–25), also functions ritualistically but in a mythical rather than personal mode. In this poem, Snyder imitates a Native American model to create an eco-logical prayer that could be recited by all citizens of Turtle Island. The human speaker of the prayer offers thanks to the earth, plants, air, wild beings, water, sun, and sky, and thus redefines the whole universe as one extended clan, the great family.

Once family has been extended to include all beings, the third sec-tion of the book, "For the Children," takes on added significance. The poems are addressed to all children, with the hope that their wis-dom will lead to a better world for future generations. What's more, the rhetorical situation shifts its focus to education, and so poems such as "What Happened Here Before" (78–81) and "Toward Climax" (82–85) are written to inform as much as to entertain the reader. The former is an account of Turtle Island from three hundred million years ago until "*now*," when poet and sons camp out and look at the stars in wonder. The latter includes ideas from ecology—a climax ecosystem is supposed to be the stable point at which it functions with most diver-sity and effectiveness—counterpointed with human culture and its ef-fect on the environment. The poem called "For the Children" (86) concludes with Snyder's often-quoted advice: "*stay together / learn the flowers / go light* [.]"

The poet as teacher is another version of the book's poet as prophet theme, and this role introduces the problem of expressing anger at America's environmental abuses while still appealing to an American audience. Many of the poems in the book's first two sections balance on this tension, and watching how Snyder alternates between critiquing American society and observing his own life can reveal interesting contrasts between different poems. Two poems in the "Manzanita" section, which are arranged as a pair on consecutive pages, treat the same subject—the speaker's anger about the expanding population developing more and more land—in different modes. "Front Lines" (18) explicitly condemns the developers and builders who intrude upon the poet's rural community; it uses direct statement and disturbing imagery to make a political statement without concern for its audience. The first two stanzas read:

> The edge of the cancer
> Swells against the hill—we feel
>   a foul breeze—
> And it sinks back down.
> The deer winter here
> A chainsaw growls in the gorge.
> Ten wet days and the log trucks stop,
> The trees breathe.
> Sunday the 4-wheel jeep of the
> Realty Company brings in
> Landseekers, lookers, they say
> To the land,
> Spread your legs.

People are separated into "us" and "them" in this poem. The expanding population is a "cancer," and the developers are invaders who rape the feminized land. Snyder's people—"we"—are members of the land community, sensitive to changes in the breeze, where the deer winter, and how the trees breathe. The last two stanzas emphasize the difference between these two sets of people:

> A bulldozer grinding and slobbering
> Sideslipping and belching on top of
> The skinned-up bodies of still-live bushes
> In the pay of a man
> From town.
>
> Behind is a forest that goes to the Arctic
> And a desert that still belongs to the Piute

And here we must draw
Our line.

"Their" technology is inappropriate to the land and corrupted by commerce—the bulldozer and chainsaw are both "personified," but the growling of the chainsaw seems to fit into the landscape in the first stanza whereas the bulldozer's grinding, slobbering, and belching reflect the rapacious greed of the developers. "We" see the region in ecological and cultural terms—an understanding that is supposed to be one of the transformations, a "bioregional" conception of place. In a 1971 interview, Snyder explains: "the boundaries drawn by national states and so forth don't represent any sort of real entity. But that kind of perception's been a theoretical perception, whereas what gives reality to this kind of thinking now is the realization, in terms of efficient and elegant associations of natural systems (if there's going to be a condition of harmonious growth rather than outrageous growth) that we need this kind of knowledge. People have to learn a sense of region, and what is possible within a region, rather than indefinitely assuming that a kind of promiscuous distribution of goods and long-range transportation is always going to be possible" (*Real Work* 24–25). In "Front Lines," Snyder makes the bioregional boundary a political boundary as well, a line drawn between "us" and "them."

The other poem in the pair, "Control Burn" (19), is just as severe in its critique of the current state of American culture, but it makes its statement more obliquely. The poem works on multiple levels: didactic, symbolic, metaphorical, and rhetorical. The speaker begins with a lesson in ethnobotany, explaining how the Native Americans used to manage the local ecology:

What the Indians
here
used to do, was,
to burn out the brush every year.
in the woods, up the gorges,
keeping the oak and the pine stands
tall and clear
with grasses
and kitkitdizze under them,
never enough fuel there
that a fire could crown.

For Snyder and the citizens of Turtle Island, this is an example of an "old way" that is better than the Western methods of forestry, better because it is appropriate to the place, a "natural" way of managing the forest ecosystem. The botanical information continues:

> Now, manzanita,
> (a fine bush in its right)
> crowds up under the new trees
> mixed up with logging slash
> and a fire can wipe out all.

The current situation, as we also saw in the poem "Affluence," is dangerous, a result of neglect and waste. The only way to remedy the situation is with what is called a "control burn." The poem concludes:

> Fire is an old story.
> I would like,
> with a sense of helpful order,
> with respect for laws
> of nature,
> to help my land
> with a burn. a hot clean
> burn.
>> (manzanita seeds will only open
>> after a fire passes over
>> or once passed through a bear)

> And then
> it would be more
> like,
> when it belonged to the Indians

> Before.

The poem has moved to the symbolic level in its description of the manzanita, which becomes a symbol for the transition between the present way of doing things and the "new/old way" of doing things. The bush is just fine in its own right but with neglect becomes a hazard. Recall that this section of the book is called "Manzanita," the initial stage of Snyder's reinhabitation of Turtle Island, a transition.

The next stanza, with the first appearance of the speaker ("I"), uses a metaphor that may not be evident right away. From one angle, the poet is talking about his desire to clear the property he owns with a controlled burn, yet, metaphorically, "my land" also refers to his country, the United States. The speaker has just made a modest proposal—a controlled burn that will purify his country—while portraying himself as perfectly calm and rational; he wants to be "helpful" and "respectful" as he does it. Snyder uses many of his strongest verse techniques in these lines in particular: the highly enjambed line breaks ("with respect for laws / of nature"), the condensed, "ideogrammatic" image or statement (the details about manzanita typographically set off from the rest of the lines), and single word lines and stanzas ("here," "Before"). These techniques allow Snyder to make his rhetorical move subtly, whereas in "Front Lines" he used direct statement for clarity and force. A "control burn" would achieve the drastic population reduction he calls for in "Four Changes," but here it has the appeal of getting the country back to a "native" condition, as it was before, by a "natural" means.

One variation Snyder performs on the poet as prophet theme is the poet as spokesman. The British Romantic poet Percy Shelley famously remarked that "poets are the unacknowledged legislators of the world," and Snyder extends this sentiment into real world politics. In a 1973 interview, he comments:

> My political position is to be a spokesman for wild nature. I take that as my primary constituency. And for the people who live in dependence on that. . . . That comes to me naturally, that position. It's a position simply of advocacy, taking the role of being the advocate for a realm for which few men will stand up. Someone must be a spokesman for that, and I think that poets are better prepared to be the spokesman for that than most people are, particularly someone with the background of myself. (*Real Work* 49)

In 1972, the United Nations held an international conference on the environment in Stockholm, Sweden, and Snyder, along with other "representatives" from indigenous groups and the counterculture, staged an alternative conference to protest the degradation of native cultures and pristine ecosystems. Snyder's friend and fellow poet, Michael McClure, recalls, "Gary Snyder and I were among the contingent of independent lobbyists . . . who took it upon themselves to represent whales, Indians, and the freedom of diversity of the environment" (33). *Time* magazine correspondent Friedel Ungeheuer reported on the conference:

To the more militant environmentalists...the official agenda offers only what some of them call "Band-Aid solutions" to dangerous problems. In a separate Environmental Forum, they are focusing on population growth and wasteful technology, which the agenda hardly mentions. The U.S.'s most articulate ecologist, Barry Commoner, urged a near Utopia. "To solve the environmental crisis," he said, "we must solve the problems of poverty, racial injustice and war."

Ungeheuer described the counterculture atmosphere of the "Environmental Forum": "the conference is also earning itself the nickname of 'Woodstockholm.' Students have set up a tent city....There are endless parades, one of which featured a large plastic whale to represent that overhunted species" (55).

A protest poem written and distributed at the conference, "Mother Earth: Her Whales" (*Turtle Island* 47–49), reveals how Snyder serves as a political representative for wild nature. One controversial issue in international environmentalism, then and now, is the tension between "first world" environmentalists who want to preserve wild ecosystems and "third world" governments who want to develop natural resources. One stanza refers to this issue, drawing on the controversies and slogans of the conference:

Brazil says "sovereign use of Natural Resources"
Thirty thousand kinds of unknown plants.
The living actual people of the jungle
      sold and tortured—
And a robot in a suit who peddles a delusion called "Brazil"
      can speak for *them*?

Snyder's anger was in fact spurred by the comments of the Brazilian representative. Another *Time* magazine account reports that "Brazil's Planning Minister João Paulo Velloso remarked in approving a polluting paper mill: 'Why not? We have a lot left to pollute' " ("Whole Earth" 73).

IMPACT

Although it may be presumptuous for a white, male poet to present himself as a spokesman for indigenous people and wild nature, Snyder uses his popularity and authority as a writer to challenge politicians and developers. He uses his poetry as a venue to raise awareness of in-justice and to rally sympathetic readers. The poem, before a lyrical conclusion, shifts into bald politicking, calling on "tree people," "bird people," "four-legged" and "two-legged" people to join in solidarity against the "robot nations."

Whether a reader accepts or rejects Snyder's politics, and thus accepts or rejects his political poetry such as "Mother Earth: Her Whales," first and last he is a poet, one of the finest and most attentive to nature in American literature, and *Turtle Island* does not lack the crystalline, con-densed nature lyrics that are his trademark. Poems such as "Pine Tree Tops" and "For Nothing" (33–34) recall some of his earliest work, which was influenced by modernists such as Ezra Pound as well as clas-sical Chinese and Japanese verse. Such contemplative lyrics express a si-multaneously material and spiritual connection to nature through pared-down phrases and immediate, sensory images. "Pine Tree Tops," for example, evokes a hike on a frosty night through plain description and simple phrases, concluding with the speaker's sense of humility be-fore the natural scene: "what do we know."

And so, the last poem, "As For Poets" (87–88), and the last essay in "Plain Talk," which is a note on this poem, embody the most basic, and the most complex, role that Snyder assumes: the poet as poet. Here, the energy of poetry alleviates the energy crisis rather than simply calling at-tention to it. In "On 'As For Poets,'" Snyder quotes William Blake's dic-tum that "Energy is Eternal Delight," and writes, "oil and coal are the stored energy of the sun locked by ancient plant-life in its cells. 'Renew-able' energy resources are the trees and flowers and all living beings of today....On these fuels contemporary nations now depend. But there is another kind of energy, in every living being, close to the sun-source but in a different way. The power within. Whence? 'Delight.'...This joy is continually reflected in the poems and songs of the world. 'As for Poets' explores the realm of delight in terms of the five elements that ancient Greek and China both saw as the constituents of the physical world. To which the Buddhist philosophers of India added a sixth, consciousness, or Mind" (113–14). The sixth stanza of the poem reads:

A Mind Poet
Stays in the house.
The house is empty
And it has no walls.
The poem
Is seen from all sides,

Everywhere,
At once.

Snyder explains:

> Now, we are both in, and outside, the world at once. The only place this can be is the *Mind*. Ah, what a poem. It is what is, completely, in the past, present, and future simultaneously, seeing being, and being seen.
>
> Can we really do this? But we do. So we sing. Poetry is for all men and women. The power within—the more you give, the more you have to give—will still be our source when coal and oil are long gone, and atoms are left to spin in peace. (114)

Turtle Island is Snyder's most complex book after *Mountains and Rivers Without End,* a book-length poem that he completed in 1995. In the three sections of poems and group of essays, Snyder uses literature as if it were a toolbox, finding in it the right tool for the right job at hand. Sometimes his task is to convince an audience or move them to take action, sometimes to express a political position or personal experience, and sometimes to represent a moment of perception into or wonder at nature's beauty. However, he does not let his readers forget that each tool, each poem or essay, exists in and of itself, and that poetry's highest purpose, even as it serves a social cause, is to give pleasure and create delight.

BIBLIOGRAPHY

Commoner, Barry. *The Closing Circle: Nature, Man and Technology*. New York: Knopf, 1971.

Ehrlich, Paul R. *The Population Bomb*. New York: Ballantine, 1968.

McClure, Michael. *Scratching the Beat Surface*. New York: Penguin, 1994.

McGuirk, Kevin. "Gary Snyder." *American Poets since World War II*, 4th series. *Dictionary of Literary Biography*. Vol. 165. Detroit: Gale Research, 1996. 254–66.

Snyder, Gary. *Earth House Hold*. New York: New Directions, 1969.

———. *A Place in Space*. Washington, DC: Counterpoint, 1995.

———. *The Real Work*. Ed. William Scott McLean. New York: New Directions, 1980.

———. *Turtle Island*. New York: New Directions, 1974.

Ungeheuer, Friedel. "Woodstockholm." *Time* 19 June 1972: 55.

"Whole Earth Conference." *Time* 22 May 1972: 73.

7

Edward Abbey,
The Monkey Wrench Gang (1975)

David Fenimore

Twenty-eight years have barely lessened the impact of Edward Abbey's *The Monkey Wrench Gang*. In fact, events of the past decade have underscored, rather than obscured, its initial relevance. First published in 1975, this bawdy saga of a tiny band of environmentalist guerillas opposing industrial development in the American Southwest still has the power to infuriate the conservative, pro-business segment of American society, while appealing to the libertarian and egalitarian streak in us that romanticizes idealism and anti-authoritarian outlawry. From Antigone and Robin Hood to the Boston Tea Party and Bonnie & Clyde, the image of the noble avenger working outside the establishment according to the dictates of a higher law is deeply etched into western civilization.

Such high-profile vigilantism has often occupied a gray area somewhere between legend and reality—did Abbey predict and perhaps inspire the formation of extremist environmental organizations such as Earth First! and Earth Liberation Front, or was he observing and abetting an existing trend in an increasingly militant American counterculture? During Abbey's early literary career, several intellectual and political strands were converging in this country. Especially in the period from 1968 to 1975, following the Civil Rights movement of the earlier 1960s and subsequent mass protests against the Vietnam War, a disorganized scattering of less principled but highly sensational acts of sabotage, robbery, and even murder were committed by shadowy underground groups such as the Weathermen and the Symbionese Liberation Army. These acts were purportedly justified by ill-defined and impossibly idealistic goals of racial and social justice, as well as opposition to the military-industrial status quo. In addition, in 1962 Rachel Carson published *Silent Spring*, a carefully researched and documented indictment of government-sanctioned environmental degradation at the hands of chemical manufacturers, which kickstarted the environmental movement as it challenged readers to ask if what was good for corporations really *was* good for the country, not to mention for ecology. *The Monkey Wrench Gang*, Abbey's fourth novel, has been blamed (and credited) for inspiring clandestine and often violent measures taken in defense of this embattled American environment. Three decades later, the word he coined, "monkey-wrenching," has entered the dictionary as a slang term for environmentally motivated sabotage, along with "ecotage," "ecoterrorism," and the more sympathetic and self-justifying "eco-defense."

HISTORICAL BACKGROUND

According to an interview with biographer James M. Cahalan, Abbey thought of the novel as early as 1963, before the publication of *Desert Solitaire*, calling its early drafts *The Wooden Shoe Gang* until his publisher talked him into the title it bears today. In one of five epigraphs to the original edition, Abbey provides a standard dictionary definition of "sabotage," referring to the eighteenth-century French weavers who tried to preserve their livelihoods by throwing wooden shoes (*sabots*) into mechanical looms. Another epigraph cites the Oxford Universal Dictionary's entry for "Ned Ludd or Lud:...a lunatic living about 1779, who in a fit of rage smashed up two frames belonging to a Leicestershire 'stockinger' " and adds a quotation from Lord Byron: "Down with all kings but King Ludd" (vi).

Two more epigraphs quote well-known American writers: "Resist much. Obey little" (Walt Whitman) and "Now. Or never" (Thoreau). As is evident from these quotes, it is not difficult to trace the beginnings of the American environmental movement back to the European Romantic movement of the nineteenth century by way of its American acolytes. Romanticism, while constructing a public reaction against Enlightenment reason, rigidity, and determinism, also placed high value on internal experience and personal subjectivity. Its proponents were often aristocrats by birth or at least financially secure and detached from the working class. It focused primarily on aesthetics, having little to do with reason or science for its own sake, and its inchoate political agenda glorified resistance to authority, albeit in emotional and poetic terms. British Romantic poet William Wordsworth found "bliss" in the French Revolution; Percy Shelley called poets like himself "unacknowledged legislators"; and his friend and fellow Romantic, the "mad and bad and dangerous" Byron, left off trysting with the wives of British peers to fight and die for the cause of European liberation.

The underlying motives of Abbey's monkeywrenchers therefore deserve close reading and discussion. Are they selfish, reckless, childish vandals—boys blowing up mailboxes for the sake of envy and excitement? Are they, as some pro-development critics claim of environmental activists, "elitists," denying livelihoods to rural communities or dooming them to jobs in a low-wage service economy to satisfy the aesthetic requirements of urban outdoor enthusiasts? "Do we know what we're doing and why?" asks one monkeywrencher early in the novel.

"No."
"Do we care?"
"We'll work it all out as we go along. Let our practice form our doctrine, thus assuring precise theoretical coherence." (65)

Aside from an explicit rejection of anarchy (70), the protagonists in *The Monkey Wrench Gang* adopt no systematic philosophy of disobedience. If anything, Abbey, who in the early 1950s wrote a master's thesis at the University of New Mexico entitled "Anarchism and the Morality of Violence," mocks any effort to seek abstract justification in environmental ethics or any preexisting moral authority other than the human heart. The main characters' ethics are shown arising on a situational basis from natural human instincts, as when Doc Sarvis impulsively declares "No guns" (69) during a planning session. Using power tools, crowbars, Karo syrup, and other low-tech mechanical and chemical weapons, they strike by night and make their escape virtually undetected. Although they take successful pains to avoid injury to human beings, their wide-ranging but sporadic destruction of billboards, mining equipment, earth-moving machinery, railroads and bridges is accomplished by stealth and subterfuge and therefore very unlike political "demonstrations" that are intended to sway the public conscience.

In the fall of 1998, an act of arson destroyed a newly constructed mountaintop lodge at the Vail ski resort in Colorado, along with several lift terminals and outbuildings. The Earth Liberation Front claimed responsibility for this nighttime attack, saying the fires were

deliberately set on behalf of lynx populations threatened by the resort's expansion into adjacent national forest lands. Incidents like this
one are often cited by pro-business spokespersons to implicate all environmentalists in a program of lawless destruction, although most
modern activists, like the members of Greenpeace and tree-sitters such
as northern Californian Julia "Butterfly" Hill, practice a form of civil
disobedience rather than secretive sabotage.

The distinction is important, especially in a modern world shocked
into awareness of politically motivated and militant terrorism by the
events of September 11, 2001. First imagined in the fifth century
BCE by the classical Greek playwright Sophocles in *Antigone,* and
elaborated both in theory and in practice by Henry David Thoreau,
Mohandas Gandhi, and Martin Luther King Jr., civil disobedience is
generally distinguished by a patient, public, nonviolent, often theatrical breaking of a particular law. In "On Civil Disobedience" (originally titled "Resistance to Civil Government"), Thoreau advises
protesters against slavery and the Mexican War to

> break the law. Let your life be a counter friction to stop the ma-
> chine.... Cast your whole vote, not a strip of paper merely, but
> your whole influence. A minority is powerless while it conforms
> to the majority; it is not even a minority then; but it is irresistible
> when it clogs by its whole weight. (103–4)

In Thoreau's influential view, public disobedience, unresisting surren-
der, and willing acceptance of whatever penalties the State imposes is
not only required of the disobedient parties but absolutely necessary
for its appeal to the general populace. In theory, this strategy is meant
to inspire an irresistible grassroots movement, leading to legal challenge of whatever unjust law has been weighed and found wanting
when measured against some higher moral standard—"natural law" in
current jurisprudence—that takes precedence over temporal legislation and economic interests.

Terrorism, at the other extreme, implies a violent, surreptitious,
and devastating action primarily designed to incite fear rather than in-
crementally encourage peaceful change. Although Abbey's "wooden
shoe people" (280) destroy machines and not lives, their actions in
some ways seem to fit the legal definition of terrorism: "premeditated,
politically motivated violence perpetrated against noncombatant targets by subnational groups or clandestine agents, usually intended to
influence an audience" (U.S. Code). In the novel, the "noncombatant

targets" are power lines, 35-ton loaders, and D-9 Caterpillars. Do the characters' actions then constitute terrorism? Perhaps sabotage is a better word after all, occupying as it does some moral middle ground between terrorism and civil disobedience. Would most Americans agree that it is a lesser crime? While qualitatively different from slaughtering thousands of civilians, destroying the private property of power companies, highway contractors, and mining interests begs the related question of why, in American culture, property seems to be as sacred, or in some cases more sacred, than life itself. In an interview, James Cahalan reports a comment made by poet Gary Snyder to Earth First! founder Dave Foreman in a 1982 letter criticizing American culture's fascination with violence and materialism: "spray as much blood as you like ... but don't violate machinery."

In real life, the borders between threatening property and threatening lives often blur. The Earth Liberation Front agents who spiked trees in the Pacific Northwest were attempting to damage or destroy chainsaws and lumber mills, but a powerful high-speed blade striking a twenty-penny nail could potentially injure a worker, enough of a threat to dissuade timber companies from continuing to cut old-growth trees in the districts said to be randomly spiked. Contrast that with Abbey's human "victims," who at worst suffer downtime while their machines are repaired or replaced. Unlike tree-spiking, monkey-wrenching does not target the lower-level operatives. It is their bosses, or rather their bosses' balance sheets, that are the enemy.

The lowest common denominator between civil disobedience, sabotage, and terrorism is a desire for attention. In this sense, all three kinds of action merit being called a form of political speech. But do the means always justify the ends? And are the ends even attainable? If Abbey's monkeywrenchers intend to physically halt development by reducing the sum total of earth-moving machines in the Southwest, their efforts are laughably inadequate, and in the long run, futile bordering on quixotic. If they intend to change the public's mind by moral example, then their secretiveness and lack of accountability undercut their educational mission. Where, a modern Thoreau might ask, is the courage of their convictions? To what natural law are they loyal?

CHARACTER DEVELOPMENT

Significantly, the four main characters in *The Monkey Wrench Gang* are not naturalists, artists, philosophers, politicians, or desert hermits.

They are united only by fierce love of the undeveloped wilderness, re-gardless of its economic potential or historic patterns of use. Two of them are radical individualists; two are medical professionals and thor-oughly middle-class urban types, "elitists" by birth and privilege. The two pairs meet for the first time on a guided trip down the Colorado River: boozy, cigar-chomping "Doc" Sarvis, an Albuquerque surgeon given to midnight extractions of unsightly roadside billboards; his sec-retary/assistant/paramour Bonnie Abzug; "Seldom Seen" Smith, a lapsed but still polygamous Mormon river guide; and George Wash-ington Hayduke III, a bearded, beer-guzzling, foul-mouthed former Green Beret and Vietnam POW working as Smith's temporary boat-man. Abbey is said to have modeled all four characters after friends and acquaintances of his, and the best-known of them, Doug Peacock ("Hayduke"), has since traded on this notoriety plus some fieldwork to become a nature writer, colorful public speaker, and environmental activist in his own right. His best-known book, *The Grizzly Years: In Search of the American Wilderness* (1990), perpetuates the Hayduke persona in the context of a plea to save the last of North America's largest land mammals.

In Abbey's tale, Hayduke is a violent extremist, reined in by the other three protagonists. One night around a riverside campfire they hatch a plot to expand Sarvis's "neighborhood beautification project" (9) into a full-blown assault on large-scale public and private projects in the Southwest, in particular Glen Canyon Dam. In the late 1960s this masterwork of the Army Corps of Engineers, a favorite rhetorical target of Abbey and other environmental writers, was constructed over the vociferous objections of the Sierra Club's David Brower. Once full, the reservoir obliterated a beloved and now-legendary flat-water stretch of Colorado River upstream of the Grand Canyon. A Jim Stiles illustration on the cover of the first edition of Abbey's essay col-lection *The Journey Home* (1977) imagines the dam, bleeding water from a huge crack across its face, ready to collapse.

First, however, they decide to warm up with a few easier targets:

"But who says we have to start with dams?" asks Hayduke. "There's plenty of other work to do."

"Good work," the doctor said. "Good, wholesome, construc-tive work.... the strip mines. And the pipelines. And the new rail-road from Black Mesa to Page. And the coal-burning power plants. And the copper smelters.... And the computer centers.

And the land and cattle companies. And the people who throw beer cans along the highways."

"I throw beer cans along the fucking highways," Hayduke said.

...Smith said "I do it too. Any road I wasn't consulted about that I don't like, I litter. It's my religion.

..."Doc," said Hayduke. "It's liberation." (64–65)

In several published essays, Abbey depicts himself tossing beer cans from his vehicle, a very Western, male, working-class, and largely despised practice humorously reinterpreted through this new ideology of individual protest. "Nature," he quotes another American social critic in a parenthetical aside to his best-known work, *Desert Solitaire* (1968), is a "place to throw empty beer cans on Sunday, said Mencken" (41). This comment hints at the exaggeration and self-parody at the center of Abbey's comic work—are we to take this buffoonery seriously? Does he mean what he says, or is dam-busting, like littering, the rhetorical gesture of a notoriety-seeking clown? The boundaries between Abbey and his larger-than-life characters are not always clear.

Having firmly planted in the reader's mind the cartoon vision of giant explosions obliterating the dam's companion bridge, thanks in part to a prologue entitled "Aftermath," and having introduced the paradoxical and anarchistic idea that destruction can be "constructive," the novel then jumps to the four gang members brainstorming equipment lists and food caches for their first operation, the destruction of heavy equipment at a road-building project. Dust and dialogue fly furiously as subsequent escapades escalate and the characters scatter and then regroup multiple times across a true-to-life and meticulously rendered Southwestern setting. The novel climaxes as three of the four are apprehended by a San Juan County sheriff's posse after an extended chase across the most rugged section of the Colorado Plateau. In a spectacular firefight at Lizard Rock, Hayduke appears to be shot to pieces and blown off a cliff thousands of feet high. The others reappear in an epilogue, paroled and peacefully settled in Green River, Utah, when one night a mysterious one-eyed masked rider (Jack Burns, the anarchist hero of Abbey's 1956 novel *Brave Cowboy*) arrives with a companion, Hayduke, in tow. The implication? "Constructive work" is continuing, Hayduke is now operating undercover as a night watchman at Glen Canyon Dam, and others have taken up the noble work of monkeywrenching, perhaps on a larger scale.

CRITICAL RECEPTION

Reviewers lost no time noticing *The Monkey Wrench Gang*. *The National Observer* called it "sad, hilarious, exuberant, vulgar." "Abbey is [the American desert's] Thoreau," claimed Larry McMurtry in *The Washington Post*. Some of the reviews also recognized the innovative nature of Abbey's accomplishment. Typical of these was the anonymous pronouncement in *Newsweek*: "a new fictional genre, the ecological caper." A few months later, novelist Jim Harrison, writing in the *New York Times*, accused *The Monkey Wrench Gang* of being a "revolutionary" manifesto for the "New Left." Nevertheless, most readers probably at first read agree with Elizabeth Ashton's opinion in the *Houston Chronicle:* "a scriptwriter's dream." Abbey's work had already been adapted by Hollywood when *Lonely Are the Brave* (1962) featured Kirk Douglas as Jack Burns, but although he was paid several sums on the order of $25,000 or more for options on the film rights, over the years potential producers have apparently shied away from the glorification of lawless guerilla activity in America's heartland. As of this writing, a film version, written by Deric Washburn (*The Deerhunter* and *Silent Running*), is listed in pre-production on the Pressman Films Web site.

The book never made the best-seller lists, but by the time of Abbey's death in 1989, it had sold 500,000 copies and 200,000 more by 1998. None of Abbey's four other novels have sold even remotely as well, and the posthumously published sequel, *Hayduke Lives* (1990), never achieved anything like the original's critical notice or notoriety, surpassed among Abbey's work only by that more ruminative and rambling set of environmental soliloquies, *Desert Solitaire*.

The sequel did attract another kind of attention when, according to the *Philadelphia City Paper*, 22-year-old Neil Godfrey tried to board a United Airlines flight one month after the September 11, 2001, terrorist attacks carrying a copy of *Hayduke Lives!*, with its lurid cover art featuring a ticking dynamite bomb. The would-be passenger was detained, searched, and interrogated while his novel was confiscated and analyzed by the National Guard, state troopers, and city police officers (Shaffer).

Aside from its sensationalist theme, the appeal of *The Monkey Wrench Gang*—some might say its danger—lies in its complete and seductive accessibility. There are no earnest environmentalist polemics or political theory here but instead an action-packed plot powered by jokes, puns, and postmodern irony. Paragraph after paragraph dances to its conclusion in sentence fragments like piled-on punch lines, often dripping with literary allusions:

> The steam spiraled up from the coffee in the shape, transient but clear, of a question mark. The question was not the practical one—Are they armed?—for if they carried weapons they kept them, like Hayduke's, concealed.... The question was: Will the sphincter hold till I get out of here and free and clear? The riddle of the sphincter. That was the question. (265)

Underground cartoonist Robert "R." Crumb illustrated a 1985 edition of the novel, and other editions feature graphic, adventurous cover art in the colorful and romantic style of an updated Frederic Remington. Abbey repeatedly claimed that "above all," he wanted to be "entertaining." Yet he is recorded as saying, to a group of students, that "if someone else wanted to do it, I'd be there holding a flashlight," and, in a 1984 interview, that he "did quite a bit of field research for that book...I spent whole nights on construction sights in Utah, putting sand in transmissions, shooting holes in truck tires and radiators." Tucked away on the verso of the first paperback edition's title page is Abbey's solemn declaration that "Everything in [this book] is real and actually happened. And it all began just one year from today" (vi). Like many writers, Abbey is a notoriously unreliable source for biographical details, and it is difficult to say where truth leaves off and personal myth-making begins. In *Desert Solitaire* he portrays his fictional, if semiautobiographical, alter-ego "Ed" casually pulling survey stakes from a road project:

> as I went I pulled up each little wooden stake and threw it away, and cut all the bright ribbons from the bushes and hid them under a rock. A futile effort, in the long run, but it made me feel good. (67)

In *The Monkey Wrench Gang,* Abbey portrays Hayduke unreflectively pulling survey stakes, "a patient, noble, resolute, sweating man doing his job" (99).

HUMOR

In *The Monkey Wrench Gang,* philosophical rumination plays second fiddle to comic narration and witty dialogue. As in *Desert Soli-*

taire, it sometimes seems as if Abbey is incapable of sustaining a gentler, more introspective tone without quickly deflating his aesthetic pretensions with humor:

> In the afternoon I watch the clouds drift past the bald peak of Mount Tukuhnikivats. (*Someone* has to do it.) (*Desert Solitaire* 46)

Abbey was reputedly difficult to pin down concerning his basic philosophy. Biographer Jack Loeffler reports Abbey calling himself "a registered anarchist."

> I asked him, "How long have you been a registered anarchist?"
>   Ed said, "Oh, about 5,000 years. In the realm of ideal politics, I'm some sort of agrarian, barefoot wilderness eco-freak anarchist...." (31)

The closest anyone gets in *The Monkey Wrench Gang* to an environmental manifesto is an exchange between Bonnie and Hayduke, who have become lovers for the duration. On the verge of vandalizing a yardfull of Georgia-Pacific equipment, a troubled Bonnie asks Hayduke how he can oppose logging if lumber is needed to build shelters.

In the opening scenes of *The Monkey Wrench Gang,* these sorts of snappy exchanges between characters, woven together by wisecracking narration and heavily caricatured descriptions, serve to lighten the darker implications of what amounts to a noble effort to save the wilderness or a criminal conspiracy to destroy private property—take your pick. Whichever it is, it's all going to be in good fun, Abbey implies. But the last of the novel's opening epigraphs cuts for a moment against this comic grain, conveying great emotional weight in lines by Southwestern naturalist, poet, and university professor Richard Shelton, which read, "...but oh my desert/yours is the only death I cannot bear." This mystical lament, combining a personal attachment to a landscape with Romanticism's "pathetic fallacy" (personifying an aspect of nature and projecting one's own feelings upon it), implies an underlying rational assessment of ecological damage to the West's arid regions.

Beneath the broad, picaresque plot of *The Monkey Wrench Gang,* a reader willing to suspend disbelief in the more extreme antics of Sarvis, Hayduke, Smith, and Abzug will find the same serious, polemic themes as in *Desert Solitaire* and disguised versions of the more soberly modulated sentiments and arguments expressed by Western writers from John Muir to Wallace Stegner: ecstatic apprecia- tion of the intricacy and beauty of desert and mountain ecosystems and mingled sorrow and rage at their desecration and destruction. If these overwhelming emotions sweep one toward a misanthropic view of human nature, so be it. People can be comic, but there is nothing funny about a mountain. Abbey comes on strong with satire, sarcasm, and cleverly allusive wordplay as he narrates his characters' exploits or mocks the state of "national parking lots" swarming with hordes of "knobby-kneed oldsters in plaid Bermudas buzz[ing] up and down the quaintly curving asphalt road on motorbikes" (*Desert Solitaire* 51), but when he shears off into pure description of Southwestern canyons, mesas, and mountain ranges, he can sound as sincere and reverent as Muir himself, at least for a paragraph or two:

> ...alone here in the wilderness, where all that is most significant takes place. (Sunset and moonrise, moaning winds and stillness, cloud transformations, the metamorphosis of sunlight, yellowing leaf and the indolent, soaring vulture....) (297)

The Monkey Wrench Gang is a far lighter and more mischievous book than *Desert Solitaire*, full of digression and irony, sustaining a satiric tone in the high tradition of Cervantes and Swift, with post- modern elaborations reminiscent of Joseph Heller and Kurt Vonnegut Jr. Readers of his other novels and essays will recognize familiar Abbeyesque themes like the shattered TV tube and the omnipresent vulture, puns ("Arches National Money-Mint"), plus stray aphorisms both quoted and original, so that some text passages resemble a tissue of references to the rest of his writing. Author Abbey is not even averse to writing himself a cameo appearance: a park ranger at Navajo Bridges National Monument who confronts the monkeywrenchers is named "Edwin P. Abbott, Jr.," a reminder that Abbey himself served several stints as a ranger at Arches in the late 1950s, as first chronicled in *Desert Solitaire*.

On the other hand, two aspects of *The Monkey Wrench Gang* that Abbey plays for laughs can seem more disturbing nearly three decades later—his sexism and his apparent contempt for the Mormon religion. The former charge revolves around the portrait of Bonnie, a nubile and feisty former New Yorker who falls for the inarticulate, unshaven, and semipsychotic Hayduke. Abbey's own problems with women are and recounted in sometimes excruciating detail by biographers such as

Loeffler and Cahalan, who each take pains to document that Abbey found it impossible until near the end of his life to remain faithful for very long to one partner. Loeffler, a close friend and Abbey apologist, writes,

> He regarded his desire to make love to many women as a bio-logical imperative that has nothing to do with chauvinism. A bil-lennia of monkey genes does not a monogam make....He was married five times, divorced thrice, widowered once, and was fi-nally reshaped by his commitment to his last wife for whom he proved to be a good husband. (35)

In *The Monkey Wrench Gang,* Abzug serves primarily as executive assistant and sexual companion to Sarvis and Hayduke, while Smith's plural marriages are played for laughs, and various other female char-acters lurk in the background as temptations or respites for the men.

Born and raised in traditionalist Appalachia back in 1927 when the American women's movement was in temporary abeyance (suffrage had been achieved, Simone de Beauvoir had yet to publish *The Second Sex* or Betty Friedan *The Feminine Mystique,* and World War II had yet to get women out of the kitchen and into the factory), Abbey was nearly 50 when he wrote *The Monkey Wrench Gang.* It may be enough to conclude that he was a product of his unenlightened time and place. Indeed, like the beer cans he throws on the highway, this aspect of himself may be written into Hayduke, who in one of his more tran-scendental immersions into nature manages to foreshadow the immi-nent tryst with Bonnie, whom he has just told to "fuck off" twice:

> Among those faraway buttes and pinnacles, rosy red against the sky, lay the promise of something intimate—the intimate in the remote. A secret and a revelation. Later, he thought, we'll get into all that. (110)

As for his apparent prejudice against The Church of Jesus Christ of Latter-Day Saints, a discussion in *Desert Solitaire* debunks the sect's theology (in company with most other major world religions) but grudgingly admires its social organization. "[M]uch to admire, much worth saving...friendly, hospitable, honest, self-reliant and self-confi-dent" (266–67)—strange conclusion for an anarchist! But wait: "Bal-ance, that's the secret," writes Abbey. "Moderate extremism. The best of both worlds" (*Desert Solitaire* 298). In *The Monkey Wrench Gang* Abbey goes to the other extreme by pinning every sin of modern corporate-industrial degradation, pollution and political hanky-panky on the novel's primary antagonist, Bishop Love, who

> ...was not only bishop of the church but also served as chairman of the county commission, planned to run for the Utah State Assembly and higher office after that, owned the Chevrolet agency in Blanding, several uranium mines active and inactive...and a half interest in the marina complex at Hall's Crossing. And eight children. (271–72)

Needless to say, Love's crusade against monkeywrenching on behalf of the miners, road builders, loggers, and land developers is motivated by the desire to make money, while he cloaks his operations in piousness and uses ecumenical authority to command a posse of vigilantes in pursuit of Sarvis, Hayduke, and company. Abbey paints this unsympathetic character by highlighting his fraud and hypocrisy and adding a few exaggerated traits of the southern redneck sheriff, rendered Western-style. Love's churchgoing cronies are portrayed at worst as thick-headed yokels; at best, as well-meaning but naïve soldiers like Love's brother Sam, who does seem at the end to be converted to a more sympathetic view of the monkeywrenchers through Doc Sarvis's self-sacrificing humanity and Hayduke's determination.

Perhaps then, in Abbey's literary West, there is hope after all. Perhaps ecoterrorism will give way, as it has to a great extent in the real West, to civil disobedience. Perhaps the power of the heart, coupled with endurance and courage, will convert rural populations one by one to a renewed appreciation of the natural world and a determination to preserve some of it despite traditional ways and local economic concerns. Or perhaps not. In a 1982 interview, Abbey speculated on what might happen if

> the conflict between conservation and development becomes more intense, and if the politicians fail to follow the popular will on the matter. I think a lot of people are going to become very angry and they're going to resort to illegal methods to try to slow down the destruction of our natural resources.... If the conflict becomes violent and physical then I'm sure the environmentalists will mostly end up in prison or shot dead in their

tracks. So I hope we can save what's left of Arizona and the United States by legal, political means and I still think we can.

As a dramatization of the conflict, Abbey's story keeps us interrogating the motives and methods of the environmental activists who campaign for our consciences on behalf of the natural world. Luis Alberto Urrea reports in his analysis of Abbey's apparent prejudice against Mexican immigrants that Ed liked to think of himself as a "gadfly...and nobody was spared." Not Mexicans, not Mormons, not Indians (either American or Asian), not cowboys, not college professors or Buddhists or beef cattle. If satire is a double-edged sword, perhaps Abbey was sticking it not only to those who would pave the last parcels of undeveloped Western land but also to those who would take reckless measures to conserve it, and even those who would write about it—himself in particular. As Plato portrays Socrates, the original self-described "gadfly" of Western civilization, saying to the Athenian jury, "I awaken, and persuade, and reproach each one of you" (82).

BIBLIOGRAPHY

Abbey, Edward. *Desert Solitaire*. 1968. New York: Ballantine Books, 1971.
———. Interview with Eric Temple. 1982. <http://www.abbeyweb.net/articles/etemple/index.html#Speak>.
———. *The Monkey Wrench Gang*. 1975. New York: Avon, 1976.
Ashton, Elizabeth. *Houston Chronicle*. 28 Sept. 1975. 8.
Cahalan, James M. *Edward Abbey: A Life*. Tucson: U of Arizona P, 2001.
———. Personal interview at Western Literature Association annual meeting. 10 Oct. 2002.
Harrison, Jim. "Two Novels." *New York Times*. 14 Nov. 1976. 267.
Hepworth, James R., and Gregory McNamee, eds. *Resist Much, Obey Little*. San Francisco: Sierra Club Books, 1996.
McMurtry, Larry. "Fertile Fictions of the American Desert." *Washington Post*. 8 Sept. 1975. C8.
"*Monkey Wrench Gang* by Edward Abbey." *The National Observer*. 6 Sept. 1975. 17.
"*Monkey Wrench Gang* by Edward Abbey." *Newsweek*. 5 Jan. 1976. 70.
Plato. *The Apology. Four Texts on Socrates*. Rev. ed. Trans. Thomas G. West and Grace Starry West. Ithaca: Cornell UP, 1998.
Pressman Films. The Edward R. Pressman Film Corporation. <http://www.pressman.com/inproduction/monkey.htm>.

Shaffer, Gwen. "Novel Security Measures." *Philadelphia City Paper.* 18–25 Oct. 2001. <http://citypaper.net/articles/101801/news.godfrey. shtml>.

Thoreau, Henry David. "On Civil Disobedience." *Five Hundred Years: Exploring American Traditions.* Ed. Scott E. Casper and Richard O. Davies. 3rd ed. Boston: Pearson Custom Publishing, 2000.

U.S. Code, Title 22, Section 2656f(d).

8

Leslie Marmon Silko, *Ceremony* (1977)

Scott Slovic

Published in 1977, Leslie Marmon Silko's novel *Ceremony* is considered one of the cornerstones of the contemporary renaissance of Native American literature. Texas State University scholar Allan Chavkin reported in 2002 that "Since its publication in 1977, more than half a million copies of the book have been sold, and it is now one of the most frequently taught contemporary novels in higher education" (Chavkin, 4). This novel tells the story of a Native American man, Tayo (pronounced "tay-yo"), who has returned to the Laguna Pueblo reservation in New Mexico after serving in the U.S. Army during World War II, where he was a prisoner of the Japanese on a Pacific Island. Half-white and half-Indian, Tayo has spent his entire life feeling isolated and estranged; and his experiences during the war have only accentuated his sense of alienation. Other soldiers returning to the reservation seek solace in alcohol and bar fights, but Tayo yearns for a deeper kind of healing. With the help of his relatives, he visits a traditional medicine man and then a more modern medicine man, trying to find a ceremony that will enable him to feel whole, to feel grounded in the place where he belongs and in the community. In a sense, the novel tells the story of a young man struggling to find—or create—a ceremony that will enable him to survive and, possibly, to be a constructive, healing presence in the world.

Silko's stylistically experimental novel progresses from scene to scene without being divided into traditional chapters. Although the narrative is presented in the third person, the story focuses on the psychological condition of the protagonist, Tayo, describes various incidents that occur after his return to Laguna Pueblo and flashbacks to earlier experiences during the war and during his childhood, and then occasionally expands to a mythic level (represented by poems centered on the pages or by omniscient prose overviews of the meaning of particular events). Readers will immediately notice the early emphasis in the book on Tayo's "sickness"—his despair, confusion, feelings of profound unbelonging—his nausea. He seems to be suffering from post-traumatic stress disorder, a condition that we now know to be fairly common among soldiers and others who have experienced terrifying and stressful conditions. In an early scene in the novel, he has actually been sent to a hospital en route home from the war, but his treatment there does not heal him. One way of reading the novel is to consider how Tayo manages gradually to recover from his mental and physical ailments, trying various routes to recovery.

Scholars and teachers of environmental literature have traditionally valued *Ceremony* because of the beautiful passages describing Tayo's growing sense of contact with the landscape of the American Southwest, his native land. For both Native American readers and nonnatives, these descriptions of personal identification with landscape seem to represent the possibility of all people to achieve deeper, more meaningful contact with place than is typical in modern, urban America. However, readers have increasingly observed that *Ceremony* is a significant work in its representation of an environmental ethos—a powerful sense of place—within the context of real-life social, political, and psychological experiences. In the pages that follow, I will explain both the traditional "environmental" reading of *Ceremony* and the new way of reading the work from the perspective of "environmental justice." The field of environmental justice is concerned with the unequal impacts of environmental destruction on poor communities and people of color.

SILKO'S LIFE AND WRITINGS

An explanation of Leslie Marmon Silko's life provides a context for understanding her novel, *Ceremony*. Silko was born on March 5, 1948, in Albuquerque, New Mexico. She is of mixed Laguna, Mexican, and Anglo ancestry, and she grew up in a rock-and-adobe house on the edge of the traditional Laguna community, her family marginalized by its mixed-blood status from the rest of the pueblo. Virginia, her mother, was a Plains Indian from Montana, and her father, Lee H. Marmon, was part white and part Laguna. Robert Gunn Marmon, Silko's great-grandfather, was a white government surveyor who married a Laguna woman, Marie Anaya, whom he met when he came to the pueblo in 1872. Silko later wrote, "I suppose at the core of my writing is the attempt to identify what it is to be a half-breed, or mixed-blooded person; what it is to grow up neither white nor fully traditional Indian. It is for this reason that I hesitate to say that I am representative of Indian poets or Indian people. I am only one human being, one Laguna woman" ("Old and New," 197).

As a child, Silko was cared for by her great-grandmother Marie, known as "Grandma A'Mooh," while her mother worked. Her father's aunt, known as "Aunt Susie," was also an important influence on Silko. Both Grandma A'Mooh and Aunt Susie were sources of stories that Silko would eventually weave into her own writing. Silko began her formal education at a Laguna school run by the Bureau of Indian Affairs, where the children were required to speak English. She later attended a private school before entering the University of New Mexico. At New Mexico, she earned a bachelor of arts degree in English in 1969 and published her first short stories, "The Man to Send Rain Clouds" and "Tony's Story." Her son Robert was born in 1966, followed by Cazimir in 1972. She completed three semesters of law school at the University of New Mexico before receiving a National Endowment for the Humanities Discovery Grant and quitting school to devote her time to writing. Her poetry collection, *Laguna Woman,* appeared in 1974, when Silko taught at Navajo Community College in Tsaile, Arizona. She and her family moved to Ketchikan, Alaska, during the 1970s, where her husband, John Silko, worked as the supervising attorney for Alaska Legal Services. This time in Silko's life was particularly difficult, and her emotional and family struggles while living in Alaska have a direct bearing on *Ceremony.* As she told interviewer Robin Cohen in 1998, she wrote the novel in order to map out her own road to recovery: "I did it because I was homesick and alienated, and of course my then-husband, his family weren't very nice to me, so there was a real social isolation, although my two sisters followed me up there. The marriage was really falling apart. I remember literally thinking, boy if I did not have this little kid, I would be out of this marriage. So the marriage was in awful shape, and so when I started *Ceremony,* I was as sick as Tayo was. I was having nausea and all kinds of weird symptoms and stuff and then as he starts to get better, of course, I was starting, so there is this parallel" ("Of Apricots," 258). The landscape in Alaska actually "triggered" or inspired her work on the novel. "There was ocean, fog, tall trees," Silko told Cohen. "I felt sort of claustrophobic. I suffered. Now they understand that there can be depressions triggered by lack of sunshine. I had a terrible kind of depression like that, and that was before I really got started writing. . . . So I literally wrote *Ceremony* to save my life. That is why it is called *Ceremony*, because I know that I could not have made it if I had not been writing *Ceremony* for those two years" ("Of Apricots," 257–58). Although her own experiences were clearly different from those of the male, war-veteran protagonist of her novel, Tayo's feelings of homesickness, isolation, and psychological stress are imaginative projections from the author's own life, with a fictional twist.

A year after *Ceremony* was published in 1977, Silko left Alaska and moved to Tucson, Arizona, where she began teaching at the University of Arizona. In August 1978, Silko received a letter from the distinguished American poet James Wright, whom she had met in 1975 at a writers conference in Michigan. Wright had just finished reading *Ceremony* and wrote to tell Silko "how much the book means to me." He wrote: "In some strange way it seems inadequate to call it a great book, though it is surely that, or a perfect work of art, though it is one. I could call *Ceremony* one of the four or five best books I have ever read about America and I would be speaking the truth. But even this doesn't say just what I mean. I think I am trying to say that my very life means more to me than it would have meant if you hadn't written *Ceremony*. But this sounds inadequate also" (Wright 3). Silko replied almost immediately, telling Wright, "Your letter came at a time when I needed it most. So many sad things have happened with my marriage and my children—it is good to know that my work means something" (4). And thus ensued a correspondence between the two writers that lasted until James Wright's death from cancer in March 1980. The encouragement and advice from James Wright helped Silko to keep up her spirits and keep working during a sad and stressful time in her life. A year after Wright's death, her collection of miscellaneous stories, poems, sketches, and photographs appeared, titled *Storyteller*. In 1981, she also received a five-year fellowship from the MacArthur Foundation that enabled her to stop teaching and devote all of her time to writing her next major novel, *Almanac of the Dead*, which eventually appeared in 1991.

During the years between the publication of *Storyteller* and the appearance of *Almanac of the Dead*, Silko produced only one book. Her correspondence with James Wright, edited by Wright's widow Anne Wright, came out in 1986, titled *The Delicacy and Strength of Lace: Letters Between Leslie Marmon Silko and James Wright*. Years later, in a conversation that would be printed in *The Bloomsbury Review*, poet and nature writer Ray Gonzalez pointed out to Silko "the connection in the earth and the landscape" that abides in both her letters to Wright and the 1991 novel, singling out the letter at the end of the collected correspondence where Silko describes seeing an owl in a Saguaro cactus on the day Wright died (Gonzalez 104). When Gonzalez asked if Silko went back and looked at *Ceremony* while writing *Almanac,* Silko replied:

> I thought they were very different until recently. The further I get away from *Almanac,* I hope I haven't written the same book twice. But in a sense, I probably have because I'm still trying to figure out where injustice comes from. Injustice I pretty much equate with evil, an imbalance and unwellness. In my mind, I was probably thinking back to *Ceremony.* If people thought that vision of good and evil ended with *Ceremony,* then what I was seeing around me in Tucson told me I could define it some more. Once I delivered *Ceremony* to the publisher, I don't think I ever read it all the way through again. (105)

It is difficult to summarize the various themes of *Almanac,* except to say that the novel's multiple narratives, which sometimes diverge and other times overlap, explore many aspects of the violence, depravity, and despair of contemporary American life, hinting that there may be profound explanations of human nature and of good and evil in a set of ancient Native American notebooks. Critic Janet M. Powers argues that *Almanac* is an allegorical work in the tradition of Dante's *Divine Comedy:* "Just as Dante does, she shows us human beings dealing with each other, with minorities, and with the earth—torturing, butchering, shooting, raping, excavating—until we can stand it no longer and cry out, 'Stop!' That is precisely Silko's strategy, what earlier mystics called the *via negativa.* If we are truly horrified, we will take steps toward change. *Almanac of the Dead* is not escape fiction.... Silko's mission in this novel is to present the horror in such a way that it cannot be shunted aside" (Powers 270–71).

Almanac is a sprawling, 763-page, unflinching look at a North America on the verge of murdering, drug-dealing apocalypse—an effort to employ the actions of individual characters in pursuit of a global, mythic explanation of the human predicament. When asked by Laura Coltelli shortly after the publication of the novel whether *Almanac* was an extension of *Ceremony,* Silko responded:

Yes, *Almanac* might be seen as an "exploded" version of *Ceremony,* but one should beware of over-simplifying *Almanac. Almanac* examines time and history in a way that *Ceremony* only begins to approach. In *Almanac,* I go farther with my thinking about the influence of spirit beings as well as animal beings. I go farther with my thinking about the power of narrative in *Almanac* when I consider the writings of Marx. I go farther in thinking about dreams and their influence over human consciousness.

Whereas *Ceremony* is about one person trying to recover his health and well-being, this is about the whole Earth trying to save herself. *Ceremony* barely hints at the activities and thinking of the Gunadeeyahs, but with Trigg, Beaufrey, the Police Chief, the Judge, and the rest, the reader gets to see what actually goes on in the minds of these Gunadeeyas, these worshippers of suffering and destruction. And of course, these "monsters" are not so different from the rest of us. (Coltelli 131–32)

It is important to know how Silko expanded and intensified certain themes from *Ceremony* in creating her next novel, but the power of *Almanac* does not diminish the brilliance and beauty and social analysis of the earlier work. While Silko tended to emphasize the ambitiousness of her new work in interviews she gave in the early 1990s, many critics, teachers, and students continued to find *Ceremony* more readable and aesthetically coherent than the new novel, in all its bleakness and experimental disjunctiveness.

Two years after the appearance of *Almanac,* Silko produced a small, handmade volume of her own black-and-white photographs, accompanied by a personal essay about experiences with water in the various places where she has spent her life, from Laguna Pueblo to Alaska to Tucson. She begins by noting that her great-grandmother, Marie Anaya, "belonged to the water clan" (*Sacred Water* 15), implying the significance of the element of water to her own life and consciousness. Although in her author's note at the end of the small book she suggests that *Sacred Water* is intended almost as the antithesis of *Almanac*—a small, informal book, made "for the sheer sensual pleasure of the paper, glue, and the copy machine images of my photographs" (80)—the themes of ominous contamination and destruction and the hope for re-purification, evident in *Almanac* and earlier in *Ceremony,* emerge in the meditation on water, too. "For a long time," she writes, "I had a great many Sonoran red-spotted toads around the rain water pool behind my house.... Hundreds of toads used to sing all night in a magnificent chorus with complex harmonies" (63). On the following page, recounting a dinner with a friend and his two boys, she mentions in a deadpan, matter-of-fact way what happened when the boys and their dog went out to the rain water pool by themselves: "Strewn all around the pool were the remains of toads smashed flat by the boys and the dog" (64). Two pages later, she expands her explanation from one scene of destruction to the broader destructive implications of industrial-technological disaster:

> I managed to keep my composure until the dinner guests and their dog had left. I never saw them again. The night-long choirs of multitudes of toads ceased. The Chernobyl nuclear reactor disaster occurred not long afterward and may also have affected the toad population. Last summer the pool had polly-wogs again, the descendants of the red-spotted toads which had survived radioactive fall-out and the boys with the dog. The night-long choirs have not resumed yet; the toads need a few years more to recover. (66)

This brief vignette, like the discussion that follows of the appearance of "a strange red algae with the texture of mucous" in her pond, offers a fine example of the author's attentiveness to the cycle of harm and recovery and to the imaginative connections between personal and global events. Readers will find these patterns, likewise, in *Ceremony* and *Almanac*, and also in Silko's 1999 novel, *Gardens in the Dunes*, which explores, among other things, the legacy of colonialism in North America, as two "Sand Lizard" (Papago) girls struggle to stay connected to their native land and their traditional knowledge of place despite the cultural forces of American society that wrench them away from the Sonoran Desert.

NARRATIVE TRADITION AND WORLD VIEW

Critics, readers, and teachers interested in the worldview represented in the novel *Ceremony* and in Silko's rationale for constructing the complex web of narratives in that work have often pointed to her essay "Landscape, History, and the Pueblo Imagination" for a helpful—if indirect—explanation of these issues. Critic Thomas K. Dean has suggested that "Very few printed documents more succinctly and eloquently express the intimate and complex relationship between nature and culture" than this essay (Dean 818), which appeared initially in the Autumn 1986 issue of *Antaeus* and was reprinted in 1996 under the title "Interior and Exterior Landscapes: The Pueblo Migration Stories" in Silko's volume *Yellow Woman and a Beauty of the Spirit: Essays on Native American Life Today,* along with 21 other pieces. Silko describes the traditional style of Pueblo storytelling as follows:

> [T]he ancient Pueblo people depended upon collective memory through successive generations to maintain and transmit an entire culture, a worldview complete with proven strategies for survival. The oral narrative, or story, became the medium through which the complex of Pueblo knowledge and belief was maintained. Whatever the event or the subject, the ancient people perceived the world and themselves within that world as part of an ancient, continuous story composed of innumerable bundles of other stories....Whatever happened, the ancient people instinctively sorted events and details into a loose narrative structure. Everything became a story. (*Yellow Woman* 30–31)

Although *Ceremony* is obviously a printed text, published by a mainstream American publisher for a broad readership, one could argue that the novel presents some of the features of traditional Pueblo narrative. The fluctuating, shifting focus of the narrative has the meandering feel of oral storytelling. The notion that story is more than simple entertainment, that it carries "strategies for survival," is hinted at in Silko's linkage of individual lives and vast cultural issues and stories—in her work, there are seldom only solitary people and small communities at stake. The fate of Culture (with a capital C), the fate of the Earth, often seems to be hanging in the balance as her characters navigate the hazy, fluid boundaries between good and evil. And finally, the notion that the big, overarching story of the universe consists of "innumerable bundles of other stories" is crucial in appreciating the multilayered texture of *Ceremony* and Silko's later novels.

Unlike the stereotypical Western (or European) perspective of "dualism," which tends to separate human viewers from each other and from other phenomena in the world, the traditional Pueblo view of landscape was "monistic," emphasizing unity rather than distinction. This monistic worldview is one of the survival strategies carried by traditional stories. Silko writes:

The narratives linked with prominent features of the landscape between Paguate and Laguna delineate the complexities of the relationship that human beings must maintain with the surrounding natural world if they hope to survive in this place. Thus, the journey [emergence myth of the Pueblo people] was an interior process of the imagination, a growing awareness that being human is somehow different from all other life—animal, plant, and inanimate. Yet, we are all from the same source: awareness never deteriorated into Cartesian duality, cutting off the human from the natural world. (*Yellow Woman* 37)

To survive as a human, from this point of view, requires achieving a delicate balance between self-awareness and awareness of one's deep connectedness to other lives. This traditional perspective finds its counterpart, in certain ways, in the views of the contemporary spiritual and philosophical movement known as "deep ecology." For instance, one of the movement's founders, Norwegian philosopher Arne Naess, who coined the term "deep ecology" in 1973, describes his concept of "biospherical egalitarianism" as follows: "To the ecological field-worker, *the equal right to live and blossom* is an intuitively clear and obvious value maxim. Its restriction to humans is an anthropocentrism with detrimental effects upon the life quality of humans themselves. This quality depends in part upon the deep pleasure and satisfaction we receive from close partnership with other forms of life" (95). In the specific context of *Ceremony,* the character Tayo's own yearning (at first unconscious and later more intentional) to make contact with the physical and animate landscape of his native New Mexico embodies this intuitive sense that Survival (with a capital "S") is contingent on having a sense of connection and on valuing the place itself and all that lives there, not only oneself and one's own species.

Another key aspect of storytelling and the sense of connection in both traditional and modern Pueblo culture is the idea that stories are not used to disenfranchise or shun any member of the community. It is important to keep this in mind when reading *Ceremony* because part of Tayo's problem is his sense of unbelonging, of marginalization. As Silko puts it,

Even now, the people at Laguna Pueblo spend the greater portion of social occasions recounting recent incidents or events that have occurred in the Laguna area. Nearly always the discussion will precipitate the retelling of older stories about similar incidents or other stories connected with a specific place. The stories often contain disturbing or provocative material but are nonetheless told in the presence of children and women. The effect of these interfamily or interclan exchanges is the reassurance for each person that she or he will never be separated or apart from the clan, no matter what might happen. Neither the worst blunders or disasters nor the greatest financial prosperity and joy will ever be permitted to isolate anyone from the rest of the group. In the ancient times cohesiveness was all that stood between extinction and survival, and while the individual certainly was recognized, it was always as an individual simultaneously bonded to family and clan by a complex bundle of custom and ritual. (38–39)

Keeping in mind this concept of story as an integrative, community-sustaining process, as a unifying ritual even, it is possible to imagine the novel *Ceremony* itself as an effort to transfer, or translate, the traditional Pueblo forms and functions of storytelling into a late-twentieth-century work of literary art, accessible not only to Native American audiences but to readers from outside the author's own culture.

THEMES AND ISSUES IN *CEREMONY*

The opening pages of *Ceremony* present a page-centered narrative that raises the context of the ensuing story to a mythic, universal level, enveloping the reader's experience within the specific details of Tayo's struggles. "Ts'its'tsi'nako, Thought-Woman, / is sitting in her room," Silko begins, "and whatever she thinks about / appears.... She is sitting in her room / thinking of a story now // I'm telling you the story / she is thinking" (1). The entire universe of physical beings and actions is portrayed as the creation of Thought-Woman. And this is serious business:

> I will tell you something about stories,
> [he said]
> They aren't just entertainment.
> Don't be fooled.
> They are all we have, you see,
> all we have to fight off
> illness and death.

You don't have anything
if you don't have the stories. (2)

The third prefatory statement, also made in centered, poetic form, is
"*What She Said:* // The only cure / I know / is a good ceremony,
that's what she said" (3). We are immediately invited into a hybrid
realm of oral informality (indicated through repetitive and vernacular
phrasing) and print-culture aesthetics (highlighted by orthography,
the centering of poetic lines on the opening pages). Before we know
anything about the ceremonies Silko will be presenting in her narrative, we learn that ceremony is a "cure" for some kind of problem that
will be presented in the text. The vagueness of the meaning of both
"ceremony" and "cure," as introduced in the novel, enables the terms
readily to take on multiple meanings, from the level of Tayo's personal
problems to a global level.

Early in the novel, we encounter an extended description of Tayo's
confusion, his "sickness," after returning to Laguna Pueblo from the
war. "Tayo didn't sleep well that night.... he could hear Uncle Josiah
calling to him.... But before Josiah could come, the fever voices
would drift and whirl and emerge again—Japanese soldiers shouting
orders to him, suffocating damp voices that drifted out in the jungle
steam, and he heard the women's voices then; they faded in and out
until he was frantic" (5–6).

In this opening prose segment of the narrative, we learn of Tayo's
illness, of his attachment to Uncle Josiah, of his experiences with his
cousin Rocky as a Japanese prisoner of war on "some nameless Pacific
island" (7), and of Tayo's prayers to make the rain stop in the jungle.
Amid his hallucinations, it is clear that Tayo feels responsible for his
cousin's safety, fearful that the unending rain may prevent the weakened Rocky from marching through the jungle and determined to
protect Rocky by willing the rain to stop. There are powerful fore-
shadowings of key scenes from later in the novel in this opening section, including his memory of Josiah telling him, "Nothing was all
good or all bad either; it all depended" (11).

Another early scene in the novel shows Tayo during his stay at a
hospital in Los Angeles on his way home to New Mexico from the Pacific. "For a long time he had been white smoke," Silko writes. "He
did not realize that until he left the hospital, because white smoke had
no consciousness of itself" (14). Tayo's invisibility, his immateriality,
seems to be part of his sickness—he is ungrounded, disconnected.
Later we learn that Tayo had grown up in his Auntie's household, the

half-breed son of her sister Laura; Auntie never missed an opportunity to put down Tayo (29, 66–70). Several early scenes in the novel emphasize Tayo's utter lack of self-esteem, describing his initial desire to return to the hospital where he could be painlessly invisible (32–33).

The traditional medicine man, Ku'oosh comes to visit Tayo at the pueblo, but his ceremony is too rigid, too traditional. As he speaks, Tayo "had to strain to catch the meaning, dense with place names he had never heard" (34). In his soft voice, Ku'oosh tells Tayo, "But you know, grandson, this world is fragile," a cryptic reference to "the responsibility that went with being human" that will ultimately inspire Tayo to take decisive action against evil (35). Although he spends too much of his time bumming around the pueblo, often drinking, with fellow veterans—Emo, Pinkie, Leroy, Harley—Tayo gradually begins to have moments where he makes vital contact with the land. These passages in the novel are crucial for readers interested in the environmental themes of the work. For instance, on an excursion one day with Harley,

> [Tayo] sat down . . . and closed his eyes. In a world of crickets and wind and cottonwood trees he was almost alive again; he was visible. The green waves of dead faces and the screams of the dying that had echoed in his head were buried.

And in the next paragraph, Silko's prose echoes Ernest Hemingway's language in "Big Two-Hearted River, Part One," where his character Nick recovers from some unnamed catastrophe by making physical contact with nature during a fishing trip in northern Michigan. Silko writes:

> The place felt good. . . . It was soothing to rub the dust over his hands; he rubbed it carefully across his light brown skin, the stark white gypsum dust making a spotted pattern, and then he knew why it was done by the dancers: it connected them to the earth. (104)

Here Tayo begins to understand the importance of recognizing one's vital connection to the earth. This reinforces earlier passages where he recalled Uncle Josiah trying to teach him the importance of feeling close to the place where one lives (45, 74). Also, we see Tayo here unconsciously decorating himself in a ritualized way, drawing on his skin with plaster dust, creating a new, personal ceremony. In a sense, this is one of the central implications of the novel: that each of us might benefit from inventing ceremonies that help us to appreciate our connection to the earth.

Tayo later visits the medicine man Betonie, who helps him to articulate his suffering. Not only does Tayo experience the catharsis of expressing his sense of guilt, his grief from the loss of his cousin, but with Betonie's counseling he begins to become more conscious of the value of his insights into the commonality, the unity, of people from across the globe. Whereas his conflation of Japanese, Spanish, and Laguna voices and Japanese and Laguna faces early in the novel had seemed to be signs of madness and confusion, it eventually becomes possible for Tayo to realize that there is a fundamental similarity between his own people and the Japanese soldiers they were fighting in the Pacific. Also, his passive, painful guilt gradually transforms into a knowledge of powerful responsibility.

Tayo's physical sensitivity, mental clarity, and social consciousness steadily increase as the novel approaches its climax. While scouting for his family's lost cattle, he finds a cut in the barbed wire at the edge of the reservation and considers the inability of white ranchers to see beyond the lie: "only brown-skinned people were thieves; white people didn't steal, because they always had the money to buy whatever they needed." Tayo realizes:

> If the white people never looked beyond the lie, to see that theirs was a nation built on stolen land, then they would never be able to understand how they had been used by the witchery; they would never know that they were still being manipulated by those who knew how to stir the ingredients together: white thievery and injustice boiling up the anger and hatred that would finally destroy the world: the starving against the fat, the colored against the white. The destroyers had only to set it into motion, and sit back and count the casualties. (191)

This scene of indignation and frustration is followed a few pages later by an apprehension of ultimate beauty and belonging, as Tayo encounters a mountain lion at night, lying upon the ground amid pine needles (another Hemingway echo here, invoking the concluding lines of *For Whom the Bell Tolls*):

> The mountain lion came out from a grove of oak trees in the middle of the clearing. He did not walk or leap or run; his motions were like the shimmering of tall grass in the wind. He came across the meadow, moving into the wind. Tayo watched it with his head against the ground, conscious of pine needles tangled in his hair. He waited for the mare to shy away from the yellow form that

moved toward them; but the horse was upwind and did not stir. . . .

Tayo got to his knees slowly and held out his hand.

"Mountain lion," he whispered, "mountain lion, becoming what you are with each breath, your substance changing with the earth and sky." The mountain lion blinked his eyes; there was no fear. He gazed at him for another instant and then sniffed the southeast wind before he crossed the stream and disappeared into the trees, his outline lingering like yellow smoke, then suddenly gone. (195–96)

Passages like these alter the traditional assignment of evil/danger in the American West. Tayo wishes white ranchers—white readers—to understand that "brown-skinned people" are not thieves, are not the source of evil. Likewise, Silko does not designate white people as the evil perpetrators of land theft and other injustices. The novel deftly refers to "the witchery" and "the destroyers" without neatly categorizing destructive forces according to ethnic boundaries.

Tayo's healing culminates in a late scene that takes place at a uranium mine called Enchanted Mesa. As critic Thomas K. Dean from the University of Iowa explains, "Tayo realizes that the place of ultimate destruction, and the place of possible reclamation of the universe through ceremony, is the uranium mine. The Europeans, through this mine, had extracted natural forces and twisted them to their own incomprehensibly destructive ends, culminating in the atomic destruction of Hiroshima and Nagasaki" (822). In the novel's climactic passage, Tayo kneels and lifts a piece of ore, "gray stone . . . streaked with powdery yellow uranium, bright and alive as pollen." He observes the patterns in the rocks and understands that "they had taken these beautiful rocks from deep within earth and they had laid them in a monstrous design, realizing destruction on a scale only *they* could have dreamed." The vague pronoun "they" remains unassigned in this passage, as the author takes pains to avoid narrowly condemning the Europeans and Euro-Americans involved in developing nuclear technology. For an interesting comparison of Western and Native American perspectives on nuclear science, see Marilou Awiakta's 1993 book, *Selu: Seeking the Corn-Mother's Wisdom*. Silko continues this climactic scene:

He cried the relief he felt at finally seeing the pattern, the way all the stories fit together—the old stories, the war stories, their stories—to become the story that was still being told. He was not

crazy; he had never been crazy. He had only seen and heard the
world as it always was: no boundaries, only transitions through
all distances and time. (246)

This revelation enables Tayo to understand that perceptions he had
once flailed against as signs of madness—transcultural, translinguistic
connections and desires to be deeply bonded to the land—were actually special insights, signs of his power to exert force against witchery.
As Jim Tarter explains in his study of *Ceremony* and environmental
justice, this scene takes place at the Jackpile-Paguate uranium mine,
which opened on the Laguna Pueblo reservation in 1952. He writes:
"At that time, the Anaconda Copper Company, a subsidiary of the
Atlantic-Richfield Corporation (now ARCO), was issued a lease by
the Bureau of Indian Affairs to 7,500 acres of Laguna Pueblo land.
The operation was comprised of a huge open-pit uranium mine, at
2,800 acres the largest of its kind in the United States, and an adjoin-
ing milling operation, which ran day and night for thirty years until
1982." In the climactic scene of *Ceremony,* explains Tarter, "Tayo has
a vision of sweeping interconnections between the mine and what was
going on beyond Laguna land, both on native land in the region and
overseas" (105–6).

Shortly after Tayo has his epiphany, Emo, Pinkie, and Leroy—all of
them drunk—drive up to the mine shaft with Tayo's friend Harley.
Pinkie and Leroy torture Harley, and Emo shouts, "Scream!...
Scream loud so he can hear you" (251). They are trying to lure Tayo
to participate in the cycle of violence, to reinforce the witchery by
fighting back in defense of Harley. Tayo can scarcely hold himself
back, but he does. Silko writes: "It had been a close call. The witchery
had almost ended the story according to its plan; Tayo had almost
jammed the screwdriver into Emo's skull the way the witchery had
wanted....Their deadly ritual for the autumn solstice would have
been completed by him" (253).

RELATED ISSUES

Ceremony raises many issues related not only to environmental and
social policy, but to the *experience* of the physical world and social responsibility in the modern world. Tayo's growing self-awareness and
sense of place enable him to play a decisive role in preventing an ongoing cascade of violence within his community. Harley and Leroy are
killed, and Emo later shoots Pinkie at a sheep camp, but he is then

banished to California by the FBI. Rather than carrying the haunting tendencies of violence with him, Tayo helps to end witchery "for now" (261).

In her study "Contested Ground: Nature, Narrative, and Native American Identity in Leslie Marmon Silko's *Ceremony*," Rachel Stein explains how Silko "revisits the American mythos of the conquest of the continent from a Native American vantage point," her characters coming to "realize that both the desperate ills of reservation life and the corruptions poisoning mainstream American society result from the way in which American national development has been predicated over and against Indian inhabitation of the land" (193). Stein echoes Barry Lopez's assertions in *The Rediscovery of North America*, in which he argues that our destructive attitudes and actions toward the land and people in America today represent our legacy from the early Europeans who arrived in North America seeking material wealth and short-term gratification rather than trying to learn from the native people and the exotic flora and fauna on this continent.

University of Arizona scholar Joni Adamson is even more explicit, in the introduction to *American Indian Literature, Environmental Justice, and Ecocriticism*, when she explains what it means to view *Ceremony* in the context of "environmental justice." She talks about her experiences teaching the book to Native American students in Tucson:

> For example, in a discussion of Leslie Marmon Silko's *Ceremony*, I might begin by drawing students' attention to Tayo's mystical connection to nature and his journey to wholeness, but my students would redirect our focus to the ways in which American Indians have been stereotyped for far too long by environmentalists and by others as the people with an ancient wisdom that alone can save the planet. Discussions of Tayo's symbolic battle with the "Destroyers" to save the earth were transformed into discussions of the novel's depiction of the literal radioactive poisoning of the Four Corners communities where many of the students live. Every time I wanted to discuss the abstract, aesthetically beautiful concept of "the earth in balance," they wanted to discuss the ways in which Tayo's mother represents the high rates of teenage pregnancy, the high rates of suicide, the high rates of alcohol abuse, and the high numbers of alcohol-related automobile accidents that occur in communities that have been racially marginalized and impoverished by the U.S. govern-

ment's reservation system. Most importantly, they wanted to discuss the underlying reasons for such imbalances. In *Ceremony,* Silko's description of human relation to the land most certainly taps into the beauty and harmony of American Indian oral traditions, but she always has her eye on power inequities that have distinct and interconnected social and environmental consequences for impoverished people-of-color communities. (xiv–xv)

Adamson's pedagogical discoveries—like the readings offered by Rachel Stein, Jim Tarter, and other scholars performing what T. V. Reed calls "environmental justice ecocriticism"—are a helpful antidote to interpretations of *Ceremony* that are overly interested in the symbolic and philosophical aspects of the novel and that buy into the stereotypes of native people as being uniquely in synch with nature. It is useful to be reminded that Silko has woven this narrative from real daily struggles at Laguna Pueblo and other, similar reservations. By combining an appreciation of the novel's stunning aesthetic achievement and its representation of painful reality, we can achieve a fuller understanding of the social and artistic significance of this novel.

BIBLIOGRAPHY

Adamson, Joni. *American Indian Literature, Environmental Justice, and Ecocriticism: The Middle Place.* Tucson: U of Arizona P, 2001.

Awiakta, Marilou. *Selu: Seeking the Corn-Mother's Wisdom.* Golden, CO; Fulcrum, 1993.

Chavkin, Allan, ed. *Leslie Marmon Silko's CEREMONY: A Casebook.* New York: Oxford UP, 2002.

Cohen, Robin. "Of Apricots, Orchids, and Wovoka: An Interview with Leslie Marmon Silko." Chavkin 257–63.

Coltelli, Laura. "*Almanac of the Dead:* An Interview with Leslie Marmon Silko." 1993. *Conversations with Leslie Marmon Silko.* Ed. Ellen L. Arnold. Jackson: U of Mississippi P, 2000. 119–34.

Dean, Thomas K. "Leslie Marmon Silko." *American Nature Writers.* Ed. John Elder. Vol. 2. New York: Scribner's, 1996. 817–27.

Gonzalez, Ray. "The Past Is Right Here and Now: An Interview with Leslie Marmon Silko." 1991. *Conversations with Leslie Marmon Silko.* Ed. Ellen L. Arnold. Jackson: U of Mississippi P, 2000. 97–106.

Lopez, Barry. *The Rediscovery of North America.* Lexington: UP of Kentucky, 1990.

Naess, Arne. "The Shallow and the Deep, Long-Range Ecology Movement." *Inquiry* 16 (1973): 95–100.

Powers, Janet M. "Mapping the Prophetic Landscape in *Almanac of the Dead*." *Leslie Marmon Silko: A Collection of Critical Essays*. Ed. Louise K. Barnett and James L. Thorson. Albuquerque: U of New Mexico P, 1999. 261–72.

Reed, T.V. "Toward an Environmental Justice Ecocriticism." *The Environmental Justice Reader: Politics, Poetics, and Pedagogy*. Eds. Joni Adamson, Mei Mei Evans, and Rachel Stein. Tucson: U of Arizona P, 2002. 145–62.

Silko, Leslie Marmon. *Ceremony*. 1977. New York: Penguin, 1988.

———. "Interior and Exterior Landscapes: The Pueblo Migration Stories." *Yellow Woman and a Beauty of the Spirit: Essays on Native American Life Today*. New York: Simon, 1996. 25–47.

———. "Old and New Autobiographical Notes." *Yellow Woman and a Beauty of the Spirit: Essays on Native American Life Today*. New York: Simon, 1996. 196–200.

———. *Sacred Water*. Tucson, AZ: Flood Plain, 1993.

Stein, Rachel. "Contested Ground: Nature, Narrative, and Native American Identity in Leslie Marmon Silko's *Ceremony*." Chavkin 193–211.

Tarter, Jim. "Locating the Uranium Mine: Place, Multiethnicity, and Environmental Justice in Leslie Marmon Silko's *Ceremony*." *The Greening of Literary Scholarship: Literature, Theory, and the Environment*. Ed. Steven Rosendale. Iowa City: U of Iowa P, 2002. 97–110.

Wright, Anne, ed. *The Delicacy and Strength of Lace: Letters Between Leslie Marmon Silko and James Wright*. Saint Paul, MN: Graywolf, 1986.

9

Barry Lopez,
Arctic Dreams (1986)

Jen Hill

When *Arctic Dreams* won the National Book Award in 1986, Barry Lopez was a well-respected but largely unknown author. The book was a bestseller that captured the nation's imagination. Subtitled *Imagination and Desire in a Northern Landscape,* it examines the landscape, flora, fauna, and peoples of the Arctic Circle. Its purpose is to ask questions about the place of the Arctic in the human imagination as well as the role of the imagination in understanding locations that resist human development and values. Lopez's hope is that once Arctic space—so long thought of as desolate and empty—becomes part of human consciousness, it will no longer be easy to exploit the natural resources of the area and contribute to the degradation of the region's environment and native cultures. The only way to fully appreciate this place, Lopez suggests, is to try to comprehend all of its parts while at the same time understanding that the Arctic's very resistance to definition and comprehension is valuable to human experience. Lopez combines a personal narrative of experience and discovery with historical, scientific, and anthropological theories and facts. The body of the book is divided into 10 sections, 8 of which focus on specific topics, themes, or species particular to the northern landscape. Just as the Arctic is composed of many stories, experiences, and different species and places, *Arctic Dreams* is a narrative made of many smaller narratives. As such, the book's structure mimics the variety and expanse of the Arctic.

BIOGRAPHICAL BACKGROUND

Born in Port Chester, New York, in 1945, Lopez moved to Southern California as a young boy. He spent his childhood in a rural area of what is now greater Los Angeles, exploring the hills and canyons. Family trips to the Grand Canyon, the Mojave Desert, and Big Bear Lake fostered his early love of and connection to the outdoors. At age 11, he left the West and moved back to New York City, where he attended a Jesuit prep school. Later, Lopez attended the University of Notre Dame, where he studied theology and philosophy and played varsity soccer. Like other environmental writers in the late twentieth century, Lopez was influenced by the political activism and social change of the 1960s and early 1970s. He considered a monastic life, and in 1966 visited Gethsemani Abbey in Kentucky, where the Trappist monk Thomas Merton lived. But the outdoors called to him and as Lopez puts it, "The work I wanted to do with my life—I didn't have anything specific in mind—I was going to do outside" (O'Connell, "Natural World" 13). He moved to Oregon to go to graduate school, where he obtained his master's degree in teaching and enrolled in a graduate English program for a year before dropping out to be a full-time writer. He has lived in Oregon ever since, although he travels extensively to research and promote his books. Lopez's concern for and connection to the outdoors, his intellectual curiosity and love of books, his deeply held views of the value of environmental protection, and his spiritual beliefs all inform *Arctic Dreams* and his other writing.

ENVIRONMENTAL ISSUES

While *Arctic Dreams* emerged from the environmental movement of the 1970s and from a renaissance in American nature writing in the 1980s (both well-documented in other essays in this collection), it remains an important work today for several reasons. *Arctic Dreams* can be considered in terms of the continuing debate about the appropriate uses of public lands. In the Arctic, the focus of the debate is on whether or not to allow gas and oil exploration and drilling in the Arctic National Wildlife Preserve. The Arctic National Wildlife Refuge is the second-largest wildlife refuge in the United States, covering 19 million acres of mountains, forests, wetlands, wild rivers, and tundra in Northeast Alaska. As early as 1923, the government established a 23-million-acre Naval Petroleum Reserve in northwestern Alaska, to which an additional 20 million acres were added during World War II. By 1952–53, government scientists were concerned about the effects of the oil and mining industries on the environment. Their report, "The Last Great Wilderness," identified the northeast of Alaska as a place worthy of protection. As a result, in 1957, access to the 20 million acres made available to gas and oil industries for lease during the war was revoked. In 1960, Secretary of the Interior Fred Seaton designated 8.9 million acres of coastal plain and mountains of northeast Alaska as the Arctic National Wildlife Range to protect its "unique wildlife, wilderness, and recreation values" (USFWS, "Conservation Values"). Oil discoveries on nearby state land in the 1960s and 1970s led to debate about whether or not this land should be opened to exploration. The political battle that ensued is detailed by the U.S. Fish & Wildlife Service, a division of the Department of the Interior that oversees administration of the Arctic National Wildlife Refuge: The U.S. House of Representatives passed legislation in 1978 and 1979 designating the entire original range, including the now-contested Arctic coastal tundra, as wilderness. The Senate's version, however, required studies of wildlife and petroleum resources and the potential impacts of oil and gas development within the northern part of the range. It postponed the decision to authorize oil and gas development or wilderness designation (USFWS, "History").

In 1980, President Carter signed the Senate's version of the bill into law. While the new Arctic National Wildlife Refuge was now doubled in size, the Senate's requirement for documentation of the resources and impact of oil and gas development led to renewed discussion about the Arctic refuge twenty years later.

Although Section 1003 of ANILCA (the bill's name) specifically states that the "production of oil and gas from the Arctic National Wildlife Refuge is prohibited," in the summer of 2000 the U.S. House of Representatives voted in favor of opening the refuge to drilling. The U.S. Senate voted in April of 2002 to reject oil drilling in the refuge. The Defenders of Wildlife, an environmental activist organization, have described the refuge and the threats to it:

> Tucked away in the state's remote northeast corner, this 19.6-million-acre wildlife sanctuary is an awe-inspiring natural wonder: A sweeping expanse of tundra studded with marshes and lagoons and laced with rivers dramatically situated between the rugged foothills of the Brooks Range and the wide, icy waters of the Beaufort Sea.
>
> ...The oil companies have their sights on the biological heart of the refuge, its Arctic Ocean coastal plain, an area critical to the survival of many birds and mammals. About 160 bird species, including species that visit each of the lower 48 states, find breed-

ing, nesting or resting places on the coastal plain. The plain is the most important on-shore denning area in the United States for polar bears. It is the principal calving ground of the 130,000-strong migratory Porcupine caribou herd, the second largest caribou herd in the United States and a key source of food, clothing and medicine for the Gwich'in Indians, one of the world's few remaining subsistence cultures. Grizzly bears, wolverines, wolves, arctic foxes, whales and other species also thrive in the region. ("Wildlife Threats")

This landscape is the setting of much of *Arctic Dreams*. Barry Lopez has not stated whether or not the debates surrounding protection of the Arctic National Wildlife Refuge contributed to his desire to visit and learn more about the Arctic. The book, however, is an attempt to make comprehensible a landscape so huge and alien that it is an almost unimaginable abstraction to people who have never visited it. These very people elect the politicians who voted to create the refuge, as well as those politicians who have more recently voted not to protect it. Because natural spaces are often physically distant from populated spaces where political power resides, they are perceived as unimportant when they are considered at all. Lopez seeks to address this lack of visibility and its effects in *Arctic Dreams*.

At the same time that wilderness in the Alaskan Arctic is under attack by the gas and oil industry, the welfare of the polar environment has another very real enemy: global warming. Debate about the greenhouse effect and global warming—fact or fiction? historical blip? caused by overpopulation? industrial gases? natural, cyclical atmospheric conditions?—is not in the scope of this article, but the fact remains that average temperatures around the globe are rising, and that this temperature shift endangers the health of the polar ice cap and its surrounding ecosystems. One worry is that the effects of global warming will be disastrous to populated, low-lying areas. Since that water will come in part from the polar ice cap, scientists are paying close attention to the effects of warming in the Arctic. Between 1978 and 1994, the Arctic ice sheet shrank almost 6%. Research in the summer of 2002 revealed that the ice cap has continued to shrink not only in geographical area, but in depth and density as well. Gale E. Christianson writes that the polar landscape is

a pristine ecology that may be on the brink of major upheaval. Predictions are that arctic temperatures could rise by as much as six degrees Celsius in summer and twelve degrees Celsius in winter during the coming decades. Should such a drastic warming take place, millions of acres of permafrost would thaw, transforming the tundra into a suppurating morass impenetrable by man or beast. At the same time, an unknown portion of the estimated 180 billion metric tons of carbon locked in the soil would be released into the atmosphere, altering the surrounding ecosystem and adding significantly to the world's climatic woes. (216)

Since global warming is linked to increasing carbon dioxide levels in the atmosphere, the additional released carbon dioxide could endanger all of us by further eroding global air quality.

Industrial pollution is the prime culprit in global warming and environmental degradation. As Miguel A. Santos notes, pollutants move with ease between air, land, and water, and pay no attention to geographical or geopolitical borders. "The transboundary movements of pollutants lead to unusual and complex economic and political difficulties. Individuals in one nation may suffer economic loss and health hazards as a result of the pollution originated in another nation, yet they may not benefit from the economic activity that caused the pollution" (59). But these regional disputes are not only limited to nations. Local indigenous peoples are often minority voices in regional or national politics, and as such go unheard. Their lives, livelihoods, and cultural histories can be threatened when it is in the best interest of national governments and international corporations to develop, exploit, and export natural resources.

World economic policy, international banking, multinational corporations, and national government contracts are complicit not only in the exploitation of natural resources but in the subjection of economically disadvantaged people. The Indian scholar and environmental activist Vandana Shiva identifies many of the poorer inhabitants of the world as being "new global environmental refugees."

For the poorer two thirds of humanity... nature's capital is their source of sustenance and livelihood. The destruction and diversion and takeover of their ecosystems in order to extract natural resources or dump waste generates a disproportionate burden for the poor. In a world of globalised, deregulated commerce in which everything is tradable and economic strength is the only determinant of power and control, resources move from the poor to the rich, and pollution moves from the rich to the poor. The result is a global environmental apartheid. (112)

Increasingly, debates about deforestation, water rights, and gas and oil leases have become debates about sovereignty and democracy for indigenous peoples in Asia, the Pacific, South America, and the Arctic. The link between environmental issues and economic exploitation has come to the attention of diverse groups that include the United Nations, the World Health Organization, and many nongovernmental organizations (NGOs) devoted to the resolution of these problems (among them the World Summit on Sustainable Development [WSSD]). The 1992 Summit in Rio on the Environment addressed serious ecological threats of the late twentieth century, yet 10 years later free trade and globalization had increased environmental pressures to the extent that in August of 2002 another international summit was held in Johannesburg, South Africa. This time the summit explicitly addressed the environmental and social impact of globalization. The Gwich'in Indians, Inuit, Yupik, Aleut, and Inupiat are only some of the indigenous natives who make their homes in the northernmost reaches of North America. Although for the most part no longer primarily nomadic, these different cultures traditionally rely on the animals and plants of the subarctic and arctic ecosystems, the same animals and plants that are threatened by gas and oil development and changing atmospheric conditions linked to world industrial pollution.

THEMATIC ANALYSIS

Lopez's writing ties environmental and political concerns to moral ones. In *Arctic Dreams* he demonstrates the deep connection between the human and nonhuman, not only by investigating land-centered native practices and knowledge but also by employing a vivid, moving first-person narrative that invites his readers to participate in this deep connection. Scott Slovic identifies Lopez as possessing a "particularized understanding," enacted in careful attention to physical detail and to his place in the world (141). The act of writing for Lopez is an ethical practice, one that reflects his deeply held belief in the sacred. For Barry Lopez, writing is linked to an idea of natural spaces as sacred or holy spaces and writing as a meditative, prayerful practice. In a 1998 interview with Nicholas O'Connell, Lopez said, "Prayer is a way to formalize the relationship between yourself and a spiritual entity. But I think of prayer as larger than that; in the monastic traditions your work is your prayer. There must be moments in your life when you are saying your prayers better, and that's what writing is for me" ("Natural World" 12). Talking about the old growth forest near his home in Oregon, Lopez said, "It's a kind of love—agape—between me and the place. I recognize God in the place and I love the place because of it" (O'Connell, "On Sacred Ground" 61).

Agape is a Greek word for love that is linked to Christianity, with connotations of unselfishness and charity. Understanding Barry Lopez's writing as an expression of agape reveals that for Lopez the stakes in environmental policy are not remote and political but deeply personal. The priest and critic Thomas Berry observes of Lopez, "He has such an intimate presence with the world of nature, with the animal world, with the landscape, with the entire range of natural phenomenon. He's deeply sensitive to how the human mind and emotions meet with the reality of the nonhuman. He understands profoundly the manner in which humans and the natural world are present in a single community of existence" (O'Connell, "Natural World" 15). As Lopez himself put it in an interview with Maureen Abood,

> I love to be in the landscape occupied by animals and to be tutored by them and their place. I may write a story about polar bears, but I'm not a naturalist in the sense that my interest ends with an understanding of the biology and ecology of polar bears. What the reader will find in that story is that I'm after something else: Why is the bear beautiful? Is the bear beautiful because of the way it's integrated into its place? The questions I'm after really have to do with love and issues of community. (21)

The definition of community as an expression of a moral and ethical framework is apparent from the very beginning of *Arctic Dreams*. In the preface, Lopez literally stumbles upon nesting golden plovers on the tundra, upsetting and stressing them. To assure them that he means no harm and to acknowledge their precedence in this landscape, he takes to bowing to them on his daily walks. "I would bow slightly with my hands in my pockets, toward the birds and the evidence of life in their nests—because of their fecundity, unexpected in this remote region, and because of the serene arctic light that came down over the land like breath, like breathing" (xx). Although the birds cannot understand Lopez's gesture, his bowing represents the humility of his desire to connect to the greater world around him.

Community, for Lopez, not only encompasses and effaces differences between people—differences having to do with ethnicity, culture, belief systems, and everyday practices—but also seeks to embrace and comprehend the nonhuman, non-civilized world. Specifically, in *Arctic Dreams,* an awareness of wilderness—something for the most part remote and incomprehensible to his housebound readers—is the first step to appreciating and valuing wilderness, which will then lead to enlarging their ideas of the world and their places in it. In addition, to attempt to fully understand a resistant landscape might help us to more completely understand our immediate surroundings and our relationship to them.

Barry Lopez seeks to counteract the over-simple binaries that traditionally shape Western interactions with wilderness: "civilized" and "savage," developed and empty, tame and wild, center and margin. These pairs are not innocent. In each, one term is usually privileged; that is to say, the term associated with "civilization" is understood to be more important and valuable than the other term. As the often unconscious set of assumptions that accompany us in our experience of new places, these binaries structure the way we comprehend our world. This is where the subtitle of Lopez's book, "Imagination and Desire in a Northern Landscape," becomes important. Lopez goes to the Arctic seeking an understanding of the place but realizes that his own desires and his own imagination are central to how he comprehends the North. On the one hand, this makes any unmediated experience of place impossible: his assumptions and desires will always accompany him. On the other hand, being aware of the role of imagination and desire in encountering space and creating meaning enables the author to look at how assumptions about the Arctic have structured human experience and expectations of this difficult space.

Even if the Arctic were the barren space popular culture perceives it to be, Lopez concludes, it would not be "empty," because we would populate it with our imaginings and our desires. Lopez's chapter titled "The Country of the Mind" examines the history and geography of Pingok Island, a remote Arctic outpost. The emptiness of the island belies the complex history of the place, one that encompasses an active life by nomadic natives, exploration expeditions by nineteenth-century European explorers, and the natural history of the many plants and animals that make their homes there. Simple geography, the mapping of the physical characteristics of a place, does not capture the truth of that place. The act of organizing space in order to comprehend it is structured and produced by biases that can only be partially comprehended. And each person's approach will be different. "No one can tell the whole story," Lopez concludes (273).

As "The Country of the Mind" demonstrates, the Arctic is not empty at all. Yet making visible the millions of human and animal inhabitants requires more than a lesson in history and geography. Three chapters of Lopez's narrative are devoted to species that have evolved to meet the demands of the difficult Arctic environment: the narwhal, the polar bear, and the musk ox. In "Banks Island," the author attempts to comprehend the nearly unclassifiable *Ovibos moschatus,* or musk ox. Their complete adaptation to the rigors of Arctic survival makes them alien to humans, but their commitment to herd behavior that values the life of each calf to the risk of adult lives is readable to Lopez as a noble trait. Still, though, musk oxen are musk oxen: they are not noble, they are not even knowable, except that Lopez observes them closely in an attempt to bridge the gap between human and animal. The only thing knowable about the Banks Island musk oxen, Lopez concludes, is that "they were so intensely good at being precisely what they were. The longer you watched, the more intricately they seemed a part of where they were living, of what they were doing. Their color, their proportions against the contours of the land, were exquisite" (75). The recognition that we cannot separate "being" from "place" resounds on almost every page.

In each of the chapters that focus on wildlife, the factual portrait of the species is interwoven with details about the Arctic ecosystem, the human history in that ecosystem, and Lopez's personal narrative of encounter. In "Tôrnârssuk," a chapter devoted to the polar bear, Lopez's title subject is the polar bear. But Lopez starts the chapter with himself, hunting with some oceanographic research scientists for seals. The hunters don't find seals but instead find another hunter: the polar bear. The similarity between the human and the bear ends there, however. For Lopez, the powerful, dangerous, self-contained polar bear is an example of alterity, that is, of an "otherness" so extreme that it demands to be acknowledged at the same time that it can't be comprehended. The polar bear represents the Arctic not just because it is the Arctic's best-known inhabitant and has evolved specifically to meet the demands of the harsh atmosphere but because its very wildness and unpredictability are the same qualities the landscape itself signifies for humans. The polar bear also has an understanding of the Arctic that is denied to humans. Lopez muses, "Even if it were possible to follow [the bear], I thought, how well could we put together what we saw? What would we miss out there?" (96). Lopez's desire to know more of the polar bear and its particulars is a desire to know both the alien animal other and to know what it knows, the specific knowledge of its experience that must be denied to humans.

Yet generalizing about humans is also a dangerous oversimplification, Lopez finds. As an anthropologist warns him, "You ignore at your peril the variety in human culture" (75). Lopez uses "Eskimo" as "an inclusive term" to refer "to descendants of the Thule cultural tradition in present-day Canada and the Punuk and Birnirk cultural traditions in modern-day Alaska" (10). As Lopez observes, "What one knows [about the Arctic] is either gathered firsthand or learned from books or indigenous observers. This information, however, is assembled differently by each individual, according to his cultural predispositions and his personality" (271). Yet Lopez is wary of romanticizing the Eskimo's relation to the land. The anthropologist Johannes Fabian points out in his important book *Time and the Other* that a common error "western" cultures make is to categorize people perceived as "less civilized" as being somehow frozen in time. Understanding civilization as a time line, then, causes us to deny indigenous peoples the same relation to time and agency (the ability "to do," to self-determine and define) that we have. This enables us to use "progress" to privilege our own cultures at the expense of others. Lopez picks up on the damaging consequences of this misunderstanding when discussing nineteenth-century exploration of the North:

> The notion of the Eskimos exploring their own lands and adapting anew at the same time Europeans were exploring the Arctic was something the Europeans were never aware of. They thought of the Arctic as fixed in time—a primitive landscape, a painting, inhabited by an attenuated people. They mistook the stillness and the cold for biological stasis. They thought nothing at all changed here. They thought it was a desert, a wasteland. (382)

Lopez's time spent traveling with Eskimo hunters challenges his own romantic ideas of native life. As a non-hunter and a non-Eskimo, he can only partially understand the Eskimos' relation to the hunt, but he comes to respect and even envy the lack of separation they have from "the world that animals occupy" (200). While spending time with the Eskimos enables Lopez to experience their world, he understands that he cannot have complete, comprehensive access to that world any more than he can to the world of the polar bear.

Barry Lopez contrasts the intimate relationship that the Eskimos have with the land with his observations of an oil company's headquarters in Prudhoe Bay, Alaska. Coming near the end of the book and at the end of his discussion of several disastrous Arctic expeditions of the nineteenth century, Lopez's portrait of this most recent incursion by the West into Arctic space is predictably bleak. In contrast to the intimacy with which natives experience the environment, the oil company's cafeteria is in "a sky-lit atrium of patrician silences, of slacks and perfume and well-mannered people, of plants in deferential attendance" (394–95). A movie theater, a games arcade, a weight room and swimming pool are all separated from the surrounding cold tundra by thick walls and carpeting. These walls and the lives that are led behind it are the physical evidence of an alienation from the environment that enables a human relationship with the land that is economic and exploitative, rather than personal. Lopez tries to explain his interest to the employee assigned to monitor his visit, saying, "I am interested mostly in the landscape, why we come here and what we see. I am not a business analyst, an economist a social planner. The engineering is astounding" (396). He concludes, "The true cost, I think, must be unknown." The oil man, we assume, computes cost in terms of the millions of dollars the pipeline cost and the price tag of the sumptuous company headquarters. Lopez's unspoken computations include the cost of a landscape irrevocably altered, the interrupted migrations of wildlife, and finally the cost of human alienation from nature. These things, we are to understand, are priceless.

CONCLUSION

When in the last paragraph of the book's epilogue, Lopez bows again, it is a bow of appreciation both for the difficult landscape he has come to comprehend and for the lessons it has taught him about himself.

> The landscape and the animals were like something found at the end of a dream. The edges of the real landscape became one with the edges of something I had dreamed. But what I had dreamed was only a pattern, some beautiful pattern of light. The continuous work of the imagination, I thought, to bring what is actual together with what is dreamed is an expression of human evolution. The conscious desire to achieve a state, even momentarily, that like light is unbounded, nurturing, suffused with wisdom

and creation, a state in which one has absorbed that very darkness which before was the perpetual sign of defeat.

Whatever world that is, it lies far ahead. But its outline, its adumbration, is clear in the landscape, and upon this one can actually hope we will find our way. (414–15)

Finally, *Arctic Dreams* forces its readers to question their relationship with the land—the Arctic specifically, but *all* land—in a way that causes them to reflect on their own values. The expectations or "dreams" with which we approach the unknown structure what we will find there. Deeply held, unconscious, and even unarticulated, our desires can overwhelm and blind us, but they are what makes us human, and they also enable our imaginations. The human capacity to imagine, Lopez argues, makes us special and allows us connection and empathy with the nonhuman.

The experience of reading *Arctic Dreams* is an experience of discovery, and what we discover is not only knowledge of a remote, unfriendly, and unforgiving place but valuable knowledge of our own place in the world. As Barry Lopez puts it in *The Rediscovery of North America*, "What does it mean to be rich? Is it to possess the material, tangible wealth of North America—the gold and the silver, the timber, the fish, and the furs? Or is real wealth, lasting wealth, something else? Most of us, I think, believe that it is something else. We have taken the most obvious kind of wealth from this continent and overlooked the more lasting, the more valuable, and sustaining experience of intimacy with it, the spiritual dimension of a responsible involvement with this place" (124). For Lopez, a healthy environment is not only the result of a healthy human spirit but its cause, and as long as we believe that, there is hope both for the environment and for ourselves.

BIBLIOGRAPHY

Abood, Maureen. "God Between the Lines." *U.S. Catholic* June 1998: 18–23.

Bullard, Robert, ed. *Confronting Environmental Racism: Voices from the Grassroots.* Boston: South End P, 1993.

Christianson, Gale E. *Greenhouse: The 200-year Story of Global Warming.* New York: Walker, 1999.

Defenders of Wildlife. "Wildlife Threats." <http://www.defenders.org/wildlife/arctic/html>.

Fabian, Johannes. *Time and the Other: How Anthropology Makes Its Object*. New York: Columbia UP, 1983.

Glotfelty, Cheryll. "Barry Holstun Lopez." *Updating the Literary West*. Fort Worth, TX: Western Literature Association, 1997. 283–88.

Lopez, Barry. *Arctic Dreams: Imagination and Desire in a Northern Land-scape*. New York: Scribner's, 1986.

———. *The Rediscovery of North America*. Lexington: UP of Kentucky, 1990.

O'Connell, Nicholas. "At One With the Natural World: Barry Lopez's Adventure with the Word and the Wild." *Commonweal* 24 March 2000: 11–17.

———. "On Sacred Ground." *Sierra* Nov.–Dec. 1998: 58–61.

Paul, Sherman. *For Love of the World*. Iowa City: U of Iowa P, 1992.

Rueckert, William H. "Barry Lopez and the Search for a Dignified and Honorable Relationship with Nature." *Earthly Words*. Ed. John Cooley. Ann Arbor: U of Michigan P, 1994. 137–64.

Santos, Miguel, E. *The Environmental Crisis*. Westport, CT: Greenwood, 1999.

Shiva, Vandana. "The World on the Edge." *Global Capitalism*. Ed. Will Hunter and Anthony Giddens. New York: New Press, 2000. 112–29.

Slovic, Scott. *Seeking Awareness in American Nature Writing: Henry Thoreau, Annie Dillard, Edward Abbey, Wendell Berry, Barry Lopez*. Salt Lake City: U of Utah P, 1992.

U.S. Fish & Wildlife Service (USFWS). "The Unique Conservation Values of the Arctic Refuge." <http://www.defenders.org/wildlife/arctic/fws/drill/usfws1.html>.

———. "History of the Arctic Refuge as it Relates to Oil in Alaska." <http:www.defenders.org/wildlife/arctic/fws/drill/upsprint1.html>.

10

Terry Tempest Williams, *Refuge* (1991)

Cheryll Glotfelty

Intense, fierce, and from the heart, Terry Tempest Williams's *Refuge: An Unnatural History of Family and Place* (1991) is a diary of pain and a record of loss. It is a memoir of seven years (1982–89), beginning with her mother's discovery of ovarian cancer and ending with her death and the deaths of both of Williams's grandmothers. At the same time as Williams's mother is diagnosed with cancer, the bird-rich marshes of a favorite freshwater inlet to the Great Salt Lake, where Williams has always gone for refuge, are being drowned by record rises in lake level. The challenge of these difficult years is to learn to adapt to change and to find refuge in her own capacity to love. Readers who have borne losses of their own will identify strongly with this book as it gives voice to pain, so often suffered in private. What gives *Refuge* more than personal significance, however, is its engagement with larger issues of place, nature, gender, religion, and citizenship. *Refuge*'s powerful epilogue, "The Clan of One-Breasted Women," further translates the personal into the political when Williams reveals that the high cancer rate and consequent mastectomies in her family may be linked to Utah's exposure to radioactive fallout during U.S. above-ground atomic testing during the 1950s and early 1960s. The book's final scene depicts Williams's arrest at the Nevada Test Site for protesting the U.S. government's continued testing of nuclear bombs.

BIOGRAPHICAL BACKGROUND

As a fifth-generation Mormon and Utahn, Williams has strong ties to the landscape and history of the Great Salt Lake basin, where *Refuge* takes place. Her ancestors on both sides were members of the Mormon "handcart pioneers," who pulled their belongings in two-wheeled handcarts from Illinois, where they suffered from religious persecution, to the Great Salt Lake, an area spurned by other emigrants, but which appeared to leader Brigham Young as a good place to make saints. "This Is the Place" is said to have been his famous declaration in 1847, and the words apply equally well to Terry Tempest Williams's family history in Utah, where the Tempest men have owned a pipeline contracting business for four generations. In *Refuge,* Williams recalls the special relationship she shared with her grandmother Mimi, who often took Terry bird watching when she was a child, planting in her the seeds of a lifelong love of birds and nature. When Williams attended the University of Utah, she wanted to combine her love of landscape with her love of language, so she majored in English and minored in biology. She later earned a master's degree in environmental education and has been employed as curator of education and naturalist-in-residence at the Utah Museum of Natural History.

During her college years, Williams worked at a local bookstore, where she met a man who shared her taste in books and who had earned a degree in biology. Terry Tempest married Brooke Williams in 1975 in the Mormon Temple in Salt Lake City; she was 19, he 23. In an interview in 1991, Williams cited her marriage as the single most important influence on her life; having a soul mate and enjoying the sense of security that this relationship provides have allowed her to take wing, take risks, and develop meaningful relationships to the land and to other people (Petersen 9). In *Refuge* Williams struggles with the decision of whether or not to have children. She fears that having her own family will deprive her of the solitude she values and will sap her creative energy and time for writing. Williams and her husband ultimately decide not to have children, a choice that strongly goes against the grain of Mormon culture and that feels to her to be paradoxically both selfish and a sacrifice. Nevertheless, Williams has been prolific in print, her books forming a large and growing family, with five books preceding her masterpiece *Refuge* and four books following it, along with three co-edited books, dozens of essays, and the narration for video documentaries. As a family, Williams's books express a fierce love for wild nature and are passionate in their defense of it; they combine the fidelity to fact of a biologist with the dexterity with language and imagery of a poet; they explore women's ways of being in the world; they reflect the Mormon magical worldview in which a spiritual realm animates the earthly kingdom; they are uncommonly and sometimes uncomfortably revealing, always pushing the boundaries of public and private; and they frequently employ story to, in her words, "bypass[ ] rhetoric and pierce[ ] the heart" (*Red* 3).

STRUCTURAL AND THEMATIC COMPONENTS

In *Refuge*, Williams writes that the landscape of the Bear River Migratory Bird Refuge is,

> a landscape so familiar to me, there have been times I have felt a species long before I saw it. The long-billed curlews that foraged the grasslands seven miles outside the Refuge were trustworthy. I can count on them year after year. And when six whimbrels joined them—whimbrel entered my mind as an idea. Before I ever saw them mingling with curlews, I recognized them as a new thought in familiar country. (21)

For many readers and literary scholars, the arrival of *Refuge* itself appears as "a new thought in familiar country," a new idea on the horizon of writing about nature. The degree to which Williams combines natural history observation with personal and familial history—aims her binoculars at birds *and* focuses attention on her family's battle with cancer—is, quite simply, unprecedented. Scientists are trained to be objective, to eliminate the use of "I" in their writing, and certainly to keep their personal lives out of their publications, while creative writers who focus on family relationships rarely include birds as relatives and almost never show the same degree of attention to the natural world that they do to the complexities of human experience. In granting equal time and importance to *Family* and *Place*, to the story of her mother's cancer and to the story of the birds and the rising Great Salt Lake, Williams no doubt created a cataloging problem for librarians and bookstores—memoir or natural history? By challenging the way we compartmentalize experience, Williams also teaches us to see life whole and to imagine our place "in the family of things" (a quotation from "Wild Geese" by Mary Oliver, a poem that serves as the epigraph to *Refuge*).

Casually leafing through *Refuge*, one finds a map of Great Salt Lake at the front of the book and a long bird list of Great Salt Lake (with both common and scientific nomenclature) at the end. Clearly, this book is very specifically placed and preoccupied with birds. A quick glance at the Contents page of *Refuge* reinforces this impression, revealing that each of its 37 unnumbered chapters is named for a species of bird or birds and that instead of dates, as one might expect from a memoir, each chapter is "dated" by a lake level, recorded in feet and accurate to two decimal places. Upon closer inspection, the reader will observe that a couple of the chapters—"Pink Flamingos" and "Birds-of-Paradise"—play with this naming convention and that the lake levels trace a gradual rise and fall throughout the course of the book. Scholars of literature have long observed that novels and plays—today, one might add films—tend to follow a pattern of rising action, climax, and denouement or resolution and falling off, creating a distinct narrative arc and a satisfying emotional trajectory for the reader. This common pattern in fiction is fairly uncommon, however, in memoir, and rarer still in natural histories. The fact that *Refuge* follows the narrative shape of fiction—externally keyed to lake levels, internally structured by events—reveals how carefully crafted this work is and partially explains its extraordinarily powerful emotional effect.

But while a strong narrative momentum drives the intertwined stories of Great Salt Lake's rising lake level, culminating in the destruction of the Bear River Migratory Bird Refuge, and Diane Tempest's failing health, culminating in her death, *Refuge* is not a continuous narrative. Rather, each chapter consists of fragments, together forming a scrapbook of undated excerpts, extracted from the 22 journals that Williams kept during these years, interspersed with brief essays on Mormon history, natural history, and family history. In form as in subject, *Refuge* is a hybrid text that invites the reader to integrate many parts into a whole. Thematically, *Refuge* explores many social issues that are unified by their relation to the environment. Some themes, such as place and nature, are obviously environmental. Others, such as gender, religion, and citizenship are more subtly linked.

In America, known for its restlessness, and in an era characterized by mobility, Williams says, "It just may be that the most radical act we can commit is to stay home. Otherwise, who will be there to chart the changes? Who will be able to tell us if the long-billed curlews have returned to the grassy vales of Promontory, Utah?" (*Unspoken Hunger* 134). In *Refuge,* Williams counterpoints images of bird wings and migration with images of tree roots and residency. She chronicles the way that she has been shaped by the landscape of the Great Salt Lake, suggesting, too, a reciprocal relationship, whereby the people who love a place have an obligation to defend it. Williams has been an active participant in contemporary heated battles over land use in the American

West, in which she has fought on the side of wilderness against those who would develop or despoil it.

Early in *Refuge* Williams establishes that "I come from a family with deep roots in the American West" (13). Not only has her family resided in Utah for five generations, sinking down genealogical roots, but she herself has been personally marked by the landscape of Utah. She writes, "The Bird Refuge has remained a constant.... The birds and I share a natural history. It is a matter of rootedness, of living inside a place for so long that the mind and imagination fuse" (21). She recalls childhood trips to the lake, where she and her brothers would float on their backs for hours, "imprinting on Great Basin skies. It was in these moments of childhood that Great Salt Lake flooded my psyche" (33). As an adult, she states the relationship more radically, writing, "I am desert. I am mountains. I am Great Salt Lake" (29), implying no separation between herself and her environment. In this way of understanding oneself-in-place, a perspective known as Deep Ecology, by defending a place one is defending oneself, because one identifies so strongly with the place that the individual self has become the more encompassing Self, which includes one's environment. It is this kind of intimate relationship to a particular landscape that Williams encourages her readers to consider and, perhaps, to desire for themselves, for out of such a close connection arises commitment.

For Williams, identification with the land is tied to the body, such that she imagines the land, like herself, to be female. Of the sand dunes at Fish Springs, Williams asserts, "And they are female. Sensuous curves—the small of a woman's back. Breasts. Buttocks. Hips and pelvis. They are the natural shapes of Earth. Let me lie naked and disappear. Crypsis" (109). Of Great Salt Lake, Williams writes, "I want to see the lake as Woman, as myself, in her refusal to be tamed. The State of Utah may try to dike her, divert her waters, build roads across her shores, but ultimately, it won't matter. She will survive us. I recognize her as a wilderness, raw and self-defined" (92). And of the Earth, Williams wonders, "How do we empathize with the Earth when so much is ravaging her?" (85). Williams's close identification of women and nature aligns her with a theoretical position and a social movement known as ecofeminism, which seeks to expose and eradicate the linked oppressions of women and nature in male-dominated cultures. Williams establishes her ecofeminist sympathies in the first pages of *Refuge* where she and a woman friend speak of "rage. Of women and landscape. How our bodies and the body of the earth have been mined" (10). Williams's love for nature arises out of a feminine and feminist sensibility, and her sense of its violation is visceral.

One of the perils of loving a landscape as intimately as Williams does is the panic you feel when that landscape is threatened. This problem is particularly acute in the American West, where the federal government owns a high percentage of the land. For example, 65% of Utah and 87% of Nevada are federally owned. Westerners, despite serious disagreements over land use among themselves, often share a sense of frustration that land management policies are set in the East, in Washington, D.C., by legislators who may never have visited the western lands whose fate they determine. As a writer, Williams has found it enormously challenging to effectively defend western wilderness:

> How can I convey the scale and power of these big wide-open lands to those who have never seen them, let alone to those who have? How can I learn to write out of my own experience, out of my deep love for wild country, while still maintaining a language that opens minds rather than closes them? How to write again and again from every conceivable angle to stay the hand of development? How to write as clearly as one can from the heart and still be credible? (*Red* 11–12)

In *Refuge,* the problem of eastern policy makers misunderstanding and mistreating the American West centers on what to make of the "blank spaces" on the map. To the U.S. military, Williams writes,

> A blank spot on the map translates into empty space, space devoid of people, a wasteland perfect for nerve gas, weteye bombs, and toxic waste.
>
> The army believes that the Great Salt Lake Desert is an ideal place to experiment with biological warfare.
>
> An official from the Atomic Energy Commission had one comment regarding the desert between St. George, Utah, and Las Vegas, Nevada: "It's a good place to throw used razor blades." (241–42)

Refuge combats this insulting view of western deserts by including page after page of personal encounters with landscapes described as sensuous and spiritual, places of profound peace and great beauty.

Williams's view is that "A blank spot on the map is an invitation to en-counter the natural world, where one's character will be shaped by the landscape....The unknown Utah that some see as a home for used razor blades, toxins, and biological warfare, is a landscape of the imag-ination, a secret we tell to those who will keep it" (244).

In 1992, a year after *Refuge* was published, Williams told an inter-viewer that she cannot imagine moving away from Utah. "I really love Utah. It's my home. I am deeply committed to it. I think it's about residency. And it's about really digging in" (Gross). Ten years after *Refuge,* in 2001, Williams's *Red: Passion and Patience in the Desert* was published, a collection of essays, stories, and letters. In the lead essay, cleverly entitled "Home Work," Williams rearticulates *Refuge's* insights on people-in-place, while pushing the implications of this re-lationship toward an ethic of political engagement:

> Each of us belongs to a particular landscape, one that informs who we are, a place that carries our history, our dreams, holds us to a moral line of behavior that transcends thought. And in each of these places, home work is required, a participation in public life to make certain all is not destroyed under the banner of progress, expediency, or ignorance. We cannot do it alone. This is the hope of a *bedrock democracy,* standing our ground in the places we love, together. (*Red* 19; emphasis Williams's)

The landscape of Williams's imagination includes both red deserts and rich wetlands. The Bear River Migratory Bird Refuge, on the northeast shore of Great Salt Lake, where the Bear River creates a freshwater marsh, was established by Congress in 1928 as America's first waterfowl sanctuary and is home or way station to more than one million birds who breed, migrate, or winter there. This bird refuge is also Williams's personal refuge, where she goes to find solace by being with the birds. The central drama of *Refuge* concerns the destruction of these wetlands—the loss of the refuge for the birds and for Williams—by rising lake levels due to an unusually wet series of years, coincidentally the same years that Williams's mother is dying of ovar-ian cancer. Williams writes, "I could not separate the Bird Refuge from my family. Devastation respects no boundaries. The landscape of my childhood and the landscape of my family, the two things I had al-ways regarded as bedrock, were now subject to change. Quicksand" (40). Ironically, the destruction of the refuge was not due to human mismanagement but to natural causes, rain and melting snow. Similarly, at the end of *Refuge,* the wetlands' gradual regeneration is also a natural process, giving Williams hope for her own recovery from grief.

In spite of the resilience of marshes under natural conditions, however, wetlands all over the world are seriously threatened by development, and *Refuge* engages this issue. Williams explains how wetlands ecosystems provide critical habitat for birds and how scientists have found "a direct statistical relationship" between loss of habitat and declining rate of bird production (113). In the American West, the numbers for some birds do not look good: "In recent years, the long-billed curlew, the largest North American shorebird, has been declining in number in the Great Basin, as it loses much of its breeding habitat to the plow and other land developments. In the midwest, it has been extirpated as a breeding species altogether. The eskimo curlew is close to extinction" (145). "Snowy plovers have shown a 50 percent decline in abundance on the California, Oregon, and Washington coasts since the 1960s, due to loss of coastal habitats" (257). "California has lost 95 percent of its wetlands over the past one hundred years" (111). One senses a note of desperation as Williams warns, "Marshes all across the country are disappearing without fanfare, leaving the earth devoid of birdsong" (112).

The grim statistics presented in *Refuge* are familiar ones; indeed, most Americans have heard them so many times that they cease to have meaning, fail to incite us to action. Just as Williams struggles to find words to convey the value of wilderness and the need to preserve it, so, too, she wonders how best to write on behalf of birds: "How do you place a value on inspiration? How do you quantify the wildness of birds, when for the most part, they lead secret and anonymous lives?" (*Refuge* 265). In *Refuge* her success in getting readers to appreciate, understand, and care about birds is nothing short of brilliant, as she breaks open a bright piñata of rhetorical strategies, including sublimation, story, poetry, and spirituality. Most obviously, Williams weaves references to and information about birds throughout the compelling story of her mother's cancer. Thus, readers who are caught up in the riveting human story learn about birds almost subliminally. In an important, related strategy Williams tells stories about birds. Stories about bird watching from bus windows as a girl with her grandmother on an Audubon field trip. Stories about how avocets and stilts "had become [her] relatives" (19). Stories about sitting on bulging black trash bags to count starlings at the Salt Lake City municipal dump for the annual Christmas bird count. Stories about how Burrowing Owls protect their young and about how the new Canadian Goose Gun Club graveled over their nesting grounds. Stories about how a flock of California Gulls miraculously saved the crops of the first Mormon settlers from an infestation of ravenous crickets and became the state bird of Utah. Stories of love. Stories of death. Stories of curiosity. Of empathy. Of kinship. Of rare sightings. Of courtship and pilgrimage. After meeting dozens of species of birds not as natural history specimens but as characters in stories, even readers with little prior interest in birds find themselves knowing a lot about these individuals, and caring about them.

While stories introduce birds as personalities, Williams's seductive lyricism entices readers to see birds as beautiful, while her spiritual worldview creates a sense of wonder and possibility. Thus, although a man at the Gun Club describes burrowing owls as " 'messy little bastards' " (12), Williams teaches the reader to see them poetically: "Just under a foot long, they have a body of feathers the color of wheat, balanced on two long, spindly legs. They can burn grasses with their stare. Yellow eyes magnifying light" (9–10). Her description of pelicans resembles an abstract painting in the precision of its spare detail: "Hundreds of white pelicans appear—white against blue. They turn, disappear. Reappear, black against blue. They turn, disappear. Reappear, white against blue" (149). A focus on birds' eyes startles the reader out of complacency by its unexpected imagery and incantatory rhythm: "The eye of the cormorant is emerald. The eye of the eagle is amber. The eye of the grebe is ruby. The eye of the ibis is sapphire. Four gemstones mirror the minds of birds, birds who mediate between heaven and earth" (95).

Often Williams draws from the vocabulary of religion—"chorus of wings" (264), "magic of birds" (18), "miracle" of migration (264), "pilgrimage" of gulls (76), birds that "mediate between heaven and earth" (18)—to encourage her readers to see birds as sacred. While in Williams's case such a view may be most indebted to the magical worldview of Mormonism, it also ties her to the beliefs of Native Americans and, as such, takes part in a larger social movement to "re-sacralize" our relationship to nature. In 1996 Williams and Stephen Trimble co-edited a collection of works by 21 prominent writers from the West who contributed pieces on behalf of wilderness; the collection, which was distributed to every member of the U.S. Congress, was entitled *Testimony* and the introduction "An Act of Faith." Reimagining the earth as "Holy Land" (*Refuge* 69) and reinstituting rituals to celebrate that vision, some argue, will not only encourage us to treat the environment more respectfully but will also heal us from the modern-day ills of alienation.

In her writings, Williams challenges the orthodoxy of the Mormon church and introduces an Earth-centered focus to religious devotion. Indeed, Williams makes her allegiances clear on a Sunday morning in April. It is the annual Mormon General Conference in which Mormons from all over the world convene in Salt Lake City to sit in the tabernacle and receive the latest doctrine from the church leaders. In contrast, Williams drives by the "cast-iron gates" of Temple Square to the bird refuge where she is "free": "I am spun, supported, and possessed by the spirit who dwells here. Great Salt Lake is a spiritual magnet that will not let me go. Dogma doesn't hold me. Wildness does" (240). After an ecstatic communion with wind and waves, Williams pulls away from the lake to "rest easily in the sanctuary of sage" (240). To orthodox Mormons, this passage depicting her escape from the community to worship privately in nature will be unsettling, bordering on heretical. Indeed, Williams has referred to herself as "a radical soul in a conservative religion" (qtd. in Anderson 973). But Williams pushes the boundaries of propriety to make two points—to remind her fellow Mormons that Mormonism "believes in personal revelation" (*Refuge* 196) and to remind them that early prophets, such as Jesus Christ and Joseph Smith, received their sacred visions in nature: "[T]heir sojourns into nature were sacred. Are ours any less?" (149).

Williams struggles to reclaim for Mormonism its historical and doctrinal ties to the natural world, and, in so doing, to make this powerful religious institution more environmentally aware and responsible. In 1998 Williams co-edited with William B. Smart and Gibbs M. Smith a landmark collection entitled *New Genesis: A Mormon Reader on Land and Community,* thus taking part in a contemporary movement within Mormonism that could fittingly be called a Latter-Day Environmental Reformation. As we have seen, in her passionate defenses of wild land and wildlife, Williams frequently employs religious language to insist on the spiritual value of wilderness, and, conversely, in her participation in Mormon culture, she strives to "return" "our worship . . . to the Earth" (241). For Williams, just as there is no separation between her mother's cancer and the flooding of Great Salt Lake, there is little separation between church and state, religion and politics.

Williams was not always so outspoken in her political views. She writes that "In Mormon culture, authority is respected, obedience is revered, and independent thinking is not. I was taught as a young girl not to 'make waves' or 'rock the boat' " (*Refuge* 285). In Mormon culture, which is patriarchal, women are expected to be obedient and quietly respectful not only to church and state but to men. As Williams's grandmother Mimi observes, Mormon women " 'are taught to sacrifice, support, and endure' " (117). Mimi asks, " 'Why is it…that we are so willing to give up our own authority?' " (116). In *Refuge* Williams will ultimately reclaim her own authority to speak, asserting that "the price of obedience has become too high" (286). Williams, characteristically, tells a story to explain her conversion from submission to radicalism. About a year after her mother's death, she tells her father that throughout her life she has had a terrifying dream of a bright flash of light in the night in the desert. To her surprise, he replies that the flash really happened. In 1957, when Williams was just barely two years old, the family was driving just north of Las Vegas, Nevada, when they happened to witness an atomic explosion, which took place an hour or so before dawn. Williams is stunned. She recalls, "It was at this moment that I realized the deceit I had been living under. Children growing up in the American Southwest, drinking contaminated milk from contaminated cows, even from the contaminated breasts of their mothers, my mother" (283). Williams learns that above-ground nuclear testing at the Nevada Test Site north of Las Vegas was a common occurrence between 1951 and 1962, when America was in the midst of the Cold War against the Soviet Union and was consumed by a fear of communism. Massive arms buildup and the development of ever more powerful atomic weapons, such as the hydrogen bomb, took place on both sides of the globe, and the U.S. government routinely detonated these bombs in its aggressive testing program. In its twelve years of atmospheric testing, the United States detonated an estimated 126 atomic bombs, each of which created a cloud of radioactive fallout that contained levels of radiation comparable to the 1986 nuclear reactor disaster in Chernobyl (Schneider xv). In contrast to the considerable press coverage that Chernobyl received, U.S. testing in the fifties took place with relatively little fanfare, and the government reassured the people in Utah who lived downwind of the explosions that they were perfectly safe. " 'Your best action,' an Atomic Energy Commission booklet read, 'is not to be worried about fallout' " (quoted in *Refuge* 284).

In light of what Williams learns about U.S. atomic testing, the deaths of her mother and six other women of her family to cancer—along with her own two biopsies for breast cancer and a small tumor between her ribs diagnosed as a borderline malignancy—come to seem tragically unnecessary. "Sheep. Dead sheep," she writes, chalking up these deaths to "fear and inability to question authority" on the part of the citizens of Utah (286). For her part, Williams told an interviewer, "I think we were used by our government, and when the Atomic Energy Commission said, 'It is virtually uninhabited desert terrain,' my family, my generation were some of the virtual uninhabitants" (Gross). In its epilogue, *Refuge* bears witness to the birth of a revolutionary as Williams concludes, "What I do know...is that as a Mormon woman of the fifth generation of Latter-day Saints, I must question everything, even if it means losing my faith, even if it means becoming a member of a border tribe among my own people. Tolerating blind obedience in the name of patriotism or religion ultimately takes our lives" (286). At the conclusion of *Refuge* Williams describes a dream in which women from all over the world dance wildly around a blazing fire in the desert, where they have come to "reclaim the desert for the sake of their children, for the sake of the land" (287). Williams's own transformation from victim to activist is suggested by a small change she made to the text of the 1991 original edition of *Refuge* as it was being prepared for paperback release in 1992. She notes that the United States still conducts nuclear tests, underground, and that she was arrested for crossing the line at the Nevada Test Site, where she was protesting these tests. In the original edition, one officer handcuffs her while another frisks her. Williams writes, "She did not find my scars" (290). In the revised paperback version, the officer who frisks her body finds a pen and a pad of paper tucked inside her left boot. Questioned by the officer, Williams replies that these are " 'Weapons.'...Our eyes met. I smiled. She pulled the leg of my trousers back over my boot" (290). *Scars* to *weapons* describes the moral arc of *Refuge* as Williams's suffering engenders a fighting spirit that is fierce in its defense of the environment.[1]

A decade later, empowered by the success of *Refuge,* which is widely acknowledged to be a classic in environmental literature, Williams is still fighting. With her trademark combination of passion, vision, and eloquence, Williams reflects on why she writes,

> I write to make peace with the things I cannot control. I write to create red in a world that often appears black and white. I write to discover. I write to uncover. I write to meet my ghosts. I write to begin a dialogue. I write to imagine things differently and in imagining things differently perhaps the world will change. I write to honor beauty....I write against power and for democ-

racy. I write myself out of my nightmares and into my dreams. I write in a solitude born out of community.... I write to remember. I write to forget.... I write to record what I love in the face of loss.... I write out of my anger and into my passion.... I write for the surprise of a beautiful sentence. I write with the belief of alchemists.... I write past the embarrassment of exposure.... I write because it is dangerous, a bloody risk, like love, to form the words, to say the words, to touch the source, to be touched, to reveal how vulnerable we are, how transient we are. I write as though I am whispering in the ear of the one I love. (*Red* 112–15)

NOTE

1. Williams shared with me the story behind the word change from "scars" in the hardcover edition to "weapons" in the paperback edition. She explained to me that the epilogue to *Refuge* originated as an essay entitled "The Clan of One-Breasted Women," published in *Northern Lights* (6.1 [Jan. 1990]). That essay concluded with the "weapons" conversation between Terry and the arresting officer, an incident that really did happen. When she wrote the essay Williams had no idea that it would eventually be incorporated into *Refuge,* but she later realized that it was an integral part of the story, so she included it as the epilogue to the book. Her editor urged her to change the final scene to the "She did not find my scars" version, thinking that it referred back to an earlier image in the book where Terry discusses her biopsy with her husband Brooke. Williams argued for her original version—the true story—but was so exhausted from the process of writing the book, she conceded. She regretted the new ending as it gave up her own power. When the book was being prepared for paperback release, Williams insisted that the original "weapons" version be reinstated, thus reclaiming her power, affirming her original instincts, and illustrating her politicalization at the moment where she learned to stand her ground and go forth not as a victim but as a warrior. (Personal communication to the author, 29 May 2002)

BIBLIOGRAPHY

Anderson, Lorraine. "Terry Tempest Williams." *American Nature Writers,* vol. 2. Ed. John Elder. New York: Scribner's, 1996. 973–88.

Gross, Terry. Interview with Terry Tempest Williams. *Fresh Air.* National Public Radio. WHYY, Philadelphia. 1 Oct. 1992.

Petersen, David. "Memory is the Only Way Home: A Conversational Interview with Terry Tempest Williams." *Bloomsbury Review* 11.8 (Dec. 1991): 8–9.

Schneider, Keith. "Foreword." *American Ground Zero: The Secret Nuclear War.* Carole Gallagher. [Cambridge: MIT Press], 1993. xv–xix.

Trimble, Stephen, and Terry Tempest Williams, eds. *Testimony: Writers of the West Speak On Behalf of Utah Wilderness.* Minneapolis: Milkweed, 1996.

Williams, Terry Tempest. Personal communication. 29 May 2002.

———. *Red: Passion and Patience in the Desert.* New York: Pantheon, 2001.

———. *Refuge: An Unnatural History of Family and Place.* New York: Pantheon, 1991. Rpt. New York: Vintage, 1992.

———. *An Unspoken Hunger: Stories from the Field.* New York: Pantheon, 1994.

———, William B. Smart, and Gibbs M. Smith, eds. *New Genesis: A Mormon Reader on Land and Community.* Salt Lake City: G. Smith, 1998.

11

Denise Levertov,
The Life Around Us (1997)

George Hart

The Life Around Us: Selected Poems on Nature brings together 60 poems on ecological themes from throughout Denise Levertov's career. The earliest poems appeared in her collections *The Jacob's Ladder* (1961) and *The Sorrow Dance* (1966), and the most recent come from the last two books published in her lifetime, *Evening Train* (1992) and *Sands of the Well* (1996). The majority of the poems are from her later work—mostly from the 1980s and 1990s—and so they reflect contemporary ecological perspectives (such as the interdependence of creatures and ecosystems) and environmental issues (such as nuclear testing, global warming, and ecological restoration). Levertov herself selected the poems for this volume, and rather than putting them in chronological order, she chose a thematic arrangement that reflects a poet's dual impulse to praise the natural world and to lament its destruction. In the foreword, she writes, "I decided not to group them separately—praise-poems in one clump, laments and fears in another—but to follow (though not always in chronological order) the natural undulations and alternations I experienced in writing now in one vein, now in another…I believe this flux and reflux echo what readers also feel in their response to 'the green world' " (xi–xii). Along with this overall order, other thematic groupings occur—travel poems, creature poems, protest poems, and, most important, a sequence near the end of the book reflecting Levertov's ongoing encounter with Mt. Rainier, outside of Seattle, Washington, which was her home in the last years of her life.

BIOGRAPHICAL BACKGROUND

Denise Levertov was born in Essex, England, in 1923; worked as a nurse during World War II; married an American ex-serviceman, Mitchell Goodman, who was also a writer; and moved with him to the United States in 1948. She had already published her first book in England, *The Double Image* (1946), and after relocating to the states she began to school herself in the American poetic tradition, especially the work of Ralph Waldo Emerson in the nineteenth century and Williams Carlos Williams in the twentieth century. Her deep familiarity with traditional British poetry and her rapid absorption of American romanticism and modernism combined to produce highly lyrical, open-form poetry, and critics praised her early work for its purity and lyricism. Levertov became a U.S. citizen in 1955 and published two more books in the late 1950s with American publishers. In 1960, she published *With Eyes at the Back of Our Heads* with New Directions, which remained her primary publisher for the rest of her career. Nature was always a prominent subject in her poetry, especially since she looked back to the Romantics as models, but it was her intense objections to the war in Vietnam during the 1960s and 1970s that defined her as a poet, and, in fact, that prepared the way for her more explicitly environmentalist poetry of the 1980s and 1990s. Levertov became a well-known political poet during the antiwar movement, and the context for all of her poetry from the sixties on is the balancing act between the lyrical impulse to sing and the political impulse to critique.

Levertov's opposition to the Vietnam War, and before that to the nuclear arms race, led her into political activism, not simply a political point of view, and at Brown University in 1975 she delivered a lecture on this topic ("On the Edge of Darkness: What Is Political Poetry?"). After describing the diversity of political poetry being written at that time—from the minority rights and gay liberation movements to the feminist, antinuclear, and environmental movements—Levertov comments on the organic relationship between poetry and politics when a poet is actively involved in a cause:

> A striking characteristic of contemporary political poetry is that, more than in the past, it is written by people who are active participants in the causes they write about, and not simply observers. It's a reciprocal phenomenon: people who are already poets in any case become involved in some aspect or aspects of these interrelated struggles, and it follows naturally that they

write poems concerned with the causes they believe in; these in turn inspire others, both to participation and to the writing of poems. Whether these poems are good or not depends on the gifts of the poet, not on the subject matter. But what is interesting historically is the greater interplay between these poets' actions and their writing. (*Light Up the Cave* 120)

That she sees this relationship as reciprocal is very important, for Levertov is also one of the major practitioners of "organic form" poetry, and to say that a subject matter was imposed on a form, or vice versa, would violate her deeply held poetic principles.

In one of her most famous essays, "Some Notes on Organic Form," she describes how organic poetry works: "I think it's like this: first there must be an experience, a sequence or constellation of perceptions of sufficient interest, felt by the poet intensely enough to demand of him their equivalence in words: *he is brought to speech*" (*The Poet in the World* 8). For Levertov, the form of the poem emerges from this initial encounter, and whether the experience or perception was political or emotional does not matter. For many critics and readers, this process works very effectively for nature poetry but not always for political poetry. How Levertov uses organic form to express her engagement with the natural world, whether personal, spiritual, or political, is a particular strength of *The Life Around Us*. Throughout Levertov's career, critics have debated whether her politics interfere with her lyrical gifts or not.

In his introduction to *Denise Levertov: Selected Criticism*, Albert Gelpi describes Levertov's approach to the natural world in her work of the early sixties, especially *The Jacob's Ladder* and *O Taste and See* (1964):

> [T]he poems again and again break into a celebration of the sacredness, even the sacramentality of temporal experience: not just the organic beauty and sublimity of natural creation but intimations of essentializing spirit breaking through even the ugly, violent brutality of urban life. (4)

This celebratory energy was blocked or diminished as Levertov became more and more stridently opposed to the war in Vietnam and wrote more openly political poetry. In a review of her Vietnam-era collection, *To Stay Alive* (1971), Marie Borroff details the change in Levertov's work and the conflict between the poetic and the moral purpose:

[T]he book is heavy with fact: names are named, places and dates are given, accusations made, praise bestowed. Its major fault—in the geological sense of a fracture-line between opposed forces—results from the attempt to absorb these materials into a specifi-cally *poetic* dramatization.... The time-honored impulse to celebrate, to wander, to sing is basic in her, and this impulse is, literally, disturbed by the knowledge that an unassimilable evil exists which must be hated and which must be fought on the level of action.... [T]he reader has an irritating sense of being made to switch back and forth between poetic and moral re-sponse. (Gelpi 30)

Other critics were not as generous as Borroff, and Levertov, as well as many other antiwar poets, was accused of betraying her art for her pol-itics.

Yet, this willingness to follow both the political as well as the poetic "muse" is what makes Levertov a poet of her time, and what makes her both a meditative, spiritual nature poet and an activist, environ-mentalist poet at the same time. In an essay from the early 1980s, "Po-etry, Prophecy, Survival," Levertov reveals that she is still negotiating the balance between politics and poetry, and that she now includes the environmental crisis among her political concerns. Discussing political poetry—or, more generally, poetry that expresses rage, anger, or protest—she writes that it "has the obvious functions of raising con-sciousness and articulating emotions for people who have not the gift of expression. But we need also the poetry of praise, of love for the world, the vision of the potential for good even in our species which has so messed up the rest of creation, so fouled its own nest" (*New and Selected Essays* 144). As Levertov's political interests expanded to include the environment, her immediate, daily surroundings changed when she moved to Seattle, and this new situation greatly affected her poetry. In the author's note to a limited edition of some of her first Pacific Northwest poems, Levertov writes:

In 1989 I moved from East to West and—though still in a city—from a congested neighborhood to one in which there are large expanses of sky and water, and where a wooded hill nearby is thronged with ancient massive Douglas Firs and cedars. Not since the summers I used to spend in Maine have I had so much daily relationship to the natural world. It was in quest of that daily blessing that I came here. These poems are some of the first that reflect it. (*Lake*)

Many of these poems make up the conclusion of *The Life Around Us*—they are the Mt. Rainier poems mostly—and they reflect Levertov's intense lyricism; they are very much poems of praise. However, the relocation to a landscape apparently more peaceful and undisturbed did not dull Levertov's political conscience or consciousness. A poem she includes early in *The Life Around Us*, "Tragic Error," comes from her first collection written after the move to Seattle, *Evening Train*, and in a diary entry she expresses the tension between the quiet, green landscape of her new home and the environmental crisis that produced a new poetry of lament for her. In her diary for September 24, 1989, shortly after she moved into her new home, Levertov writes,

[t]he place I have come to is as beautiful, and essentially calm, as I dreamed [...]. The weather so far continues golden; perfect fall weather.

   But "dread is with me" too; for the New Yorker article by Bill McKibben about global warming is the *most* chilling news I have ever read, worse than all the information on violence, war, torture, injustice, nuclear threat—I've ever read, because according to him human interference with nature has *already* gone so far that the *best* we can hope for is only a partial alleviation of irreversible damage already done, the world's climate *already* changed, with all that that will mean to every aspect of life. Pray God he is not right. Pray God for mercy. (Papers)

The article she refers to is Bill McKibben's "The End of Nature," a version of his book by the same title published that year. Levertov was responding to passages such as this, quoted from the *New Yorker* article:

We have changed the atmosphere, and that is changing the weather. The temperature and rainfall are no longer entirely the work of some uncivilizable force but instead are in part a product of our habits, our economies, our way of life.... The world outdoors will mean the same thing as the world indoors, the hill the same thing as the house. An idea can become extinct, just like an animal or a plant. The idea in this case is "nature"—the wild province, the world apart from man, under whose rules he was born and died. We have not ended rainfall or sunlight. The wind still blows—but not from some other sphere, some inhuman place. It is too early to tell how much harder the wind will blow, how much hotter the sun will shine. That is for the future. But their *meaning* has already changed. (70)

In her diary, on the page following the entry previously quoted, Levertov began a draft of "Tragic Error" (12), which laments humanity's mistaking of the biblical command to subdue the earth with the idea that we have complete power over creation.

One distinct feature of the later work in the collection is that it is urban nature poetry. Many poems discuss Mt. Rainier, a forest path with Douglas firs and cedars, a lake, and so on, but the setting is Seward Park—a peninsula extending into Lake Washington—not a rural backcountry or wilderness area. The environment Levertov describes is both intimate and public, daily and timeless, urban and natural. For many environmentalists, urban nature does not have the political importance that wilderness does. Preserving and protecting large wilderness areas, sensitive, relatively undisturbed ecosystems, and remote, inaccessible landscapes such as the Arctic National Wildlife Refuge are the environmental causes that receive most attention. Levertov's activism regarding global and national politics focused on causes such as the nuclear threat and human rights rather than strictly environmental issues. Nonetheless, she found local issues that combined her advocacy for nature and her commitment to political activism. The poem "Salvation" addresses the issue of ecosystem restoration in an urban setting. In the mid-nineties, urban planners in Seattle considered restoring Ravenna Creek, which had been turned into an underground channel that connected with the sewage system. The poem begins, "They are going to / *daylight* a river here—/ that's what they call it, noun to verb" (56).

In keeping with her political principles, Levertov combined her poetic celebration of restoration with activism. On June 4, 1996, she wrote to the chairperson of Seattle's Parks, Public Grounds and Recreation Commission:

I am writing to urge that you do support the Ravenna Creek restoration project.

...Not only will this model project give pleasure and relief to busy people now, but coming generations will bless us—bless *you*—for having the foresight to fund the "daylighting" of the stream....

A sense that Seattle has a stronger and better relationship to the natural world around it than that of most modern cities is precisely what gives it much of its charm. And here is a small opportunity to continue that relationship (and, importantly, one which is not in conflict with the desperate need to provide housing for the poor and homeless). (Papers)

In her letter, Levertov appeals to the practical and human benefits that "daylighting" Ravenna Creek will yield, and she balances environmental restoration with her concern for human rights. In the poem, she embraces the idea of restoration and gives it a religious significance by calling it "salvation." Thus, treating the idea of restoration metaphorically, she can project her imagination farther into the potential of the situation, envisioning the project not just as a blessing for future generations but as a blessing for the creek itself. The second and last stanza of the poem, which playfully reverses the daylighting idea by imaging the creek at night, reads:

> At night, stars or at least streetlamps
>   will gleam in it,
> fish and waterbugs swim again in its ripples;
>   and though its course,
> more or less the old one it followed before its
>   years of humiliation,
> will pass near shops and the parking lot's
>   glittering metallic desert, yet
> this unhoped-for pardon will once more permit
>   the stream to offer itself at last
> to the lake, the lake will accept it, take it
>   into itself,
> the stream restored will become pure lake.

Guided by the poetic impulse to celebrate, Levertov can use personification to grant natural objects feelings and purpose—the stream can feel humiliated, the lake can intentionally accept the stream, and so on—and so she can offer another justification for the human action she advocates. Ironically, a *Seattle Times* editorial from August 28, 1995, which supported consideration of the restoration plan, closed with this sentence: "Just imagine the poetry a born-again creek could bring to an otherwise-prosaic shopping center" ("What price"). Although not yet completed, the Ravenna creek restoration is underway and a 480-foot portion of the creek corridor may be daylighted by summer 2004.

Levertov's social politics inform her nature poetry in other significant ways as well. Occasionally, ideas and language from her social commitments inform her experience in the natural world, and often nature poems emerge from her activism on behalf of nonviolence. An example of the former is "In the Woods." Even though nature's diversity is threatened, the speaker of this poem takes heart that every day evidence of its continuing existence "presents itself." She says:

> Everything answers the rollcall,
> and even, as is the custom,
> speaks for those that are gone.
> —Clearly, beyond sound:
> that revolutionary '*Presente!*' (48)

This poem, probably written in response to one of Levertov's walks in the woods in Seward Park, combines lament and celebration in explicitly political terms. The poet thinks of the loss of species and habitat throughout the world even as she admires the lush Pacific Northwest forest. The paradoxical combination of absence and presence takes on a political, even revolutionary, aspect in Levertov's imagination. In an interview, she explains the reference to the "rollcall":

> ...it is customary in Latin America to include in roll call those who have been killed in resistance, and so one includes Archbishop Romero, and everyone will shout "*presente!*" Just as those who have died as martyrs in Latin America are considered to be present when roll call is taken, so the disappeared things in nature, killed off by us, still answer "*presente!*" (Archer 68)

"In the Woods" seamlessly joins Levertov's sense of social justice and awareness of political struggle with her appreciation of and concern for nature; each informs the other, establishing a continuum between the human and the natural, the political and the environmental, a connection that shows readers that there is no clear line between the two.

Sometimes, on the other hand, political activism yields nature poetry. Throughout her life, Levertov was most involved in the antinuclear movement, protesting against nuclear power, nuclear testing, and the threat of nuclear war. Over the years, the character of the protests in which she was involved changed, but many were acts of civil disobedience. In *Light up the Cave,* she describes her activity with a group called the Seabrook Natural Guard, which was opposed to the construction of a nuclear power plant in Seabrook, New Hampshire, in 1978. The protest centered around a "die-in"—a dramatic enactment of the impact of a meltdown—which resulted in many of the activists, including Levertov, being arrested and spending a night in jail. She felt that this event signaled a new kind of activism, distinct from the angry and violent protests of the sixties and early seventies. According to Levertov, the members of the Natural Guard mostly "come from the environmental movement; many have Earth Days and backpacking trips as memories from high school years. They've evolved a gentle, unpretentious, civilized style of daily life, and they seem to me more mature than the people of the same average age—early twenties—that I knew and acted with nine or ten years ago" (*Light up the Cave* 165). In a section called "Age of Terror," in her book *Candles in Babylon* (1982), Levertov wrote many poems based on her activism against the nuclear threat, including one titled "Psalm: People Power at the Die-in" (*Candles in Babylon* 84–85). Another poem from this section is included in *The Life Around Us.* "What It Could Be" describes uranium mining as the rape of a feminized landscape, and then goes on to imagine that *not* extracting this power from the earth would be a sign of "the continuing act of / *non*violence, of passionate / reverence, active love" (24).

As she became more explicitly environmentalist in her politics in the 1980s and 1990s, Levertov also found her way to a revitalized religious faith. (New Directions published *The Stream and the Sapphire,* a collection of her religious poems, as a companion volume to *The Life Around Us.*) Attracted to its ritual and tradition as well as certain factions' commitment to social justice, Levertov was received into the Roman Catholic Church in 1990. Her activities as a socially conscious Catholic continued her civil disobedience on behalf of the environment and human rights. In 1990, she participated in a Lenten protest against nuclear testing at the Nevada Test Site, and the following year she was cited and fined for trespassing, along with, among others,

Archibishop Helder Camara from Brazil ("Nevada"). "Protesting at the Nuclear Test Site" reflects some of these experiences, and it is also a meditation on her response, as one of the "lovers of lakes and trees" (21), to an arid and alien landscape. Again, the poet imagines uranium mining as a violation of the earth, a rape, and realizes the legacy of such violence is the ugliness she perceives, not the desert itself. In particularly Christian imagery, alluding to St. Francis, the poem ends:

> Slowly,
> revulsion unstiffened itself, I learned
> almost to love
> the dry and hostile earth, its dusty growth
> of low harsh plants, sparse in unceasing wind;
> could almost have bent
> to kiss that leper face. (22)

She could only "almost" love the desert landscape, but her response to the forests and mountains of the Pacific Northwest was less qualified if still somewhat contradictory and complex. Fifteen poems near the end of *The Life Around Us* describe Mt. Rainier as it appears from the vantage of Seward Park, which is some 50 miles to the north and west. The arrangement of the poems is by season, beginning in the autumn, running through spring and summer into another fall. The sequence begins when she moves to Seattle permanently, described in the poem "Settling," and it concludes with three poems that express clearly her feelings about the mountain and how it should be seen. The majority of the poems are lyrical evocations of the mountain as the poet sees it in her daily walks in the park; some of the poems are haiku-like in their clarity and brevity.

These poems are mostly descriptive, the poet's attention focused on the mountain and the weather rather than her feelings or circumstances, but they are not completely objective. Levertov is in fact developing a relationship with Mt. Rainier, and the ways she imagines the mountain as an entity are important to defining the nature of that relationship. The relationship is primarily spiritual, or even religious, but she does not see the mountain as a god exactly. The mountain has a divine presence—it is a symbol of divinity but in complex and various ways. In his essay "The Poet," Emerson, who Levertov studied intensely in her transition from a British to American tradition, remarked that "all symbols are fluxional." For Emerson, as for Levertov, the difference between the poet and the mystic is that the latter "nails a symbol to one sense, which was a true sense for a moment, but soon becomes old and false" (463). In an interview with Emily Archer, Levertov remarked on this kind of symbol-making:

> A symbol doesn't have to abstract, but the outlook that appropriates the mountain, let's say, as a symbol, denies the mountainness of the mountain. A true symbol enlarges, but that denial reduces. (Archer 68)

In writing about Mt. Rainier as a symbol of the divine, Levertov wants to enlarge her encounter with it, not reduce it to a mere figure of speech that says "mountain" = "God." At the same time, however, her insistence that the proper way to view the mountain is from a distance, and that a direct experience of the mountain destroys the mystery that gives it its divine aspect, brings into question her ability to express the "mountain-ness of the mountain." This tension between the mountain as thing-in-itself and mountain as symbol or apparition makes the Mt. Rainier poems some of the most interesting in the book.

Levertov uses a natural fact—the foggy and wet climate of the Pacific Northwest—to render this theme in contrasting images of presence and absence. From day to day, hour to hour even, she did not know if she would see Rainier or not as she walked in the park. The variable climate also produces a range of ways she could see the mountain—through rain, mist, or fog, in clear or stormy weather—not to mention the times of day she viewed it, in sunlight, in moonlight, and so on. One poem is called "Presence," and throughout the sequence the mountain is a "vast presence" (58), a "majestic presence" (62), and a "witnessing presence" (71). On the other hand, sometimes the mountain is completely "absent" (60), or sometimes hidden "in veils of cloud" (71), or "revok[ed] by the clouds" (66). Between this binary of presence/absence—"seen or unseen" (58)—is a middle ground of ambiguity, when the mountain mirrors something else in nature, not a divine entity: it can itself look like a cloud or a wave, air or foam, a "moonflower" or a moth, or it can suggest sound, a whisper.

To describe such various effects, Levertov has to be an acute observer of the facts of the scene, aware of the mountain-as-mountain, but these natural facts also allow her to make spiritual associations with the mountain. For example, "Effacement" combines the theme of presence and absence with this middle ground:

Today the mountain
is cloud,
pale cone of shadow
veiled by a paler scrim—
majestic presence become
one cloud among others,
humble vapor,
barely discernible,
like the archangel walking
with Tobias on dusty roads. (61)

The three stanzas organize three levels of symbolism. The first describes the scene with a metaphor, the mountain *is* cloud, and an image to explain how it can be so, the theatrical device of a scrim. The second stanza evokes the idea of effacement, which implies rubbing out or erasing but also can mean to behave inconspicuously. The third stanza (which in her diary entry she worried about being forced) connects the mountain with divinity through a simile—it is *like* the archangel Raphael in the apocryphal Book of Tobit, who disguised himself in order to protect Tobias as he traveled the road to Media. In the poem, the mountain is not quite present, but neither is it absent; it is a divine protector but one only known through the indirection of figurative language and literary allusion.

For Levertov, this sense of indirection, ambiguity, or distance is the operative factor in her relationship to Mt. Rainier. In two poems at the end of the sequence, "Open Secret" and "Against Intrusion," she speaks directly about her belief that the best way to honor this mountain is to leave it alone. In the former, she writes, "This mountain's power / lies in the open secret of its remote / apparition" (70). The latter associates visiting the mountain, especially driving and climbing on it, with disrespect and indulgent curiosity; it concludes:

What does it serve to insist
on knowing more than that a mountain,
forbearing—so far—from volcanic rage,
blesses the city it is poised above, angelic guardian
at rest on sustaining air; and that its vanishings
are needful, as silence is to music? (72)

This attitude may distinguish Levertov from most other nature poets, certainly other West Coast poets, such as Gary Snyder, among whom wilderness excursions and mountain-climbing play an important role in their relationship to the environment. It may also be a mark of her urban nature poetry and an indicator that her sensibilities were formed not in the West, but in the East and in England.

The poem that brings the volume to a close, "Sojourns in the Parallel World," explicitly discusses the effect that nature has upon us, a revealing comment after her many poems lamenting the effect that humans have had upon nature. If, as Levertov learned when she read Bill McKibben's article, human interference and modification has changed nature irrevocably, perhaps then nature can change humans who have become too involved in the world they control. Levertov knows that mostly we live in the world of human emotions and concerns but that at times "we lose track of our own obsessions" (75) and connect with nature, a parallel and overlapping world. We must return to "our own sphere," she admits, "but we have changed, a little" (76). These parallel yet overlapping worlds are much like the presence and absence of Mt. Rainier. Levertov does not believe that humans can break from culture and return to nature, but the slight oscillation between the two poles, if one looks for it, provides opportunity for small changes that with community effort, like restoring a creek or protesting nuclear testing, might counter some of the wholesale damage done to the environment. The poet's job for Levertov (as for Emerson) is to celebrate and lament, to praise and condemn, when she is moved by experience to sing.

BIBLIOGRAPHY

Archer, Emily. "A Conversation with Denise Levertov." *Image: A Journal of the Arts and Religion* 18 (1997–98): 55–72.

Emerson, Ralph Waldo. *Essays and Lectures*. Ed. Joel Porte. New York: Library of America, 1983.

Gelpi, Albert, ed. *Denise Levertov: Selected Criticism*. Ann Arbor: U of Michigan P, 1993.

"King County completes new pipeline for Seattle's Revenna Creek restoration project." 22 March 2004. *Metropolitan King County Council*. Online. <http://dnr.metrokc.gov/dnrp/press/2004/0322ravenna.htm>. 10 May 2004.

Levertov, Denise. *Candles in Babylon*. New York: New Directions, 1982.

———. *Lake, Mountain, Moon*. N.p.: Tangram, 1990.

———. *The Life Around Us*. New York: New Directions, 1997.

———. *Light up the Cave*. New York: New Directions, 1981.

————. *New and Selected Essays.* New York: New Directions, 1992.

————. Papers, ca. 1918–1996. Department of Special Collections, Stanford University Libraries.

————. *The Poet in the World.* New York: New Directions, 1973.

McKibben, Bill. "The End of Nature." *The New Yorker* 11 Sept 1989: 47–105.

"Nevada Desert Experience." Online. <http://www.NevadaDesertExperience .org>. 24 June 2002.

"What price for babble in Ravenna's lost creek?" Opinion page. *The Seattle Times* 28 Aug 1995.

Suggested Additional Readings

This list of suggested readings is intended merely as a starting point, signaling the range and vitality of American and international environmental writing and scholarship. Many fine authors and scholars work in this field in addition to those whose works are represented here, and many of the included writers have published numerous works in addition to the texts we have space to mention.

PRIMARY TEXTS

United States

Abbey, Edward. *Desert Solitaire: A Season in the Wilderness* (fiction/nonfiction, 1968).

Ackerman, Diane. *A Natural History of the Senses* (nonfiction, 1990).

———. *The Rarest of the Rare* (nonfiction, 1996).

Alarcon, Francisco. *Snake Poems: An Aztec Invocation* (poetry, 1992).

Ammons, A. R. *Collected Poems, 1951–1971* (poetry, 1972).

———. *Garbage: A Poem* (poetry, 1993).

Anaya, Rudolfo. *Bless Me, Ultima* (fiction, 1972).

Anzaldúa, Gloria. *Borderlands/La Frontera* (nonfiction/mixed genre, 1987).

Awiakta, Marilou. *Selu: Seeking the Corn-Mother's Wisdom* (fiction/nonfiction/poetry, 1993).

Baca, Jimmy Santiago. *Black Mesa Poems* (poetry, 1989).

Bartram, William. *Travels* (nonfiction, 1791).

Bass, Rick. *The Book of Yaak* (nonfiction, 1996).

———. *Fiber* (fiction/nonfiction, 1998).

Bedichek, Roy. *Adventures with a Texas Naturalist* (nonfiction, 1947).

Berry, Wendell. *Collected Poems, 1957–1982* (poetry, 1985).

———. *The Memory of Old Jack* (fiction, 1974)

———. *The Unsettling of America: Culture and Agriculture* (nonfiction, 1977).

Beston, Henry. *The Outermost House: A Year of Life on the Great Beach of Cape Cod* (nonfiction, 1928).

Bishop, Elizabeth. *The Complete Poems: 1927–1979* (poetry, 1984).

Blum, Arlene. *Annapurna: A Woman's Place* (nonfiction, 1980).

Boyle, T. Coraghessan. *Tortilla Curtain* (fiction, 1996).

Bruchac, Joseph. *Dawn Land* (fiction, 1993).

Burroughs, John. *Wake-Robin* (nonfiction, 1871).

Butler, Octavia. *The Parable of the Talents* (fiction, 2000).

Carrighar, Sally. *One Day on Beetle Rock* (nonfiction, 1944).

Carson, Rachel. *The Sea Around Us* (nonfiction, 1951).

Castillo, Ana. *So Far from God* (fiction, 1993).

Cather, Willa. *My Ántonia* (fiction, 1918).

Childs, Craig. *The Secret Knowledge of Water* (nonfiction, 2000).

Cokinos, Chris. *Hope Is a Thing with Feathers: A Personal Chronicle of Vanished Birds* (nonfiction, 2000).

Cooper, Susan Fenimore. *Rural Hours* (nonfiction, 1850).

Crevecoeur, J. Hector St. John de. *Letters from an American Farmer* (nonfiction, 1782).

Daniel, John. *The Trail Home: Nature, Imagination, and the American West* (nonfiction, 1992).

Davis, Mike. *Ecology of Fear* (nonfiction, 1998).

DeLillo, Don. *White Noise* (fiction, 1985).

Deming, Alison Hawthorne. *The Monarchs: A Poem Sequence* (poetry, 1997).

———. *Temporary Homelands: Essays on Nature, Spirit, and Place* (nonfiction, 1994/1996).

DeVoto, Bernard, ed. *The Journals of Lewis and Clark* (nonfiction, 1953).

Dickey, James. *Deliverance* (fiction, 1970).

Dickinson, Emily. *The Poems of Emily Dickinson.* Ed. Thomas Johnson (poetry, 1955).

Dillard, Annie. *Pilgrim at Tinker Creek* (fiction/nonfiction, 1974).

———. *Teaching a Stone to Talk* (nonfiction, 1982).

Dodd, Elizabeth. *Archetypal Light* (poetry, 2001).

Douglas, Marjory Stoneman. *The Everglades: River of Grass* (1947).

Duane, Daniel. *Caught Inside: A Surfer's Year on the California Coast* (nonfiction, 1996).

Duncan, David James. *The River Why* (fiction, 1983).

Ehrlich, Gretel. *Islands, the Universe, Home* (nonfiction, 1991).

———. *The Solace of Open Spaces* (nonfiction, 1985).

Elder, John. *Reading the Mountains of Home* (nonfiction, 1998).

Emerson, Ralph Waldo. *Nature* (nonfiction, 1836).

Farber, Thomas. *On Water* (nonfiction, 1994).

Faulkner, William. *Go Down, Moses* (fiction, 1942).

Finch, Robert. *Common Ground: A Naturalist's Cape Cod* (nonfiction, 1981).

Fletcher, Colin. *The Man Who Walked Through Time* (nonfiction, 1967).

Fox, William L. *The Void, the Grid, and the Sign: Traversing the Great Basin* (nonfiction, 2000).

Franklin, Tom. *Poachers* (fiction, 1999).

Frost, Robert. *The Poetry of Robert Frost: The Collected Poems, Complete and Unabridged*. Ed. Edward Connery Lathem (poetry, 1969).

Galvin, James. *The Meadow* (fiction, 1992).

Glück, Louise. *The Wild Iris* (poetry, 1992).

Gonzalez, Ray. *Memory Fever: A Journey Beyond El Paso del Norte* (nonfiction, 1993).

Griffin, Susan. *Made from this Earth: An Anthology of Writings by Susan Griffin* (nonfiction/poetry, 1982).

Gruchow, Paul. *The Necessity of Empty Places* (nonfiction, 1988).

Haines, John. *News from the Glacier: Selected Poems 1960–1980* (poetry, 1982).

———. *The Stars, the Snow, the Fire: Twenty-Five Years in the Alaska Wilderness* (nonfiction, 1989).

Hanson, Susan. *Icons of Loss and Grace: Moments from the Natural World* (nonfiction, 2004).

Harjo, Joy. *She Had Some Horses* (poetry, 1983).

Harper, Michael. *Images of Kin: New and Selected Poems* (poetry, 1977).

Harrigan, Stephen. *A Natural State: Essays on Texas* (nonfiction, 1994).

Harris, Eddy L. *Mississippi Solo—A River Quest* (nonfiction, 1988).

Hass, Robert. *Human Wishes* (poetry, 1989).

Hasselstrom, Linda M. *Between Grass and Sky: Where I Live and Work* (nonfiction, 2002).

Hay, John. *A Beginner's Faith in Things Unseen* (nonfiction, 1994).

———. *Nature's Year: The Seasons of Cape Cod* (nonfiction, 1961).

Heinrich, Bernd. *Ravens in Winter* (nonfiction, 1989).

Hemingway, Ernest. *In Our Time* (fiction, 1925).

Hoagland, Edward. *Walking the Dead Diamond River* (nonfiction, 1973).

Hogan, Linda. *The Book of Medicines: Poems* (poetry, 1993).

———. *Dwellings: A Spiritual History of the Living World* (nonfiction, 1995).

———. *Solar Storms: A Novel* (fiction, 1997).

———. *The Woman Who Watches Over the World: A Native Memoir* (nonfiction, 2001).

Hongo, Garrett. *Volcano: A Memoir of Hawaii* (nonfiction, 1995).

Hopes, David Brendan. *A Sense of the Morning: Inspiring Reflections on Nature and Discovery* (nonfiction, 1988).

House, Freeman. *Totem Salmon: Life Lessons from Another Species* (nonfiction, 1999).

Hubbell, Sue. *A Country Year: Living the Questions* (nonfiction, 1983).

Hurston, Zora Neale. *Mules and Men* (nonfiction, 1935).

———. *Their Eyes Were Watching God* (fiction, 1937).

Janovy, John, Jr. *Keith County Journal* (nonfiction, 1978).

———. *Ten Minute Ecologist: 20 Answered Questions for Busy People Facing Environmental Issues* (nonfiction, 1997).

Jeffers, Robinson. *The Selected Poetry of Robinson Jeffers.* Ed. Tim Hunt (poetry, 2000).

Jewett, Sarah Orne. *The Country of the Pointed Firs* (fiction, 1896).

Johnson, Charles. *Middle Passage* (fiction, 1990).

Kerouac, Jack. *The Dharma Bums* (fiction, 1958).

Kingsolver, Barbara. *Animal Dreams* (fiction, 1991).

———. *High Tide in Tucson: Essays from Now or Never* (nonfiction, 1995).

Kingston, Maxine Hong. *Hawai'i One Summer* (nonfiction, 1998).

Kittredge, William. *Owning It All* (nonfiction, 1987).

———. *Taking Care: Thoughts on Storytelling and Belief* (nonfiction, 1999).

Krutch, Joseph Wood. *The Best Nature Writing of Joseph Wood Krutch* (nonfiction, 1970/1995).

———. *The Desert Year* (nonfiction, 1951).

Kumin, Maxine. *Nurture* (poetry, 1989).

———. *Women, Animals, and Vegetables: Essays and Stories* (nonfiction/fiction, 1994).

Kutchins, Laurie. *The Night Path* (poetry, 1997).

LaBastille, Anne. *Woodswoman* (nonfiction, 1976).

Lamberton, Ken. *Wilderness and Razorwire: A Naturalist's Observations from Prison* (nonfiction, 2000).

Least Heat-Moon, William. *Blue Highways: A Journey into America* (nonfiction, 1982).

———. *PrairyErth (a deep map)* (nonfiction, 1991).

Leeson, Ted. *The Habit of Rivers: Reflections on Trout Streams and Fly Fishing* (nonfiction, 1994).

Legler, Gretchen. *All the Powerful Invisible Things: A Sportswoman's Notebook* (nonfiction, 1995).

Leopold, Aldo. *A Sand County Almanac* (nonfiction, 1949).

London, Jack. *The Call of the Wild* (fiction, 1903).

Lopez, Barry. *Field Notes: Crossing Open Ground* (nonfiction, 1988).

———. *The Rediscovery of North America* (nonfiction, 1990).

Maclean, Norman. *A River Runs Through It* (fiction, 1976).

Masumoto, David Mas. *Epitaph for a Peach* (nonfiction, 1995).

———. *Four Seasons in Five Senses: Things Worth Savoring* (nonfiction, 2003).

Mathews, John Joseph. *Talking to the Moon* (nonfiction, 1945).

Matthiessen, Peter. *The Snow Leopard* (nonfiction, 1978).

———. *Wildlife in America* (nonfiction, 1959).

McClure, Michael. *Scratching the Beat Surface* (nonfiction, 1982).

———. *Selected Poems* (poetry, 1986).

McKibben, Bill. *The Age of Missing Information* (nonfiction, 1992).

———. *The End of Nature* (nonfiction, 1989).

———. *Maybe One: A Personal and Environmental Argument for Single-child Families* (nonfiction, 1998).

McNamee, Gregory. *Gila: The Life and Death of an American River* (nonfiction, 1994).

McPhee, John. *Basin and Range* (nonfiction, 1981).

———. *Encounters with the Archdruid* (nonfiction, 1971).

Meloy, Ellen. *Raven's Exile: A Season on the Green River* (nonfiction, 1994).

Melville, Herman. *Moby-Dick* (fiction, 1851).

Merwin, W. S. *The Rain in the Trees* (poetry, 1988).

Mitchell, John Hanson. *Living at the End of Time* (nonfiction, 1990).

Moore, Kathleen Dean. *Holdfast: At Home in the Natural World* (nonfiction, 1999).

———. *Riverwalking: Reflections on Moving Water* (nonfiction, 1995).

Mora, Pat. *Agua Santa/Holy Water* (poetry, 1994).

Morrison, Toni. *Beloved* (fiction, 1987).

———. *The Bluest Eye* (fiction, 1970).

———. *Paradise* (fiction, 1998).

———. *Song of Solomon* (fiction, 1977).

———. *Tar Baby* (fiction, 1981).

Muir, John. *The Mountains of California* (nonfiction, 1894).

———. *My First Summer in the Sierra* (nonfiction, 1911).

Nabhan, Gary Paul. *Cultures of Habitat: On Nature, Culture, and Story* (nonfiction, 1997).

———. *The Desert Smells Like Rain* (nonfiction, 1982).

Neely, Barbara. *Blanche Cleans Up* (fiction, 1998).

Nelson, Richard K. *The Island Within* (nonfiction, 1989).

Nichols, John. *Dancing on the Stones: Selected Essays* (nonfiction, 2000).

———. *The Milagro Beanfield War* (fiction, 1974).

Norris, Kathleen. *Dakota: A Spiritual Geography* (nonfiction, 1993).

O'Brien, Dan. *The Rites of Autumn: A Falconer's Journey Across the American West* (nonfiction, 1988).

———. *Spirit of the Hills* (fiction, 1988).

O'Brien, Tim. *In the Lake of the Woods* (fiction, 1994).

Oliver, Mary. *New and Selected Poems* (poetry, 1992).

Olson, Sigurd. *The Singing Wilderness* (nonfiction, 1956).

Ortiz, Simon J. *Out There Somewhere* (poetry, 2002).

———. *Woven Stone* (poetry, 1992).

Peterson , Brenda, and Linda Hogan, *Sightings: The Gray Whales' Mysterious Journey* (nonfiction, 2002).

Pollan, Michael. *The Botany of Desire: A Plant's-Eye View of the World* (nonfiction, 2001).

———. *Second Nature: A Gardener's Education* (nonfiction, 1991).

Pyle, Robert Michael. *Where Bigfoot Walks: Crossing the Dark Divide* (nonfiction, 1995).

———. *Wintergreen: Rambles in a Ravaged Land* (nonfiction, 1986)

Quammen, David. *The Song of the Dodo: Island Biogeography in an Age of Extinctions* (nonfiction, 1996).

Ray, Janisse. *Ecology of a Cracker Childhood* (nonfiction, 2000)

Raymo, Chet. *Natural Prayers* (nonfiction, 1999).

———. *The Soul of the Night: An Astronomical Pilgrimage* (nonfiction, 1985).

Robinson, Kim Stanley. *Blue Mars* (fiction, 1996).

Robinson, Marilynne. *Housekeeping* (fiction, 1981).

Rogers, Pattiann. *Song of the World Becoming: Poems, New and Collected, 1981–2001* (poetry, 2001).

Sanders, Scott Russell. *Staying Put: Making a Home in Restless World* (nonfiction, 1993).

Saner, Reg. *The Four-Cornered Falcon: Essays on the Interior West and the Natural Scene* (nonfiction, 1993).

Shelton, Richard. *Of All the Dirty Words* (poetry, 1972).

Silko, Leslie Marmon. *Gardens in the Dunes* (fiction, 1999).

———. *Yellow Woman and a Beauty of the Spirit: Essays on Native American Life Today* (nonfiction, 1996).

Smiley, Jane. *A Thousand Acres* (fiction, 1991).

Snyder, Gary. *Mountains and Rivers Without End* (poetry, 1996).

———. *No Nature: New and Selected Poems* (poetry, 1992).

———. *The Practice of the Wild* (nonfiction, 1990).

Solnit, Rebecca. *Savage Dreams: A Journey into the Landscape Wars of the American West* (nonfiction, 1994).

Soto, Gary. *Living Up the Street: Narrative Reflections* (nonfiction, 1992).

Stafford, Kim. *Lochsa Road: A Pilgrim in the West* (nonfiction, 1991).

Stafford, William. *The Darkness Around Us Is Deep: Selected Poems of William Stafford* (poetry, 1994).

Stegner, Wallace. *Where the Bluebird Sings to the Lemonade Springs: Living and Writing in the West* (nonfiction, 1992).

Steinbeck, John. *The Log from the Sea of Cortez* (nonfiction, 1941).

Sullivan, Robert. *The Meadowlands: Wilderness Adventures at the Edge of a City* (nonfiction, 1998).

Tally, Ted. *Terra Nova* (drama, 1981).

Teale, Edwin Way. *Wanderings Through Winter* (nonfiction, 1966).

Thomas, Lewis. *The Lives of a Cell: Notes of a Biology Watcher* (nonfiction, 1974).

Thoreau, Henry David. *The Maine Woods* (nonfiction, 1864).

———. *Walden* (fiction/nonfiction, 1854).

Toomer, Jean. *Cane* (fiction/poetry, 1925).

Twain, Mark. *Roughing It* (nonfiction, 1872).

Van Dyke, John C. *The Desert* (nonfiction, 1901).

Wagoner, David. *Collected Poems 1956–1976* (poetry, 1976).

Walker, Alice. *Her Blue Body Everything We Knowy: Earthling Poems 1965–1990 Complete* (poetry, 1993).

Waters, Frank. *The Man Who Killed the Deer: A Novel of Pueblo Indian Life* (fiction, 1942).

———. *People of the Valley* (fiction, 1941).

Weiner, Jonathan. *The Beak of the Finch: A Story of Evolution in Our Time* (nonfiction, 1994).

White, E. B. *Essays of E.B. White* (nonfiction, 1977).

Whitman, Walt. *Leaves of Grass* (poetry, 1855).

Wideman, John Edgar. *All Stories Are True* (fiction, 1993).

Williams, Terry Tempest. *Leap* (nonfiction, 2000).

———. *Red: Passion and Patience in the Desert* (nonfiction, 2001).

Williams, William Carlos. *Paterson* (poetry, 1946–51, 1958).

Wilson, Edward O. *Biophilia* (nonfiction, 1984).

———. *Naturalist* (nonfiction, 1994).

Wood, William. *New England's Prospect* (nonfiction, 1634/1977).

Yamashita, Karen Tei. *Through the Arc of the Rain Forest: A Novel* (fiction, 1990).

———. *Tropic of Orange: A Novel* (fiction, 1997).

Zepeda, Ofelia. *Ocean Power: Poems from the Desert* (poetry, 1995).

Zwinger, Ann. *Rock: Downcanyon* (nonfiction, 1995).

———. *Run, River, Run* (nonfiction, 1975).

International

Albán, Laureano. *Autumn's Legacy* (Costa Rica, poetry, 1982).

Arguedas, José María. *Deep Rivers* (Peru, fiction, 1958/1978).

Aridjis, Homero. *Eyes to See Otherwise.Ojos, de otro mirar: Selected Poems* (Mexico, poetry, 2001).

Astley, Thea. *An Item from the Late News* (Australia, fiction, 1982).

Atwood, Margaret. *Surfacing* (Canada, fiction, 1972).

Bail, Murray. *Eucalyptus* (Australia, fiction, 1998).

Ballard, J.G. *The Drought* (United Kingdom, fiction, 1965).

Boland, Eavan. *Collected Poems* (Ireland, poetry, 1995).

Breytenbach, Breyten. *The Memory of Birds in Times of Revolution* (South Africa, nonfiction, 1996).

Burns, Robert. *Robert Burns: Selected Poems* (Scotland, poetry, 1993).

Butala, Sharon. *The Perfection of the Morning: An Apprenticeship in Nature* (Canada, nonfiction, 1994).

Byatt, A.S. *Angels and Insects* (United Kingdom, fiction, 1992).

Cardenal, Ernesto. *Quetzalcóatl* (Nicaragua, poetry, 1990).

Carpentier, Alejo. *The Lost Steps* (Cuba, fiction, 1956).

Coetzee, J.M. *The Lives of Animals* (South Africa, fiction, 2001).

Collis, Brad. *The Soul Stone* (Australia, fiction, 1993).

Cook, James. *A Voyage to the Pacific Ocean* (United Kingdom, nonfiction, 1784).

Darwin, Charles. *Journal of Researches into the Geology and Natural History of the Various Countries Visited by the H.M.S. Beagle Round the World* (United Kingdom, nonfiction, 1839).

———. *The Origin of Species* (United Kingdom, nonfiction, 1859).

David-Neel, Alexandra. *My Journey to Lhasa* (France, nonfiction, 1927).

Davidson, Robyn. *Tracks* (Australia, nonfiction, 1980).

Davis, Jack. *Black Life: Poems* (Australia, poetry, 1992).

Devi, Mahasweta. *Imaginary Maps* (India, fiction, 1995).

Dinesan, Isak. *Out of Africa* (Denmark, nonfiction, 1937).

Diski, Jenny. *Rainforest* (United Kingdom, fiction, 1987).

Eliot, George. *Middlemarch* (United Kingdom, fiction, 1872).

Engel, Marian. *Bear* (Canada, fiction, 1976).

Farmer, Beverly. *The Seal Woman* (Australia, fiction, 1992).

Findley, Timothy. *Not Wanted on the Voyage* (Canada, fiction, 1984).

Flanagan, Richard. *The Sound of One Hand Clapping* (Australia, fiction, 1997).

Flannery, Tim. *Throwim Way Leg: Tree-Kangaroos, Possums, and Penis Gourds—on the Track of Unknown Animals in Wildest New Guinea* (Australia, nonfiction, 1998).

Forster, E. M. *The Longest Journey* (United Kingdom, fiction, 1907).

Fowles, John. *The Tree* (United Kingdom, nonfiction, 1979).

Franklin, Sir John. *Narrative of a Journey to the Shores of the Polar Sea, in the Years 1819, 20, 21, and 22* (United Kingdom, nonfiction, 1823).

Frison-Roche, Roger. *First on the Rope* (France, fiction, 1949).

Fukuoka, Masanobu. *The One-Straw Revolution* (Japan, nonfiction, 1975).

Gay, John. *Trivia: or, the Art of Walking the Streets of London* (United Kingdom, poetry, 1716).

Gayton, Don. *Landscapes of the Interior: Re-explorations of Nature and the Human Spirit* (Canada, nonfiction, 1996).

Giono, Jean. *The Man Who Planted Trees* (France, fiction, 1954).

Goldsworthy, Peter. *Wish* (Australia, fiction, 1995).

Gordimer, Nadine. *The Conservationist* (South Africa, fiction, 1976).

Gowdy, Barbara. *The White Bone* (South Africa, fiction, 1999).

Haig-Brown, Roderick L. *A River Never Sleeps* (Canada, nonfiction, 1946).

Hardy, Thomas. *The Return of the Native* (United Kingdom, fiction, 1878).

———. *The Woodlanders* (United Kingdom, fiction, 1887).

Hawkes, Jacquetta. *A Land* (United Kingdom, nonfiction, 1951).

Head, Bessie. *When Rain Clouds Gather* (Botswana, fiction, 1968).

Heaney, Seamus. *Field Work* (Ireland, poetry, 1979).

Herzog, Maurice. *Annapurna* (France, nonfiction, 1952).

Hoban, Russell. *Turtle Diary* (United Kingdom, fiction, 1977).

Hopkins, Gerard Manley. *A Hopkins Reader* (United Kingdon, poetry, 1966).

Hughes, Ted. *River* (United Kingdom, poetry, 1983).

Hulme, Keri. *The Bone People* (New Zealand, fiction, 1983).

Humboldt, Alexander von. *Views of Nature* (Germany, nonfiction, 1808).

Ishimure, Michiko. *Paradise in the Sea of Sorrow* (Japan, fiction/nonfiction, 1972/1990).

Jefferies, Richard. *Landscape with Figures* (United Kingdom, nonfiction, 1983).

———. *The Story of My Heart: My Autobiography* (United Kingdom, nonfiction, 1883).

Kafka, Franz. *The Metamorphosis* (Bohemia/Austria, fiction, 1915).

Karm, Dun. *Dun Karm, Poet of Malta* (Malta, poetry, 1961).

Kingsley, Charles. *The Water-Babies* (United Kingdom, fiction, 1863).

Kinkaid, Jamaica. *A Small Place* (Antigua, nonfiction, 1988).

Kipling, Rudyard. *The Jungle Book* (United Kingdom, fiction, 1894).

Kroetsch, Robert. *A Likely Story: The Writing Life* (Canada, nonfiction, 1995).

Lawrence, D.H. *Lady Chatterley's Lover* (United Kingdom, fiction, 1928).

Lines, William. *Open Air* (Australia, nonfiction, 2001).

Llosa, Mario Vargas. *The Storyteller* (Peru, fiction, 1987/1989).

Malouf, David. *An Imaginary Life* (Australia, fiction, 1978).

Marty, Sid. *Leaning on the Wind: Under the Spell of the Great Chinook* (Canada, nonfiction, 1995).

Mendes, Chico. *Fight for the Forest: Chico Mendes in His Own Words* (Brazil, nonfiction, 1989).

Minhinnick, Robert. *The Dinosaur Park* (Wales, poetry, 1985).

———. *Life Sentences* (Wales, poetry, 1983).

Miyazawa, Kenji. *Milky Way Railroad* (Japan, fiction, 1958/1996).

———. *Once and Forever: The Tales of Kenji Miyazawa* (Japan, fiction, 1969/1993).

Morgan, Sally. *My Place* (Australia, nonfiction, 1987).

Mowat, Farley. *Never Cry Wolf* (Canada, nonfiction, 1961).

Mudrooroo (Colin Johnson). *Doctor Wooreddy's Prescription for Enduring the Ending of the World* (Australia, fiction, 1983).

Murray, Les. *Subhuman Redneck Poems* (Australia, poetry, 1996).

Neruda, Pablo. *Art of Birds* (Chile, poetry, 1985).

———. *The Heights of Macchu Picchu* (Chile, poetry, 1966).

Novalis. *The Novices of Saïs* (Germany, fiction, 1800).

Park, Geoff. *Ngä Urora: The Groves of Life* (New Zealand, nonfiction, 1995).

Paz, Octavio. *The Collected Poems of Octavio Paz, 1957–1987* (Mexico, poetry, 1987).

Pilkington, Doris. *Rabbit-Proof Fence* (Australia, nonfiction, 1996).

Prishvin, Mikhail. *Nature's Diary* (Russia, nonfiction, 1951).

Rolls, Eric. *From Forest to Sea: Australia's Changing Environment* (Australia, nonfiction, 1993).

Rousseau, Jean-Jacques. *The Confessions* (France, nonfiction, 1781–88).

Roy, Arundhati. *The God of Small Things* (India, fiction, 1997).

———. *Power Politics* (India, nonfiction, 2001).

Ruskin, John. *Modern Painters* (United Kingdom, nonfiction, 1856).

Saint-Exupery, Antoine de. *Wind, Sand, and Stars* (France, nonfiction, 1940).

Sakaki, Nanao. *Break the Mirror: The Poems of Nanao Sakaki* (Japan, poetry, 1987).

Saro-Wiwa, Ken. *Adaku and Other Stories* (Nigeria, fiction, 1989).

———. *A Month and Day: A Detention Diary* (Nigeria, nonfiction, 1995).

Soyinka, Wole. *The Open Sore of a Continent: A Personal Narrative of the Nigerian Crisis* (Nigeria, nonfiction, 1996).

Stow, Randolph. *Tourmaline* (Australia, fiction, 1963).

Tagore, Rabindranath. *Selected Poems* (India, poetry, 1985).

Thomas, Edward. *The Country* (United Kingdom, nonfiction, 1913).

———. *The Heart of England* (United Kingdom, nonfiction, 1906).

Thomson, James. *The Seasons* (United Kingdom, poetry, 1726–1740).

Walker, Kath. *Stradbroke Dreamtime* (Australia, poetry, 1972).

Webb, Mary. *Gone to Earth* (United Kingdom, fiction, 1917).

Wharton, Thomas. *Icefields* (Canada, fiction, 1995).

White, Gilbert. *The Natural History of Selbourne* (United Kingdom, nonfiction, 1788).

White, Patrick. *Voss* (Australia, fiction, 1957).

Williamson, Henry. *Tarka the Otter: His Joyful Water-Life and Death in the Country of the Two Rivers* (United Kingdom, fiction, 1927).

Winton, Tim. *Dirt Music* (Australia, fiction, 2001).

———. *That Eye, the Sky* (Australia, fiction, 1986).

Wolcott, Derek. *Omeros* (St. Lucia, poetry, 1990).

Wolf, Christa. *Accident: A Day's News* (Germany, fiction, 1987).

Woolf, Virginia. *The Waves* (United Kingdom, fiction, 1931).

Wordsworth, William. *The Prelude* (United Kingdom, poetry, 1799, 1805, 1850).

Wright, Judith. *Birds* (Australia, poetry, 1962).

Zurita, Raúl. *Purgatorio, 1970–1977* (Chile, poetry, 1985).

RELEVANT SCHOLARSHIP

Abram, David. *The Spell of the Sensuous: Perception and Language in a More-than-Human World* (1996).

Adam, Barbara. *Timescapes of Modernity: The Environment and Invisible Hazards* (1998).

Adamson, Joni. *American Indian Literature, Environmental Justice, and Ecocriticism: The Middle Place* (2001).

———, Mei Mei Evans, and Rachel Stein, eds. *The Environmental Justice Reader: Politics, Poetics, and Pedagogy* (2002).

Alaimo, Stacy. *Undomesticated Ground: Recasting Nature as Feminist Space* (2000).

Allister, Mark. *Refiguring the Map of Sorrow: Nature Writing and Autobiography* (2001).

———, ed. *Eco-Man: New Perspectives on Masculinity and Nature* (2004).

Andrews, Richard N. L. *Managing the Environment, Managing Ourselves: A History of American Environmental Policy* (1999).

Armbruster, Karla, and Kathleen R. Wallace, eds. *Beyond Nature Writing: Expanding the Boundaries of Ecocriticism* (2001).

Basso, Keith. *Wisdom Sits in Places: Landscape and Language among the Western Apache* (1996).

Bate, Jonathan. *Romantic Ecology: Wordsworth and the Environmental Tradition* (1991).

———. *Song of the Earth* (2000).

Bender, Bert. *The Descent of Love: Darwin and the Theory of Sexual Selection in American Fiction, 1871–1926* (1996).

Bennett, Michael, and David Teague, eds. *The Nature of Cities: Ecocriticism and Urban Environments* (1999).

Bergman, Charles. *Orion's Legacy: A Cultural History of Man as Hunter* (1996).

Berry, Thomas. *The Dream of the Earth* (1988).

Branch, Michael P., Rochelle Johnson, Daniel Patterson, and Scott Slovic, eds. *Reading the Earth: New Directions in the Study of Literature and Environment* (1998).

Branch, Michael P., and Scott Slovic, eds. *The ISLE Reader: Ecocriticism, 1993–2003* (2003).

Bryant, Bunyan, and Paul Mohai, eds. *Race and the Incidence of Environmental Hazards: A Time for Discourse* (1992).

Bryson, Scott J. *Ecopoetry: A Critical Introduction* (2002).

Buell, Lawrence. *The Environmental Imagination: Thoreau, Nature Writing, and the Formation of American Culture* (1995).

———. *Writing for an Endangered World: Literature, Culture, and the Environment in the U.S. and Beyond* (2001).

Bullard, Robert D. *Unequal Protection: Environmental Justice and Communities of Color* (1997).

Callicott, J. Baird. *In Defense of the Land Ethic: Essays in Environmental Philosophy* (1989).

Carr, Glynis, ed. *New Essays in Ecofeminist Literary Criticism* (2000).

Cartmill, Matt. *A View to a Death in the Morning: Hunting and Nature Through History* (1993).

Chaudhuri, Una. *Staging Place: The Geography of Modern Drama* (1995).

Cohen, Michael P. *The Pathless Way: John Muir and American Wilderness* (1984).

Comer, Krista. *Landscapes of the New West: Gender and Geography in Contemporary Women's Writing* (1999).

Conley, Verena Andermatt. *Ecopolitics: The Environment in Poststructuralist Thought* (1997).

Coupe, Laurence, ed. *The Green Studies Reader: From Romanticism to Ecocriticism* (2000).

Cronon, William, ed. *Uncommon Ground: Toward Reinventing Nature* (1995).

Crosby, Alfred W. *Ecological Imperialism: The Biological Expansion of Europe 900–1900* (1986).

Daly, Herman. *Beyond Growth: The Economics of Sustainable Development* (1996).

Devall, Bill, and George Sessions. *Deep Ecology: Living as if Nature Mattered* (1985).

Diamond, Jared. *Guns, Germs, and Steel: The Fates of Human Societies* (1997).

Dixon, Melvin. *Ride Out the Wilderness: Geography and Identity in Afro-American Literature* (1987).

Durning, Alan Thein, and John C. Ryan. *Stuff: The Secret Lives of Everyday Things* (1997).

Eckersley, Robyn. *Environmentalism and Political Theory: Toward an Ecocentric Approach* (1992).

Ehrenfeld, David. *The Arrogance of Humanism* (1978).

Elder, John. *Imagining the Earth: Poetry and the Vision of Nature* (1985/1996).

———. *Reading the Mountains of Home* (1998).

———, ed. *American Nature Writers*, 2 vols. (1996).

Ensign, Robert Taylor. *Lean Down Your Ear upon the Earth, and Listen: Thomas Wolfe's Greener Modernism* (2003).

Evernden, Neil. *The Social Creation of Nature* (1992).

Feld, Steven, and Keith H. Basso, eds. *Senses of Place* (1996).

Fritzell, Peter A. *Nature Writing and America: Essays upon a Cultural Type* (1990).

Gaard, Greta, ed. *Ecofeminism: Women, Animals, Nature* (1993).

———, and Patrick D. Murphy, eds., *Ecofeminist Literary Criticism: Theory, Interpretation, Pedagogy* (1998).

Gifford, Terry. *Green Voices: Understanding Contemporary Nature Poetry* (1995).

———. *Pastoral* (1999).

Glotfelty, Cheryll, and Harold Fromm, eds. *The Ecocriticism Reader: Landmarks in Literary Ecology* (1996).

Goldsmith, Arnold L. *The Modern American Urban Novel: Nature as "Interior Structure"* (1991).

Gottlieb, Robert. *Forcing the Spring: The Transformation of the American Environmental Movement* (1993).

Griffin, Susan. *Woman and Nature: The Roaring Inside Her* (1978).

Grove, Richard. *Green Imperialism: Colonial Expansion, Tropical Island Eden, and the Origins of Environmentalism, 1600–1860* (1996).

Gupta, Akhil, and James Ferguson. *Culture, Power, Place: Explorations in Critical Anthropology* (1997).

Haraway, Donna J. *Primate Visions: Gender, Race, and Nature in the World of Modern Science* (1989).

———. *Simians, Cyborgs, and Women: The Reinvention of Nature* (1991).

Harrison, Robert Pogue. *Forests: The Shadow of Civilization* (1992).

Harvey, David. *Justice, Nature, and the Geography of Difference* (1996).

Hay, Peter. *Main Currents in Western Environmental Thought* (2002).

Herndl, Carl G., and Stuart C. Brown, eds. *Green Culture: Environmental Rhetoric in Contemporary America* (1996).

Heyne, Eric, ed. *Desert, Garden, Margin, Range: Literature on the American Frontier* (1992).

Hochman, Jhan. *Green Cultural Studies: Nature in Film, Novel, and Theory* (1998).

Hofrichter, Richard, ed. *Toxic Struggles: The Theory and Practice of Environmental Justice* (1993).

Holmes, Steven. *The Young John Muir: An Environmental Biography* (1999).

hooks, bell. *Sisters of the Yam: Black Women and Self-Recovery* (1993).

Huth, Hans. *Nature and the American: Three Centuries of Changing Attitudes* (1957).

Ingram, David. *Green Screen: Environmentalism and Hollywood Cinema* (2001).

Jamieson, Dale, ed. *A Companion to Environmental Philosophy* (2001).

Kartiganer, Donald M., and Ann J. Abadie, eds. *Faulkner and the Natural World* (1999).

Kerridge, Richard, and Neil Sammels, eds. *Writing the Environment: Ecocriticism and Literature* (1998).

Killingsworth, M. Jimmie, and Jacqueline S. Palmer. *Ecospeak: Rhetoric and Environmental Politics in America* (1992).

Kolodny, Annette. *The Land Before Her: Fantasy and Experience of the American Frontiers, 1630–1860* (1984).

———. *The Lay of the Land: Metaphor as Experience and History in American Life and Letters* (1975).

Krall, Florence. *Ecotone: Wayfaring on the Margins* (1994).

Krech, Shepard, III. *The Ecological Indian: Myth and History* (1999).

Kroeber, Karl. *Ecological Literary Criticism: Romantic Imagining and the Biology of Mind* (1995).

Kuletz, Valerie. *The Tainted Desert: Environmental and Social Ruin in the American West* (1998).

LaDuke, Winona. *All Our Relations: Native Struggles for Land and Life* (1999).

Limerick, Patricia. *The Legacy of Conquest: The Unbroken Past of the American West* (1988).

Love, Glen A. *Practical Ecocriticism: Literature, Biology, and the Environment* (2003).

Luke, Timothy. *Ecocritique: Contesting the Politics of Nature, Economy, and Culture* (1997).

MacDonald, Scott. *The Garden in the Machine: A Field Guide to Independent Films about Place* (2001).

Marsh, George Perkins. *Man and Nature* (1864).

Marshall, Ian. *Peak Experiences: Walking Meditations on Literature, Nature, and Need* (2003).

———. *Story Line: Exploring the Literature of the Appalachian Trail* (1998).

Marx, Leo. *The Machine in the Garden: Technology and the Pastoral Ideal in America* (1964).

Mazel, David. *American Literary Environmentalism* (2000).

———. *A Century of Early Ecocriticism* (2001).

McColley, Diane Kelsey. *A Gust for Paradise: Milton's Eden and the Visual Arts* (1993).

Meeker, Joseph. *The Comedy of Survival: Studies in Literary Ecology* (1972).

Merchant, Carolyn. *The Death of Nature: Women, Ecology, and the Scientific Revolution* (1980).

———. *Earthcare: Women and the Environment* (1995).

———. *Ecological Revolutions: Nature, Gender, and Science in New England* (1989).

Moser, Mary Anne. *Immersed in Technology: Art and Virtual Environments* (1996).

Murphy, Patrick D. *Farther Afield in the Study of Nature-Oriented Literature* (2000).

———. *Literature, Nature, and Other: Ecofeminist Critiques* (1995).

———, ed. *Literature of Nature: An International Sourcebook* (1998).

Nash, Roderick Frazier. *The Rights of Nature: A History of Environmental Ethics* (1989).

———. *Wilderness and the American Mind,* third ed. (1982).

Nelson, Barney. *The Wild and the Domestic: Animal Representation, Ecocriticism, and Western American Literature* (2000).

Nicholsen, Shierry Weber. *The Love of Nature and the End of the World: The Unspoken Dimensions of Environmental Concern* (2002).

Norwood, Vera. *Made from This Earth: American Women and Nature* (1993).

Oelschlaeger, Max. *Caring for Creation: An Ecumenical Approach to the Environmental Crisis* (1994).

————. *The Idea of Wilderness: From Prehistory to the Age of Ecology* (1991).

O'Grady, John P. *Pilgrims to the Wild: Everett Ruess, Henry David Thoreau, John Muir, Clarence King, Mary Austin* (1993).

Orr, David. *Earth in Mind: On Education, Environment, and the Human Prospect* (1994).

————. *Ecological Literacy: Education and the Transition to a Postmodern World* (1992).

Peck, H. Daniel. *Thoreau's Morning Work: Memory and Perception in A Week on the Concord and Merrimack Rivers, the Journal, and Walden* (1990).

Peiffer, Katrina Schimmoeller. *Coyote at Large: Humor in American Nature Writing* (2000).

Peña, Devon G. *The Terror of the Machine: Technology, Work, Gender and Ecology on the U.S.-Mexico Border* (1997).

————, ed. *Chicano Culture, Ecology, Politics: Subversive Kin* (1998).

Phillips, Dana. *The Truth of Ecology: Nature, Culture, and Literature in America* (2003).

Plumwood, Val. *Feminism and the Mastery of Nature* (1993).

Pratt, Mary Louise. *Imperial Eyes: Travel Writing and Transculturation* (1992).

Pulido, Laura. *Environmentalism and Economic Justice: Two Chicano Struggles in the Southwest* (1996).

Pyne, Stephen J. *Fire in America: A Cultural History of Wildland and Rural Fire* (1982).

Quigley, Peter, ed. *Coyote in the Maze: Tracking Edward Abbey in a World of Words* (1998).

Robertson, David. *Real Matter* (1997).

Rolston, Holmes, III. *Philosophy Gone Wild: Essays in Environmental Ethics* (1986).

Ronald, Ann. *The New West of Edward Abbey* (1982/2001).

————. *Reader of the Purple Sage* (2003).

Roorda, Randall. *Dramas of Solitude: Narratives of Retreat in American Nature Writing* (1998).

Rosendale, Steven, ed. *The Greening of Literary Scholarship: Literature, Theory, and the Environment* (2002).

Ross, Andrew. *The Chicago Gangster Theory of Life: Nature's Debt to Society* (1994).

Roszak, Theodore. *Person/Planet: The Creative Disintegration of Industrial Society* (1979).

————. *The Voice of the Earth* (1992).

————, Mary Gomes, and Allen Kanner, eds. *Ecopsychology* (1995).

Rothenberg, David. *Hand's End: Technology and the Limits of Nature* (1993).

Ryden, Kent C. *Landscape with Figures: Nature and Culture in New England* (2001).

———. *Mapping the Invisible Landscape: Folklore, Writing, and the Sense of Place* (1993).

Sack, Robert David. *Homo Geographicus: A Framework for Action, Awareness, and Moral Concern* (1997).

Sale, Kirkpatrick. *The Green Revolution: The American Environmental Movement, 1962–1992* (1993).

Satterfield, Terre. *Anatomy of a Conflict: Identity, Knowledge, and Emotion in Old-Growth Forests* (2002).

———, and Scott Slovic, eds. *What's Nature Worth? Narrative Expressions of Environmental Values* (2004).

Scheese, Don. *Nature Writing: The Pastoral Impulse in America* (1996).

Scholtmeijer, Marian. *Animal Victims in Modern Fiction* (1993).

Scigaj, Leonard. *Sustainable Poetry: Four American Ecopoets* (1999).

Seager, Joni. *Earth Follies: Coming to Feminist Terms with the Global Environmental Crisis* (1993).

Sewall, Laura. *Sight and Sensibility: The Ecopsychology of Perception* (1999).

Shabecoff, Philip. *A Fierce Green Fire: The American Environmental Movement* (1993).

Shepard, Paul. *The Only World We've Got: A Paul Shepard Reader* (1996).

———. *The Others: How Animals Made Us Human* (1996).

Shiva, Vandana. *Staying Alive: Women, Ecology, and Development* (1989).

Shutkin, William. *The Land that Could Be: Democracy and Environment in the Twenty-First Century* (2000).

Singer, Peter. *Animal Liberation: A New Ethics for Our Treatment of Animals* (1975).

Slovic, Scott. *Seeking Awareness in American Nature Writing: Henry Thoreau, Annie Dillard, Edward Abbey, Wendell Berry, Barry Lopez* (1992).

Soper, Kate. *What Is Nature?* (1995).

Soulé, Michael, and Gary Lease. *Reinventing Nature? Responses to Postmodern Deconstruction* (1995).

Spirn, Anne Whiston. *The Language of Landscape* (1998).

Spretnak, Charlene. *States of Grace: The Recovery of Meaning in the Postmodern Age* (1991).

Stein, Rachel. *Shifting the Ground: American Women Writers' Revisions of Nature, Gender, and Race* (1997).

Sturgeon, Noël. *Ecofeminist Natures* (1998).

Sweet, Timothy. *American Georgics: Economy and Environment in Early American Literature* (2002).

Tallmadge, John. *Meeting the Tree of Life: A Teacher's Path* (1997).

———, and Henry R. Harrington, eds. *Reading Under the Sign of Nature: New Essays in Ecocriticism* (2000).

Teague, David W. *The Southwest in American Literature and Art: The Rise of a Desert Aesthetic* (1997).

Thomashow, Mitchell. *Bringing the Biosphere Home: Learning to Perceive Global Environmental Change* (2002).

———. *Ecological Identity: Becoming a Reflective Environmentalist* (1995).

Tuan, Yi-Fu. *Escapism* (1998).

———. *Topophilia: A Study of Environmental Perception, Attitudes, and Values* (1974).

Turner, Jack. *The Abstract Wild* (1996).

Voros, Gyorgyi. *Notations of the Wild: Ecology in the Poetry of Wallace Stevens* (1997).

Warren, Karen J., ed. *Ecological Feminist Philosophies* (1996).

Weaver, Jace. *Defending Mother Earth: Native American Perspectives on Environmental Justice* (1996).

Weltzien, O. Alan, ed. *The Literary Art and Activism of Rick Bass* (2001).

Westling, Louise. *The Green Breast of the New World* (1996).

White, Richard. *The Organic Machine: The Remaking of the Columbia River* (1995).

Wilkinson, Charles. *The Eagle Bird: Mapping a New West* (1992).

Williams, Raymond. *The Country and the City* (1973).

Wilson, Alexander. *The Culture of Nature: North American Landscape from Disney to the Exxon Valdez* (1992).

Worster, Donald. *Nature's Economy: A History of Ecological Ideas* (1977).

———. *The Wealth of Nature: Environmental History and the Ecological Imagination* (1993).

SELECTED ANTHOLOGIES

Anderson, Lorraine, ed. *Sisters of the Earth: Women's Prose and Poetry about Nature* (1991, second edition 2004).

———, Scott Slovic, and John P. O'Grady, eds. *Literature and the Environment: A Reader on Nature and Culture* (1999).

Banting, Pamela, ed. *Writing the Land* (1998).

Barron, Patrick, and Anna Re, eds. *Italian Environmental Literature: An Anthology* (2003).

Bly, Robert, ed. *The News of the Universe: Poems of Twofold Consciousness* (1980).

Branch, Michael P., ed. *Reading the Roots: American Nature Writing before Walden* (2004).

Chipasula, Frank Mkalawile, ed. *When My Brothers Come Home: Poems from Central and Southern Africa* (1985).

Chisholm, A. H., ed. *Land of Wonder: The Best of Australian Nature Writing* (1964).

Colchie, Thomas, ed. *A Hammock Beneath the Mangoes: Stories from Latin America* (1991).

Conron, John, ed. *The American Landscape: A Critical Anthology of Prose and Poetry* (1973).

Dixon, Terrell F., ed. *City Wilds: Essays and Stories about Urban Nature* (2002).

Elder, John, and Hertha D. Wong, eds. *Family of Earth and Sky: Indigenous Stories of Nature from around the World* (1994).

Finch, Robert, and John Elder, eds. *The Norton Book of Nature Writing*, second edition (2002).

Gutkind, Lee, ed. *On Nature: Great Writers on the Great Outdoors* (2002).

Halpern, Daniel, ed. *On Nature: Nature, Landscape, and Natural History* (1987).

Hongo, Garrett, ed. *The Open Boat: Poems from Asian America* (1993).

Ihimaera, Witi Tame, and D. S. Long, eds. *Into the World of Light: An Anthology of Maori Writing* (1982).

Jordan, Teresa, and James Hepworth, eds. *The Stories that Shape Us: Contemporary Women Write about the West* (1995).

Lyon, Thomas J., ed. *This Incomperable Lande: A Book of American Nature Writing* (1989).

Merrill, Christopher, ed. *The Forgotten Language: Contemporary Poets and Nature* (1991).

Murray, John A., ed. *A Republic of Rivers: Three Centuries of Nature Writing from Alaska and the Yukon* (1990).

Olson, W. Scott, and Scott Cairns, eds. *The Sacred Place: Witnessing the Holy in the Physical World* (1996).

Orfalea, Gregory, and Sharif Elmusa, eds. *Grape Leaves: A Century of Arab American Poetry* (1988).

Pack, Robert, and Jay Parini, eds. *Poems for a Small Planet: Contemporary American Nature Poetry* (1993).

Paz, Octavio, ed. *Mexican Poetry: An Anthology* (1958).

Pichaske, David R., ed. *Late Harvest: Rural American Writing* (1996).

Ronald, Ann, ed. *Words for the Wild* (1987).

Sauer, Peter, ed. *Finding Home: Writing on Nature and Culture from* Orion Magazine (1992).

Slovic, Scott, ed. *Getting over the Color Green: Contemporary Environmental Literature of the Southwest* (2001).

———, and Terrell F. Dixon, eds. *Being in the World: An Environmental Reader for Writers* (1993).

Stewart, Frank, ed. *A World Between Waves* (1992).

Tredinnick, Mark, ed. *A Place on Earth: An Anthology of Nature Writing from Australia and North America* (2003).

Trimble, Stephen, ed. *Words from the Land: Encounters with Natural History Writing* (1988/1995).

Index

About the Contributors

Kathleen Boardman is associate professor of English and associate dean of the College of Liberal Arts at the University of Nevada, Reno, where she directed the Core Writing Program until 2004. She has written several essays on Loren Eiseley and is currently editing a collection of critical articles on western American autobiography and memoir.

Michael P. Cohen teaches ecocriticism and environmental literature at the University of Nevada, Reno. He is the author of *The Pathless Way: John Muir and American Wilderness* (1984), which won the Mark H. Ingraham Prize at the University of Wisconsin Press, and *The History of the Sierra Club, 1892–1970* (Sierra Club Books, 1988). His most recent book, *A Garden of Bristlecones: Tales of Change in the Great Basin* (University of Nevada Press, 1999), was a finalist for the Western States Book Award in creative nonfiction.

Jane Detweiler is associate professor of English and director of the Core Writing Program at the University of Nevada, Reno. A specialist in rhetoric and composition, she teaches a range of courses (writing at all levels, rhetorical theory, narrative theory, women in literature, gender and sexual identity in literature) and conducts research into narrative as a genre and a form of human understanding, the intersections of public and professional discourse, and rhetoric of the disciplines.

David Fenimore recently held the position of University Distinguished Professor of the Humanities at the University of Nevada, Reno, where he has taught British and American literature and core humanities courses since 1989. His publications include the nonfiction account *Bicycling Across America* (Pinedrop Press, 1989) and a two-act play, *A Bad Boy Grown Up: The Life and Times of Zane Grey* (Capitol Theater, 1993).

Cheryll Glotfelty is associate professor of literature and environment at the University of Nevada, Reno. She co-edited with Harold Fromm *The Ecocriticism Reader: Landmarks in Literary Ecology* (University of Georgia Press, 1996), and is cofounder, past president, and former executive secretary of the Association for the Study of Literature and Environment. She has published numerous essays on women writers, ecocriticism, and Western American literature and is currently editing an anthology of Nevada literature.

George Hart was a National Endowment for the Humanities Postdoctoral Fellow in Literatures of the Environment at the University of Nevada, Reno (2000–2002) and is currently assistant professor of English at California State University, Long Beach. He is the co-editor of *Jeffers Studies*, and has published articles on the poetry of Adrienne Rich, William Everson, Robinson Jeffers, H.D., Kenneth Rexroth, Ronald Johnson, and Larry Eigner.

Jen Hill is assistant professor of English at the University of Nevada, Reno, where she teaches Victorian and Romantic literature. She is the editor of *An Exhilaration of Wings: The Literature of Birdwatching* (Viking Press, 1999; Penguin, 2001). Her research interests include the literature of Arctic exploration and American natural history writing.

Susan Palwick is associate professor of English at the University of Nevada, Reno, where she teaches creative writing and literature. She has a longtime interest in science fiction and fantasy, which she also writes professionally.

Scott Slovic is professor of literature and environment and chair of the graduate program in literature and environment at the University of Nevada, Reno. From 1995 to 2002, he directed Nevada's Center for Environmental Arts and Humanities. He is the author of numerous articles in the field of ecocriticism and environmental literature and has written, edited, or co-edited 10 books, including most recently *The ISLE Reader: Ecocriticism, 1993–2003* (University of Georgia Press, 2003) and *What's Nature Worth? Narrative Expressions of Environmental Values* (University of Utah Press, 2004). He served as founding president of the Association for the Study of Literature and

Environment from 1992 to 1995, and since 1995 he has edited ASLE's journal, *ISLE: Interdisciplinary Studies in Literature and Environment.*

Mary Webb teaches writing and literature courses in the English Department at the University of Nevada, Reno. Her interests are land use and landscape representations in nonfiction. She recently published *A Doubtful River* with collaborating photographers Robert Dawson and Peter Goin (University of Nevada Press, 2000). This collection of essays and photographs traces cultural perspectives on arid land and historical attitudes toward the Truckee River, the primary water source in western Nevada.